9/05

Global Economic Prospects

Trade, Regionalism, and Development

2005

Contents

Foreword   vii

Acknowledgments   ix

Overview   xi

Abbreviations   xix

Frequently Cited Regional Trading Agreements and the Parties to Them   xxiii

Chapter 1 Global Outlook and the Developing Countries   1
   The Global Economy: From Recovery to Expansion   3
   Commodity Markets   6
   World Trade   8
   International Finance   10
   Risks and Policy Ppriorities   12
   Long-Term Growth, Structural Change, and Poverty   14
   Structural Changes over Two Decades   16
   Structural Change in the Future   19
   Poverty Forecast   21
   Concluding Remarks   23
   Notes   23
   References   25

Chapter 2 Regional Trade and Preferential Trading Agreements:
A Global Perspective   27
   The Proliferation of Regional Preference Systems   28
   Trends in Trade and Growth by Region   42
   Changing Export Composition and the Rise of Global Production Networks   46
   Preferential Trade and Regional Outcomes   49
   Conclusion   53
   Notes   53
   References   54

Chapter 3 Regional Trade Agreements: Effects on Trade   57
   The Impact of RTAs on Merchandise Trade and Incomes   57
   Ingredients of Success   66

Conclusions: Preferential Trade Agreements and Economic Development   72
Notes   74
References   74

Chapter 4 Beyond Trade Policy Barriers: Lowering Trade Costs Together   77
The Costs of Trade   78
Regional Agreements to Facilitate Trade and Transport   79
Standards, Conformity Assessments, and RTAs   85
Trade-Related Regional Cooperation Agreements   91
Conclusions   92
Notes   93
References   94

Chapter 5 Beyond Merchandise Trade: Services, Investment, Intellectual Property, and Labor Mobility   97
Services, Investment, and IPRs in Regional Agreements   98
Economic Consequences of Services, Investment, and IPR Provisions in RTAs   104
RTAs and Provisions for Movement of Labor   111
Conclusions: Beyond Merchandise Trade   117
Notes   119
References   121

Chapter 6 Making Regionalism Complementary to Multilateralism   125
Preferential Agreements within the Global Context   126
Building Blocks versus Stumbling Blocks   133
The Competitive Liberalization Game: The Case of Doha   136
Multilateral Disciplines on Regional Arrangements   140
Making Open Regionalism Work for Development   144
Notes   148
References   150

Figures
1.1   A record year for developing countries in 2004   4
1.2   Strong growth across most regions   5
1.3   Tradable price developments   6
1.4   Terms of trade impacts from higher commodity prices, 2001–04   7
1.5   The oil-important burden for selected countries   7
1.6   Crude oil prices, 1960–2004   8
1.7   World trade rebounds   8
1.8   Export performance, percent change in market share since 2000   9
1.9   Trade balances in major regions   10
1.10   Developing countries' debt and interest payments easing downward since 1999   10
1.11   Rising U.S. dollar reserves   11
1.12   Impact of a 200 basis point increase in interest rates   12
1.13   First year impacts of a $10 increase in oil prices   14
1.14   A rise in services   17
1.15   Rising openness to trade   18

1.16   Increased urbanization   19
1.17   Growth rate of labor supply declining   19
2.1   Number of RTAs exploded in the 1990s   29
2.2   Spaghetti and rigatoni: Multiple, overlapping RTAs, 2004   39
2.3   Trade within RTAs   41
2.4   Trade performance has differed across regions   43
2.5   Composition of trade has changed   47
2.6   Evolving trading blocs   50
3.1   Evolution of the share of intra-regional imports in total imports, 1960–2000   58
3.2   The ratio of external and intra-regional trade to GDP   59
3.3   Intra-regional trade grows faster when world trade growth is positive   60
3.4   Simulated welfare impact of various FTAs involving Chile   62
3.5   RTAs that divert imports tend to export less to global markets   64
3.6   Not all regions are open   66
3.7   Preferential tariffs in tandem with all tariffs in Latin America   68
3.8   Rules of origin in North–South agreements are more restrictive than in South–South
            agreements   70
4.1   More efficient customs are associated with more trade   80
5.1   Share of EU nationals in total population, for selected EU countries and Norway,
            1985–2000   112
6.1   Global outcomes dominate alternatives   131
6.2   Global reform dominates North–South agreements   133
6.3   Global reform dominates South–South agreements   133

Tables
1.1   The Global outlook in summary   2
1.2   Current account balances   11
1.3   Long-term prospects: Forecast growth of world GDP per capita   17
1.4   Labor market structure, 2005–15   20
1.5   Regional breakdown of poverty in developing countries   21
2.1   Most countries belong to more than one RTA   30
2.2   RTAs cover many topics besides merchandise trade   35
3.1   Implementation of tariff commitments by type of agreement, 1960–1999   69
5.1   Services, investment, and intellectual property: A comparison   99
5.2   Additional services liberalization in U.S. FTAs   100
5.3   Summary of agreements by degree of labor mobility   111
6.1   Comparison of bilateral agreements to global trade reform   128
6.2   Comparison of bilateral agreements with global trade reform   129

Boxes
1.1   The aggregation paradox   16
2.1   RTAs and types of trade liberalization   28
2.2   Reporting RTAs to the WTO   29
2.3   EPAs become the EU's trade and development instrument: An experiment in
            "North-South-South" integration   32
2.4   Labor in U.S. FTAs   33

2.5   Trade agreements and the environment   36
2.6   Can RTAs prevent conflict?   38
2.7   Regional versus multilateral and unilateral liberalization:
            What's more important?   42
3.1   A primer on modeling of RTAs   61
3.2   Regional trade agreements in gravity models: A meta-analysis   63
3.3   Implementation matters   65
3.4   Restrictive rules of origin under NAFTA—the case of clothing   71
3.5   Monitoring implementation of preferential trade agreements:
            "Single Market Scoreboard" in the European Union   73
4.1   Trading can be costly   79
4.2   Border delays tax trade   80
4.3   Standardization and simplification can increase trade volumes: The case of the
            Trans-Kalahari Corridor   82
4.4   Logistics costs in Europe have fallen in the last two decades   83
4.5   The case of the Northern Corridor Stakeholders Consultative Forum   84
5.1   Not all investment is good investment   106
5.2   Do more investor protections mean more investment? Lessons from bilateral
            investment treaties   107
5.3   Illegal migration: A growing global phenomenon   113
5.4   U.S. temporary admission programs under NAFTA and unilateral policies   116
6.1   Impacts of the new GTAP database   127
6.2   Regional trade agreements, structural change, and congruence   132
6.3   Choosing partners: Selection criteria for U.S. RTAs   137
6.4   Sequencing of RTAs: Is there a good practice?   139
6.5   RTAs and WTO disciplines   141
6.6   Tunisia's Association Agreement with the European Union   146

Foreword

THIS YEAR—2004—is shaping up to be the healthiest year for developing countries in the last three decades. East Asia has come out of the crisis of 1997–98 stronger and more vibrant than ever, the countries of Europe and Central Asia are now almost completely out of the long shadow of transition from socialism and are growing more rapidly; and South Asian countries, on the strength of continuing reforms, are performing well. Moreover, countries in Latin America, Sub-Saharan Africa, and the Middle East and North Africa had a much better year. To be sure, some countries within each region have not enjoyed the fruits of this recovery, and these countries remain a source of concern. But in aggregate, economic growth in 2004 was impressive. This performance reflects a fortuitous combination of (1) long-term secular trends built on a foundation of better macroeconomic management and (2) an improved domestic investment climate converging with a cyclical recovery of the global economy.

This is no time for complacency. Lingering imbalances in the global economy associated with the rising twin deficits in the United States, a delayed recovery in Europe, high and volatile oil prices, and questions about the path of China's economy constitute risks to the pace of growth in developing countries over the medium term. Sustaining this pace is essential for the fate of millions of the world's poor.

World trade grew by 10.2 percent in 2004, and has played an important role in this year's exemplary performance. On the policy side, the WTO discussions in August recouped the ground that was lost in late 2003 (after the Cancun WTO ministerial), when governments concluded an agreement that provides a framework for pursuing the Doha Development Agenda. The framework, however, is only an outline—the actual agreement is still to come. Whether the final agreement contains provisions that will provide a meaningful impulse to development remains to be seen.

In the meantime, this year's *Global Economic Prospects* examines the evidence on an important development that is reshaping the architecture of the world trading system: The dramatic proliferation of regional trade agreements (RTAs). These take various forms of preferential reciprocal treaties—they can be bilateral or plurilateral free trade agreements or, less commonly, customs unions. In according preferential access to members, regional arrangements necessarily discriminate against nonmembers. Even though arrangements in some instances can promote development, it is important to recognize that they also can lead to trade diversion in a way that hurts both member countries and excluded countries. Hence this year's report identifies ways to design and implement preferential trading agreements to maximize their benefits for participants and minimize their costs to nonmember developing countries. The key to making regional agreements complementary to a nondiscriminatory multilateral system is to strive for "open regionalism"—that is, agreements with low external barriers to trade, nonrestrictive rules of origin, liberalized service markets, and a strong focus on reducing transaction costs at borders.

The international community working together can leverage the August framework to achieve an ambitious Doha deal. Multilateral liberalization has a greater positive impact on development than do the myriad regional arrangements now being spawned seemingly in every corner of the globe. Moreover, multilateral oversight of inherently discriminatory RTAs must be strengthened, and the first step is to increase transparency by empowering the WTO to collect and regularly make public full details of all arrangements. If Doha can succeed in bringing down border protection in agriculture and manufactures, it will reduce the discriminatory effects of regional agreements and lower the probability of costly trade diversion for participating countries. Said differently, a strong Doha arrangement can contribute to open regionalism.

Along with other bilateral and multilateral institutions, the World Bank continues to promote the integration of developing countries into the world economy so that the benefits of globalization can extend to the poor. The Bank now has 91 trade-related projects approved or planned in 75 countries for the three-year fiscal period 2004–06. The actual and projected commitments for new trade operations are at $2.9 billion—larger than the commitments of all ongoing operations approved over the preceding eight-year period of fiscal 1996–2003 ($2.4 billion). For trade facilitation the growth is even larger. Projected commitments over fiscal 2004–06, at more than $1.2 billion, triple the commitments of ongoing trade facilitation operations approved between fiscal 1996–2003. To guide this lending and to provide policy advice, the World Bank research program in trade works for client countries all over the world, and the program continues to be ambitious.

There is still a lot to be done. Poverty remains high—with 2.7 billion people living on less than $2 dollars per day—and the global trading system is still riddled with obstacles that prevent the products of the world's poor from reaching markets. Pursuing these challenges through multilateral, unilateral, and regional policies can contribute to poverty reduction around the world, which will pay high dividends for generations to come.

François Bourguignon
Chief Economist
World Bank

November 2004

Acknowledgments

THIS REPORT WAS produced by staff from the World Bank's Prospects Group and from the World Bank Trade Department. Richard Newfarmer was the lead author and manager of the report, under the direction of Uri Dadush. The principal authors of chapter 1 were Andrew Burns and Dominique van der Mensbrugghe. Chapter 2 was written by Paul Brenton, Carolina Diaz Bonilla, Denis Medvedev, and Philip Schuler; chapters 3 and 4 were written by Paul Brenton; chapter 5 was written by Richard Newfarmer; and chapter 6 was written by Bernard Hoekman, Jeffrey Lewis, and Dominique van der Mensbrugghe. Carolina Diaz Bonilla and Denis Medvedev provided research assistance that informed all chapters. The Global Outlook—the on-line twin publication of *Global Economic Prospects*—was led by Fernando Martel Garcia. Several reviewers, including Michael Finger, Julio Nogues, Guillermo Perry, and Jeffrey Schott, as well as Alan Winters and Jaime De Melo, offered extensive and enormously useful comments. The report was produced under the general guidance of François Bourguignon.

Several people contributed substantively to the various chapters. In chapter 1, the Global Trends Team, under Hans Timmer's leadership, was responsible for the projections, with contributions from John Baffes, Maurizio Bussolo, Betty Dow, Himmat Kalsi, Robert Keyfitz, Annette De Kleine, Fernando Martel Garcia, Donald Mitchell, Mick Riordan, and Shane Streifel, and for the poverty numbers, Shaohua Chen and Martin Ravallion. For chapter 2, Vlad Manole, Will Martin and Francis Ng, Sherman Robinson and Carolina Diaz Bonilla, Maurice Schiff and Yanling Wang provided background papers and notes. For chapter 3, Souleymane Coulibaly provided statistical analysis for the gravity model work, and Takako Ikezuki contributed background material. In chapter 4, Enrique Aldaz-Carroll, Gael Raballand, and Luc de Wulf wrote background papers. In chapter 5, Ximena Clark and William Shaw, Carsten Fink and Patrick Reichenmiller, Howard Mann and Aaron Cosbey, Aaditya Mattoo, and Beatriz Nofal provided background papers. Maurice Schiff and Alan Winters wrote papers for chapter 6. The Global Outlook benefited from the efforts of several specialists, among them Abhijeet Dwivedi, Sabeera Kulkarni, Bulent Ozbilgin, and Carlos Rossel. Awatif H. Abuzeid was the senior staff assistant, who, together with Katherine Rollins, produced the several drafts of the report and managed the writing stage. Dorota Nowak worked with the World Bank's Office of the Publisher to manage the publication and dissemination process.

Many people provided written contributions and/or comments: Frederick Abbott, Hakim Ben Hamouda and staff at the Economic Commission for Africa, Carlos Braga, Harry Broadman, Aaron Cosbey, Robert Devlin and the staff of the Inter-American Development Bank, Peter Draper, Dorothy Dworskin and the staff at the U.S. Treasury and U.S. Trade Representative;

Philip English, Antoni Estevadeordal, Alan Gelb, Caroline Freund, Mary Hallward-Driemeier, Lawrence Hinkle, Elena Ianchovichina, Roumeen Islam, Alejandro Jara, Sebastien Jean, Stephen Karingi, Odin Knudsen, Hans Peter Lankes, Patrick Low, Nuno Limao, Muthukumara Mani, Howard Mann, Daniel Muller-Jentsch, Mustafa Nabli, Caglar Ozden, John Panzer, Carmen Pont-Vieira, Jean-Francois Rischard, Kamal Saggi, Maurice Schiff, Raj Soopramanien, Peter Van Den Heuvel and staff of the EU Commission, Stephen Woolcock, and Gianni Zanini.

Overview

THE PROLIFERATION OF regional trade agreements (RTAs) is fundamentally altering the world trade landscape. The number of agreements in force now surpasses 200, and it has risen sixfold in just two decades. Today more than one-third of global trade takes place between countries that have some form of reciprocal RTA.[1] The European Union (EU) and United States are playing a prominent role in this proliferation (figure 1).

This report addresses two questions:

- What are the characteristics of agreements that strongly promote—or hinder—development for member countries?
- Does the proliferation of agreements pose risks to the multilateral trading system, and how can those risks be managed?

Identifying What Works: Open Regionalism

RTAs are often one component of a larger political effort to deepen economic relations with neighboring countries.[2] As such, they can create opportunities to expand trade through joint action to overcome institutional as well as policy barriers to trade. At a basic level, it is often easier to motivate reciprocal reductions in border barriers when the participants are fewer and the policymakers feel more

in control of outcomes. Moreover, RTAs have the flexibility to pursue trade-expanding policies not addressed well in multilateral trading rules. Trade agreements therefore usually go beyond slashing tariffs to include measures to reduce trade impediments associated with standards, customs and border crossings, and services regulations—as well as broader rules that improve the overall investment climate. Finally, these agreements often form cornerstones of larger economic and political efforts to increase regional cooperation. RTAs can help motivate and reinforce broader reforms in domestic policy; they can be designed to contribute to a political environment that is more conducive to stability, investment, and growth.

Not all agreements create new trade and investment. Those RTAs with high external border protection are particularly susceptible to the adverse effects of trade diversion (figure 2). In fact, a statistical analysis based on findings from several econometric studies suggests that many agreements cost the economy more in lost trade revenues than they earn, because they discriminate against efficient, low-cost suppliers in nonmember countries. Of course, this finding does not take into account the potential dynamic gains, the positive effects associated with services liberalization, or any of the benefits from adopting new regulations. But it does underscore the point that regional agreements carry risks that merit close scrutiny by would-be participants.

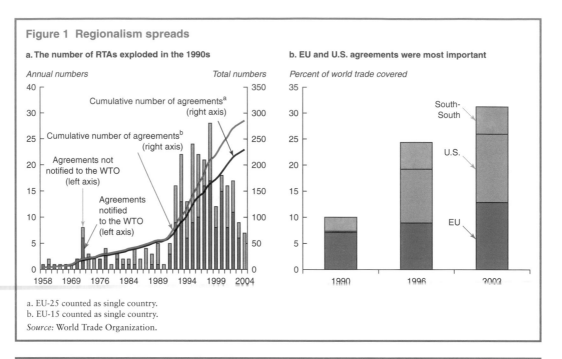

Figure 1 Regionalism spreads

a. The number of RTAs exploded in the 1990s

b. EU and U.S. agreements were most important

a. EU-25 counted as single country.
b. EU-15 counted as single country.
Source: World Trade Organization.

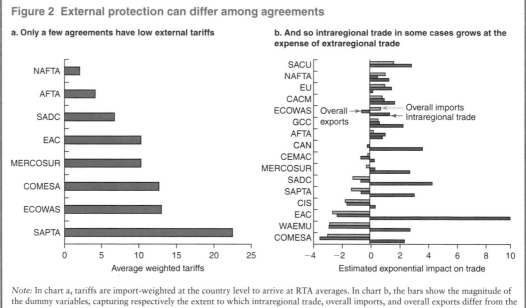

Figure 2 External protection can differ among agreements

a. Only a few agreements have low external tariffs

b. And so intraregional trade in some cases grows at the expense of extraregional trade

Note: In chart a, tariffs are import-weighted at the country level to arrive at RTA averages. In chart b, the bars show the magnitude of the dummy variables, capturing respectively the extent to which intraregional trade, overall imports, and overall exports differ from the "normal" levels predicted by the gravity model on the basis of economic size, proximity, and relevant institutional and historical variables, such as a common language.
Source: World Bank staff using UN TRAINS, accessed through WITS.

As agreements proliferate, a single country often becomes a member of several different agreements. The average African country belongs to four different agreements, and the average Latin America country belongs to seven agreements. This creates a "spaghetti bowl" of overlapping arrangements (figure 3). Each agreement has different rules of origin,

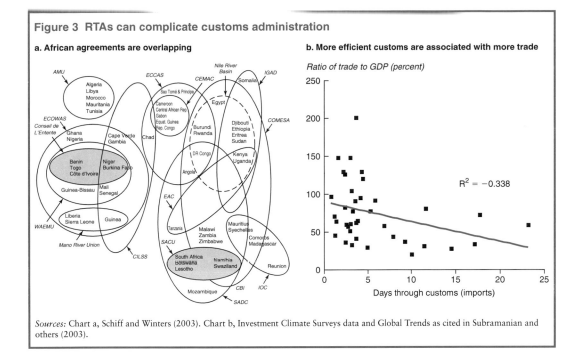

Figure 3 RTAs can complicate customs administration

a. African agreements are overlapping

b. More efficient customs are associated with more trade

Ratio of trade to GDP (percent)

$R^2 = -0.338$

Days through customs (imports)

Sources: Chart a, Schiff and Winters (2003). Chart b, Investment Climate Surveys data and Global Trends as cited in Subramanian and others (2003).

different tariff schedules, and different periods of implementation, and together they complicate customs administration. Customs agents report that it takes longer to process goods covered by preferential arrangements, and longer processing times drive up the cost of trade. In general, the longer the delays in customs, the smaller the role of trade in GDP.

So what characteristics lead to expanded trade and development? A prerequisite for the success of any trade policy is that it be integrated into a sound domestic policy framework. It is virtually impossible for entrepreneurs to take advantage of new opportunities—whether they originate in market access through an RTA, through a multilateral agreement, or other sources—if the domestic investment climate is not supportive. Macroeconomic stability, basic property rights, and adequate infrastructure regulation are all key. Indeed, trade agreements can reinforce positive elements in the domestic reform program by anchoring policy to the agreement itself. But an RTA cannot substitute for sound domestic policies.

With prerequisites in place, the RTAs most likely to increase national incomes over time are those designed with:

- Low external MFN tariffs,
- Few sectoral and product exemptions,
- Nonrestrictive rules-of-origin tests that build toward a framework common to many agreements,
- Measures to facilitate trade,
- Large ex-post markets,
- Measures to promote new cross-border competition, particularly in services, and
- Rules governing investment and intellectual property that are appropriate to the development context.

Low external tariffs and wide coverage minimize the risks of trade diversion, while nonrestrictive rules of origin allow for increased trade. The practice of excluding many agricultural products is common, and it can limit development payoffs. Trade facilitation measures, though worthwhile in and of themselves, receive more policymaker attention when they are embedded in an RTA, and they often have positive trade-creating effects for all trade partners.

Well designed agreements are of limited value if they are not implemented, and many RTAs have more life on paper than in reality. Weak implementation often afflicts South-South agreements. Monitoring mechanisms are often inadequate and do not receive the sustained high-level political attention necessary to drive institutional improvements in, for example, adherence to tariff reduction schedules, customs, and border crossings.

Against these benchmarks of success, it is difficult to give universally high marks to any single category of agreement. In general, North-South agreements score better on implementation than South-South agreements. Because North-South agreements can integrate economies with distinct technological capabilities and other different factor proportions, and because they usually result in larger post-agreement markets, the potential gains are usually greater. However, tighter rules of origin, more restrictive exclusions for particular sectors (such as agriculture), and a preoccupation with rules not calibrated to development priorities can undercut these benefits (figure 4). North-South agreements, particularly those with the United States, have been more effective in locking in new services liberalization; they have pressed intellectual property rights beyond World Trade Organization (WTO) rules; and expanded the sphere of investment protections; but they contain few provisions to liberalize the temporary movement of labor.

Some South-South agreements are better at focusing on merchandise trade, minimizing exclusions, adopting less restrictive rules of origin, and lowering the border costs. For example, the Caribbean Community (CARICOM) and the Common Market of Eastern and Southern Africa (COMESA) have had some success in reducing border costs. But in general, South-South agreements have not adhered to implementation schedules, and they suffer from their small market size and

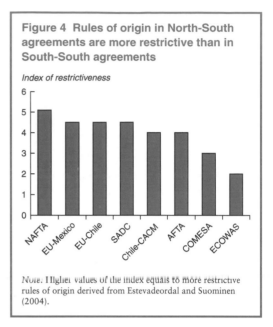

Figure 4 Rules of origin in North-South agreements are more restrictive than in South-South agreements

Index of restrictiveness

Note: Higher values of the index equals to more restrictive rules of origin derived from Estevadeordal and Suominen (2004).

economic similarity. And like the North-South agreements, South-South agreements rarely provide for the temporary movement of labor.

Consequences for the Multilateral System

The development consequences of RTAs are not limited to their effects on members—they also have cumulative effects on the multilateral system. In one sense, RTAs are a step toward greater openness in the whole system, by promoting more trade and generating new domestic constituencies with an interest in openness. Moreover, some regional trade policies are effectively nondiscriminatory, such as measures to improve customs, speed transactions at ports or border crossings, or in some cases open services markets. These measures can complement unilateral and multilateral policies.

However, this view overlooks the effects that RTAs can have on excluded countries. Preferences for some countries mean discrimination against others. Indeed, the General Agreement on Tariffs and Trade (GATT), borne out of the sad experience of discrimination in the prewar years, was founded on the principle of nondiscrimination. Today, the adverse consequences for the excluded countries are much less severe than at GATT's inception, because tariffs and other barriers have come down sharply, mitigating the exclusionary effects of regional arrangements. The exception—and it is not trivial—is agriculture. Another mitigating factor is that many countries excluded by trade agreements between the United States and the EU enjoy some degree of preferential access through voluntary preference schemes, such as the Generalized System of Preferences (GSP), America's Growth and Opportunity Act (AGOA), and the EU's Everything But Arms (EBA) program. To be sure, these programs lack the certainty of market access that MFN agreements and RTAs provide, because preferences are voluntary and subject to political whim, but they do mitigate the effects of exclusions for selected, very low-income countries. Finally, some developing countries—the spokes in the hub-and-spoke analogy—are signing bilateral agreements with each other and with other hubs.

Inevitably some countries get left out of trade agreements, either because they are not favored politically, because they cannot afford the costs of many separate negotiations, or because their neighborhood is less open. Countries as diverse as Bolivia, India, Mongolia, Pakistan, and Sri Lanka do not enjoy the same level of access to the United States or the EU as Chile, Jordan, or Mexico, and they see their trade diminished when bilateral agreements are signed.

RTAs can also undercut the incentives of governments to press for multilateral liberalization, which would improve global trade rules. This study finds little evidence that major players in the current WTO negotiations have changed their negotiating positions or retreated from the multilateral process, even as they avail themselves of regional trade deals. However, as the discussions become politically difficult, the risk is ever present that even they will abandon multilateralism in favor of "satisficing regionalism." One

consequence of the spread of regional agreements is that many poorer developing countries have diverted scarce negotiating resources to regional negotiations at the expense of more active participation in the Doha discussions. The average developing country belongs to five separate RTAs and is negotiating more all the time. In the future, will countries that now enjoy preferences fight multilateral liberalization, or even oppose further regional liberalization, to keep their privileged market access? A few small developing countries are indeed likely to lose advantages in preferential markets, and they may scuttle a deal if their legitimate concerns are not addressed.

The Importance of Doha to Open Regionalism

The policy solution to these twin concerns—the need to design regional agreements that create trade and regional agreements that have minimal exclusionary effects—comes together in the form of low MFN tariffs and other border barriers. An agreement that lowers border protection around the world promotes open regionalism by mitigating trade diversion. At the same time, it would diminish the exclusionary effects of discriminatory preferences built into regional agreements. The first order of business for the international community is to accelerate progress on the Doha Agenda and to fill in the blanks of the August 2004 framework agreement with reductions in protection, especially for products produced by the world's poor.

For Developing Countries, a Three-Part Strategy

Developing countries wishing to harness trade to their development strategy should see regional integration as one element in a three-pronged strategy that includes unilateral liberalization, multilateral liberalization, and regional liberalization.

Historically, *unilateral liberalization,* which is usually linked to a broader program of domestic reform, has accounted for most of the reductions in border protection. Most comprehensive trade reforms among large countries (Argentina, Brazil, and China in the early 1990s, and more recently, India) were primarily unilateral reforms that were undertaken to increase the productivity of the domestic economy. The same process took place in many small countries as well. In fact, of the 21 percentage point cuts in average weighted tariffs of all developing countries between 1983 and 2003, unilateral reforms account for roughly two-thirds of the reduction. Tariff reductions associated with the multilateral commitments in the Uruguay Round accounted for about 25 percent, and the proliferation of regional agreements amounted to about 10 percent of this reduction (see figure 5).

Autonomous liberalization promotes global competitiveness by lowering costs of inputs, increasing competition from imports to drive productivity growth, and integrating the national economy into the global economy. Autonomous trade reform is, ironically, more important than ever in the presence of RTAs; low border barriers minimize the risks of trade and investment diversion. Low external barriers promote trade in world markets, and this is highly correlated

with increases in intraregional trade, irrespective of the presence of an RTA.

Multilateral liberalization leverages domestic reforms into increased market access around the world. Developing countries collectively stand to gain much more in the WTO arena than in any smaller regional market. Moreover, this multilateral forum is the only place that developing countries, working together, can press for more open markets in agriculture and can seek disciplines on trade-distorting agricultural subsidies and on contingent protection.

Some have argued that RTAs can be an alternative to multilateral liberalization. They are not. Gains for all developing countries from these agreements, even under the most generous of assumptions, are usually only a fraction of those from full multilateral liberalization. Of course, if one of the partner countries is a high-income, large-market economy, and if most other countries are excluded from preferential access, the countries signing the first trade agreement may benefit individually and substantially—but those benefits wither as new countries sign additional agreements. In fact, the scenarios in this study show that all developing countries would collectively lose if they were all to sign preferential agreements with the Quad (Canada, the EU, Japan, and the United States) (figure 6). Therefore, developing countries have a powerful collective interest in an effective Doha Agenda—even if they all are scrambling to gain preferential market access to the Quad.

Forging policies on *open regionalism* is the third component of trade policy strategy. Desirable as multilateral liberalization is, the Doha Round is likely to realize only part of its development potential. For some types of policy, collective regional actions may be the first, best course, and may result in effective nondiscriminatory benefits.[3] For example, RTAs can reduce regional political tensions, take advantage of scale economies in infrastructure provision, and lead to joint programs to improve border crossings or to motivate liberalization in services. But countries should sign on with

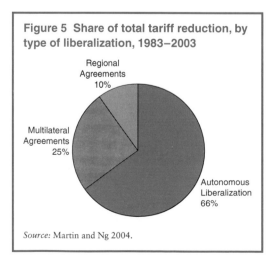

Figure 5 **Share of total tariff reduction, by type of liberalization, 1983–2003**

Regional Agreements 10%

Multilateral Agreements 25%

Autonomous Liberalization 66%

Source: Martin and Ng 2004.

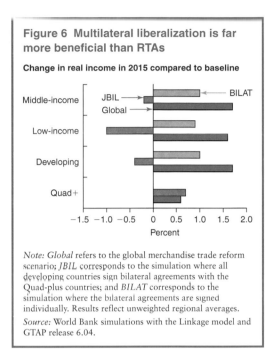

Figure 6 Multilateral liberalization is far more beneficial than RTAs

Change in real income in 2015 compared to baseline

Note: Global refers to the global merchandise trade reform scenario; *JBIL* corresponds to the simulation where all developing countries sign bilateral agreements with the Quad-plus countries; and *BILAT* corresponds to the simulation where the bilateral agreements are signed individually. Results reflect unweighted regional averages.

Source: World Bank simulations with the Linkage model and GTAP release 6.04.

their eyes wide open. The lessons of this study (and others before it[4]) are that, much as with unilateral or multilateral policies, design and implementation determine the ultimate effects. It is important to use trade policy to leverage domestic reforms that promote growth. For South-South agreements, it is essential that the focus be on some combination of full trade liberalization behind low external border protection, greater services deregulation and competition, and proactive trade facilitation measures that together positively affect both intra- and extra-regional trade.

High-Income Countries and Development

High-income countries, in order to realize their broad development objectives, must intensify their efforts to realize the development promise of the Doha Agenda. This has the potential to open up trade, particularly in agriculture, in a way that would benefit low-income groups around the world. Because the high-income countries are the large

players in the system, they have a special interest in—and responsibility for—using effective multilateral reforms to discipline the discretionary aspects of the regional agreements.

Allowing developing countries to concentrate scarce negotiating resources on the multilateral agenda may require that high-income countries decelerate their efforts at expanding RTAs. Irrespective of the pace of new agreements, high-income countries could consider the following rules of thumb when designing agreements to promote development. First, reducing the extensive exclusions for agriculture would transfer the income gains to rural areas in participating developing countries. Second, adopting more common and nonrestrictive rules of origin across agreements would reduce the administrative barriers that often undermine agreements and that increase the burden on customs administration. Third, working with prospective partners to ensure that new regulations regarding investment and intellectual property are appropriate to the level of development would reduce risks of undue enforcement costs. Finally, providing trade-related technical assistance, not only in the implementation phase but also in the negotiating phase, would promote greater liberalization of services and lower MFN tariffs.

Acting Collectively to Mute the Effects of Discrimination

To minimize the discriminatory effects of RTAs at the multilateral level, all countries must assume greater responsibility for maintaining the multilateral system. The international community, working through the WTO, should revisit Article V of its charter. If the stated disciplines cannot be enforced in the near term for collective political reasons, then increasing transparency and information should become a priority. At present, the WTO collects little if any information updating specific provisions, their implementation, and the trade consequences. It even fails to take advantage of extant public monitoring efforts in specific regions, which could inform their data collection effort. Collecting and publishing specific information on RTAs would allow members that find themselves excluded to challenge these agreements in the court of public opinion. Even the more modest goal of transparency will require building a new consensus and providing the staff of the WTO with more resources than they have currently available.

Nonetheless, WTO members should consider enhancing the existing rules to ensure that regional agreements have positive development and systemic outcomes. This could include (based on a modest tightening of current practice) setting quantitative indicators that define "substantially all trade." It could include efforts to simplify and harmonize the rules of origin that are applied to both developed and developing countries. These items are on the Doha Agenda and may be ready for action.

Organization of This Study

As is customary, chapter 1 of this study presents the World Bank's view of the global economy. The short-term section analyzes the main forces shaping the global outlook and the implications for developing countries; the long-term analysis focuses on structural changes in the global economy that will affect poverty rates and the prospects for attaining the Millennium Development Goals. A novel feature of this year's report is the introduction of a companion online feature (see www.worldbank.org/prospects), where the reader can find additional information on regional trends and commodity prices, and tools to design scenarios to his or her own specifications.

Chapter 2 introduces the issues associated with regional trade agreements and provides an overview of regional trading trends. Subsequent chapters focus on the content and consequences of regional agreements for trade creation (chapter 3), trade facilitation (chapter 4), and services, investment, intellectual property rights, and labor mobility (chapter 5). Chapter 6 returns to the issue of making regional agreements more compatible with a nondiscriminatory multilateral system.

Notes

1. Negotiated as bilateral or multicountry treaties, regional trade agreements grant members assured preferential market access, usually at zero tariffs for eligible products. Following WTO convention, the term "regional trade agreement" includes both reciprocal bilateral free trade or customs areas and multicountry (plurilateral) agreements. These are distinct from nonreciprocal voluntary agreements, such as the generalized system of preferences (GSP). Also, for statistical purposes, unless otherwise noted, intra-EU trade is excluded from quantitative trade analysis. The EU is defined as including the 15 countries that belonged to the union before its enlargement in 2004.

2. See Devlin and Estevadeordal (2004) and Schiff and Winters (2003), among others.

3. See Robert Lawrence (1997), who develops the idea of subsidiarity as applied to regional agreements.

4. See Schiff and Winters (2003).

References

Devlin, Robert and Antoni Estevadeordal. 2004. Trade and Cooperation: A Regional Public Goods Approach. In *Regional Public Goods: From Theory to Practice,* eds. A. Estevadeordal, Brian Frantz, and Tam Robert Nguyen. Washington, DC: Inter-American Development Bank.

Lawrence, Robert. 1997. Preferential Trading Arrangements: The Traditional and the New. In *Regional Partners in Global Markets: Limits and Possibilities of the Euro-Med Agreements,* eds. A. Galal and B. Hoekman. London: Center for Economic Policy Research/Egyptian Center for Economic Studies.

Martin, W., and F. Ng. 2004. Sources of Tariff Reductions. Background paper.

Schiff, Maurice, and L. Alan Winters. 2003. *Regional Integration and Development.* Washington, DC: World Bank.

Abbreviations

ACP	African Caribbean and Pacific states
ACPEU	African Caribbean and Pacific states European Union
AFTA	ASEAN Free Trade Area
AGOA	African Growth and Opportunity Act
ANZCERTA	Australia-New Zealand Closer Economic Relations Trade Agreement
APEC	Asia Pacific Economic Cooperation
ASEAN	Association of Southeast Asian Nations
BITS	Bilateral investment treaties
CAFTA	Central America Free Trade Agreement
CARICOM	Caribbean Community
CEC	Commission for Environmental Cooperation
CEMAC	Economic and Monetary Community of Central Africa
CEPR	Center for Economic and Policy Research
CGE	Computable general equilibrium
CIS	Commonwealth of Independent States
COMESA	Common Market for Eastern and Southern Africa
CRTA	Committee on Regional Trade Agreement
EAC	East African Community
EBA	Everything but arms
EC	European Community
ECO	Economic Cooperation Organization
ECOWAS	Economic Community of West African States
EEC	European Economic Community
EFTA	European Free Trade Association
EPAs	Economic Partnership Agreements
EU	European Union
FDI	Foreign direct investment

FTAA	Free Trade Area of the Americas
GAO	General Accounting Office
GATS	General Agreement on Trade in Services
GATT	General Agreement on Tariffs and Trade
GCC	Gulf Cooperation Council
GDP	Gross domestic product
GSP	Generalized System of Preferences
GTAP	Global Trade Analysis Project
HS	Harmonized system
IDB	Inter-American Development Bank
IFC	International Finance Corporation
IISD	International Institute for Sustainable Development
IMF	International Monetary Fund
INS	Immigration and Naturalization Services
IOM	International Organization for Migration
IPR	Intellectual Property Rights
IRCA	Immigration and Regularization Control Act
IRPA	Immigration and Refugee Protection Act
LAFTA	Latin America Free Trade Area
LDCs	Least developed countries
MDGs	Millennium Development Goals
MERCOSUR	Southern Lone Common Market
MFN	Most favored nation
MRA	Mutual recognition agreement
NAFTA	North America Free Trade Agreement
NBER	National Bureau of Economic Research
OECD	Organisation for Economic Co-operation and Development
PRSP	Poverty Reduction Strategy Paper
PTAs	Preferential trade agreements
RTAs	Regional trade agreements
SAARC	South Asia Association for Regional Cooperation
SACU	South African Customs Union
SAD	Single administrative document
SADC	Southern African Development Community
SAPP	Southern African Power Pool
SAFTA	South Asian Free Trade Area
SAPTA	South Asia Preferential Trade Agreement
SPS	Sanitary and phyto-sanitary standards

TBT	Technical barriers to trade
TFP	Total factor productivity
TRIM	Trade-related investment measures
TRIPS	Trade-related aspects of intellectual property rights
TTF	Transport and trade facilitation
UEMOA/WAEMU	West African Economic and Monetary Union
UNCTAD	United Nations Conference for Trade and Development
UNESCAP	United Nations Economic and Social Commission for Asia and the Pacific
USAID	United States Agency for International Development
USTR	United States Trade Representative
WCO	World Customs Organization
WIPO	World Intellectual Property Organization
WTO	World Trade Organization

Frequently Cited Regional Trading Agreements and the Parties to Them

Agreement	Full name	Members
AFTA	ASEAN Free Trade Area	Brunei, Darussalam, Cambodia, Indonesia, Lao People's Democratic Republic, Malaysia, Myanmar, Philippines, Singapore, Thailand, Vietnam
APEC	Asia Pacific Economic Cooperation	Australia, Brunei, Canada, Chile, China, Hong Kong (China), Indonesia, Japan, Korea, Malaysia, Mexico, New Zealand, Papua New Guinea, Peru, Philippines, Russia, Singapore, Taiwan (China), Thailand, United States, Vietnam
CACM	Central American Common Market	Costa Rica, El Salvador, Guatemala, Honduras, Nicaragua
CAFTA	Central America Free Trade Area	United States, Costa Rica, El Salvador, Guatemala, Honduras, Nicaragua, Dominican Republic
CAN	Andean Community	Bolivia, Colombia, Ecuador, Peru, República Bolivariana de Venezuela
CARICOM	Caribbean Community and Common Market	Antigua and Barbuda, Bahamas, Barbados, Belize, Dominica, Grenada, Guyana, Haiti, Jamaica, Monserrat, Trinidad and Tobago, St. Kitts and Nevis, St. Lucia, St. Vincent and the Grenadines, Suriname
CEFTA	Central European Free Trade Agreement	Bulgaria, Czech Republic, Hungary, Poland, Romania, Slovak Republic, Slovenia
CEMAC	Economic and Monetary Community of Central Africa	Cameroon, Central African Republic, Chad, Republic of Congo, Equatorial Guinea, Gabon
CER (ANZCERTA)	Closer Economic Relations Trade Agreement	Australia, New Zealand

Agreement	Full name	Members
CIS	Commonwealth of Independent States	Azerbaijan, Armenia, Belarus, Georgia, Moldova, Kazakhstan, Russian Federation, Ukraine, Uzbekistan, Tajikistan, Kyrgyz Republic
COMESA	Common Market for Eastern and Southern Africa	Angola, Burundi, Comoros, Democratic Republic of Congo, Djibouti, Arab Republic of Egypt, Eritrea, Ethiopia, Kenya, Madagascar, Malawi, Mauritius, Namibia, Rwanda, Seychelles, Sudan, Swaziland, Uganda, Zambia, Zimbabwe
EAC	East African Community	Kenya, Tanzania, Uganda
ECOWAS	Economic Community of West African States	Benin, Burkina Faso, Cape Verde, Gambia, Ghana, Guinea, Guinea-Bissau, Côte d'Ivoire, Liberia, Mali, Niger, Nigeria, Senegal, Sierra Leone, Togo
EEA	European Economic Area	EU, Iceland, Liechtenstein, Norway
EFTA	European Free Trade Association	Iceland, Liechtenstein, Norway, Switzerland
EMFTA	Euro-Mediterranean Free Trade Area	EU, Algeria, Cyprus, Egypt, Israel, Jordan, Lebanon, Malta, Morocco, Syrian Arab Republic, Tunisia, Turkey, Palestinian Authority
FTAA	Free Trade Area of the Americas	Antigua and Barbuda, Argentina, Bahamas, Barbados, Belice, Bolivia, Brazil, Canada, Chile, Colombia, Costa Rica, Dominica, Dominican Republic, Ecuador, El Salvador, Grenada, Guatemala, Guyana, Haiti, Honduras, Jamaica, Mexico, Nicaragua, Panama, Paraguay, Peru, St. Kitts and Nevis, St. Lucia, St. Vincent and the Grenadines, Suriname, Trinidad and Tobago, United States, Uruguay, Venezuela
GAFTA	Greater Arab Free Trade Area	Bahrain, Egypt, Iraq, Jordan, Kuwait, Lebanon, Libya, Morocco, Oman, Palestine, Qatar, Saudi Arabia, Somalia, Sudan, Syria, Tunisia, United Arab Emirates, Yemen
GCC	Gulf Cooperation Council	Bahrain, Kuwait, Oman, Qatar, Saudi Arabia, United Arab Emirates
MERCOSUR	Southern Common Market	Argentina, Brazil, Paraguay, Uruguay
NAFTA	North American Free Trade Agreement	Canada, Mexico, United States
SACU	Southern African Customs Union	South Africa, Botswana, Lesotho, Swaziland, Namibia

SADC	Southern African Development Community	Angola, Botswana, Democratic Republic of Congo, Lesotho, Malawi, Mauritius, Mozambique, Namibia, South Africa, Swaziland, Seychelles, Tanzania, Zambia, Zimbabwe
SAFTA	South Asian Free Trade Area	Bangladesh, Bhutan, India, Maldives, Nepal, Pakistan, Sri Lanka
SAPTA	South Asian Preferential Trade Arrangement	Bangladesh, Bhutan, India, Maldives, Nepal, Pakistan, Sri Lanka
WAEMU	West African Economic and Monetary Union	Benin, Burkina Faso, Côte d'Ivoire, Guinea Bissau, Mali, Niger, Senegal, Togo

1

Global Outlook and the Developing Countries

World growth accelerated sharply in 2004, with GDP advancing an estimated 4 percent (table 1.1). All developing regions are now growing faster than their average growth rates of the 1980s and 1990s. The ongoing economic boom in China was a major factor, as were the surges in activity registered in Japan and the United States. The economic recovery was slower to take hold among European high-income countries, which contributed to the less marked increase in growth rates there. Meanwhile, very strong import demand—because of the torrid expansion in China and the continued tendency for domestic demand in the United States to substantially exceed production—contributed to an exceptional 10.2 percent increase in world trade volumes.

Economic growth is expected to slow in 2005 and 2006, expanding by 3.2 percent in each year. Several factors are likely to contribute to this more moderate pace of activity. First, the investment cycle in the United States has likely peaked, implying a slowdown in growth there.[1] Second, world demand has outstripped supply, resulting in substantial increases in oil and other commodity prices that have cut into incomes, moderating demand in many countries. Third, higher interest rates will slow investment growth as central banks continue shifting monetary policy from a loose to a more neutral stance. Fourth, the large fiscal impulse that has helped propel the U.S. economy in recent years will weaken in 2004—although the deficit will remain high; and in Europe, budgetary policy is expected to tighten as countries seek to regain control over deficits, which in many cases exceed Maastricht limits. Finally, efforts in China to bring growth down to a more sustainable pace should also contribute to weaker, but still strong, demand over the medium term.

Given this external environment and especially the less rapid expansion of trade, growth in most low- and middle-income countries is also expected to moderate but remain strong. The extent of the slowdown should be mitigated because of the far-reaching structural reforms carried out in many countries, which have contributed to recent gains in market share and economic growth. Recent efforts to reduce general government and current account deficits and to pay down debt should enable most developing countries to withstand the higher interest rates expected over the next few years without excessive adjustment costs. However, there is little room for complacency—especially for the more highly indebted countries.

These favorable prospects for the next two years represent a solid starting point for longer-term growth through 2015 and increase the likelihood that developing countries meet the Millennium Development Goals (MDGs). Improvements in macroeconomic fundamentals, enhanced structural flexibility, a stronger investment climate, and further progress toward reducing trade barriers should, if sustained, support the ability of developing

Table 1.1 The global outlook in summary

Percentage change from previous year, except interest rates and oil prices

	2002	2003	2004e	Forecast	
				2005	2006
Global Conditions					
World Trade Volume	3.7	5.5	10.2	8.4	7.8
Consumer Prices					
G-7 Countries[a,b]	1.0	1.6	1.7	1.4	1.2
United States	1.6	2.3	2.7	2.2	1.7
Commodity Prices (USD terms)					
Non-oil commodities	5.3	10.2	17.0	−3.1	−4.2
Oil Price (World Bank average)[c]	24.9	28.9	39.0	36.0	32.0
Oil price (percent change)	2.4	15.9	35.0	−7.7	−11.1
Manufactures unit export value[d]	−1.3	7.4	5.2	−0.8	−0.3
Interest Rates					
$, 6-month (percent)	1.8	1.2	1.6	3.5	4.7
€, 6-month (percent)	3.3	2.3	2.1	2.4	3.6
Real GDP growth[e]					
World	1.7	2.7	4.0	3.2	3.2
Memo item: World (PPP weights)[f]	2.9	3.9	4.9	4.2	4.1
High income	1.3	2.1	3.5	2.7	2.7
OECD Countries[g]	1.3	2.0	3.5	2.6	2.6
Euro Area	0.9	0.5	1.8	2.1	2.3
Japan	−0.3	2.5	4.3	1.8	1.6
United States	1.9	3.0	4.3	3.2	3.3
Non-OECD countries	2.2	3.1	5.9	4.6	4.4
Developing countries	3.4	5.2	6.1	5.4	5.1
East Asia and Pacific	6.7	7.9	7.8	7.1	6.6
Europe and Central Asia	4.6	5.9	7.0	5.6	5.0
Latin America and the Caribbean	−0.6	1.6	4.7	3.7	3.7
Middle East and North Africa	3.2	5.7	4.7	4.7	4.5
South Asia	4.6	7.5	6.0	6.3	6.0
Sub-Saharan Africa	3.1	3.0	3.2	3.6	3.7
Memorandum items					
Developing countries					
excluding transition countries	3.2	5.1	5.9	5.4	5.1
excluding China and India	2.1	3.8	5.4	4.6	4.3

Note: PPP = purchasing power parity; e = estimate.
a. Canada, France, Germany, Italy, Japan, the United Kingdom, and the United States.
b. In local currency, aggregated using 1995 GDP weights.
c. The World Bank average is the unweighted mean of one barrel of West Texas Intermediate, Brent, and Dubai oil.
d. Unit value index of manufactured exports from major economies, expressed in U.S. dollars.
e. GDP in constant dollars at 1995 prices and market exchange rates.
f. GDP measured at 1995 PPP weights.
g. Now excludes the Republic of Korea, which has been reclassified as high-income OECD.
Source: World Bank.

countries to achieve rapid and sustained per capita growth at a level of 3.5 percent per annum between 2006 and 2015—double the growth rate of the 1990s. Such growth would enable many developing countries to halve the incidence of extreme poverty by 2015, which is a key development goal. However, even if the higher growth of recent periods were sustained, some regions, notably Sub-Saharan Africa, will fail to reduce poverty to this degree. In Sub-Saharan Africa, per capita growth has been slow, and progress to reduce poverty has been minimal. It would take implausibly high growth rates during the next 10 years to achieve the poverty target along with substantial enhancements to pro-poor policies and significantly more assistance. Finally, even if many regions are expected to achieve the MDG to reduce poverty, many are off track for reaching other important MDGs, such as reducing child and maternal mortality. In many cases economic growth is not enough. A more targeted approach and a realignment of spending priorities are also necessary.

Despite the relatively positive picture for both medium- and long-term prospects, downside risks are ever present and could have negative impacts in the near future and in the long term. An additional rise in oil prices, or a failure of them to moderate, could further restrain global demand and reduce incomes in most less developed countries. While oil prices are expected to decline from present highs, especially given substantial efforts to increase supply by oil exporting countries, existing demand conditions are such that a significant increase cannot be ruled out. Such a rise would have important negative effects on all oil-importing economies, particularly those of low- and middle-income countries that face current account constraints. For these countries, difficulties accessing international finance mean that they cannot absorb the increased costs associated with higher oil prices by increasing their current account deficit. Instead, the additional costs must be accommodated by lower imports, consumption, and investment volumes—implying a significant real-side adjustment. For the most vulnerable of such countries, an additional $10 a barrel increase in oil prices could reduce domestic incomes by as much as 4 percent. On average, incomes of oil-importing low-income countries would fall by about 1 percent of GDP.

Financing requirements of the U.S. current account and government deficits, and renewed downward pressure on the dollar, may cause long-term interest rates to rise more than forecasted. If interest rates rise, short- to medium-term impacts might include a slowing in world economic growth, sharply increased financing costs, and economic hardship for heavily indebted countries. Increased financial-market turbulence might also ensue—especially for those developing countries most exposed to the U.S. dollar. Over the medium- to long-term,

failure to rein in the U.S. budget deficit, which would also tend to reduce its current account deficit, could result in an ever increasing stock of dollar-denominated debt and rising future financing burdens. Moreover, higher interest rates would depress investment levels, provoking a prolonged slowing in the rate of increase of potential output. All of these factors heighten the risk of a resurgence in protectionist sentiment, which would thwart the pace at which developing countries are able to achieve their poverty reduction objectives.

Finally, if current efforts to slow the unsustainable pace of growth in China fail, major disruptions could result. Currently, investment levels may be unsustainably high, and there are some signs that rapidly rising food-price increases are feeding into production costs, which could ultimately choke off competitiveness, (although for the moment there are no clear indications that this is happening). Either problem could provoke a much more abrupt slowdown than described in the baseline. Given China's growing importance as a driver of world trade growth, such a sharp slowdown could have a significant damping effect on global economic activity, particularly among China's major trading partners.

The Global Economy: From Recovery to Expansion

The world economy accelerated sharply in 2004, expanding by an estimated 4 percent (figure 1.1). The United States and Japan, whose economies grew by more than 4 percent, continued to lead Europe in the recovery. Even stronger growth was experienced by a number of large developing countries, notably China (8.8 percent), Russia (8.0 percent), and India (6.0 percent). Their performance helped power developing countries as a whole to an anticipated 6.1 percent growth rate in 2004—an expansion without precedent over the past 30 years. Moreover, it marks a second year of very strong growth, and it may be the first time that recovery in developing countries preceded, rather than followed, recovery in high-income

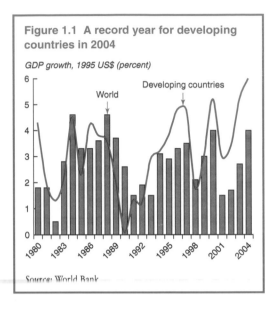

Figure 1.1 A record year for developing countries in 2004

GDP growth, 1995 US$ (percent)

Source: World Bank

countries. In contrast to the United States, where the surge was initially led by investment and household consumption, exports were the main source of growth in Europe and Japan—and much of the increase in external demand came from developing countries.

Across the developing world virtually every region enjoyed solid growth, and rapidly rising trade volumes played an important role. Even excluding China, India, and Russia, economic activity in developing countries is expected to have risen 5 percent in 2004. While easy credit contributed to China's remarkable performance, the benefits of WTO accession were also a major factor, and the increase of over 30 percent in Chinese import demand helped underpin growth among neighboring East Asian countries. Russia and the oil-producing countries in the Middle East and North Africa Region benefited from very strong oil revenues, which were reflected in strong import demand and the solid export performance of their trading partners. Increasing market shares, following substantial inward investment flows associated with the accession of many of the Europe and Central Asian Region's members to the EU, also contributed to these positive outcomes. Elsewhere, a strong cyclical recovery

is under way in Latin America, and there are signs of a more modest recovery in Sub-Saharan Africa.

Growth should moderate in 2005 and 2006, led by a slowing of the expansion among developed countries. In the United States, as the output gap closes, productivity growth is projected to slow and unit labor costs to rise; these factors, in addition to external inflationary pressures from commodity prices, likely reflect the Fed's decision to tighten monetary conditions. This, plus the maturation of the investment cycle, a tailing off of fiscal stimulus, and the impact of higher oil costs, will contribute to slowing growth. Similar factors explain the anticipated slowdown in Japan, where output is expected to increase at about trend rates. In contrast, because of its later start and the fact that investment is only now beginning to recover, Europe's growth is expected to continue gaining momentum through 2005 and into 2006, notwithstanding fiscal tightening and a slowdown in the rate of growth of world demand. Overall estimates suggest that the hike in oil prices already observed can be expected to dampen output in 2005 by about 0.5 percent of GDP.

Moderating growth in the OECD economies and a soft landing in China should translate into slower but still buoyant growth in developing countries (figure 1.2).

- In *East Asia*, efforts to stem the flow of credits into selected sectors of the Chinese economy are already having observable effects (figure 1.2a). The growth of imports of raw materials such as steel, copper, and various ores have moderated significantly in recent months. Steel imports have collapsed, although iron ore import volumes were growing by more than 25 percent (year/year) in September. However, there are indications that consumption demand continues to grow rapidly, and the Chinese authorities report that GDP increased 9.1 percent in the third quarter. The baseline forecast predicts that a soft landing (growth slowing to 7.1 percent by 2006) will be

Figure 1.2 Strong growth across most regions

a. East Asia and Pacific

Growth of real GDP (percent)

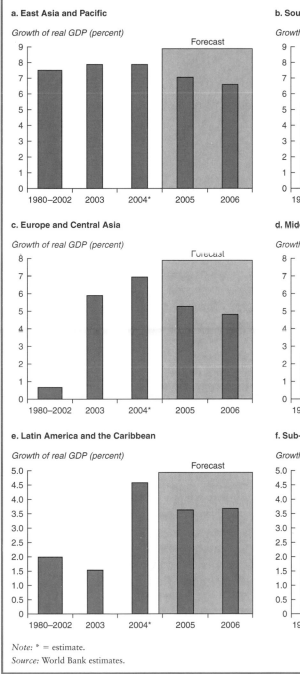

b. South Asia

Growth of real GDP (percent)

c. Europe and Central Asia

Growth of real GDP (percent)

d. Middle East and North Africa

Growth of real GDP (percent)

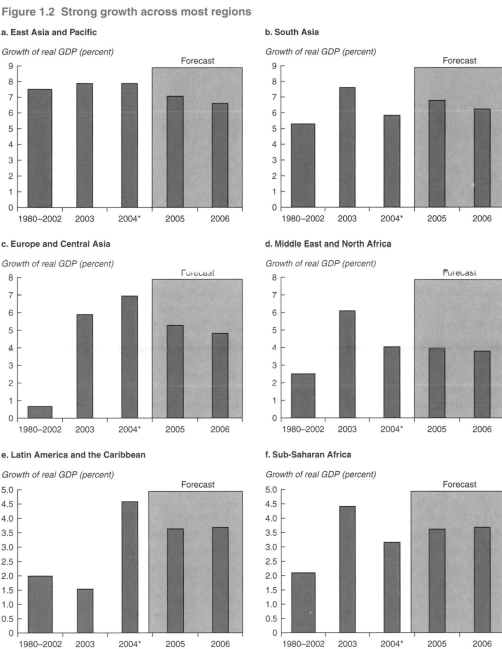

e. Latin America and the Caribbean

Growth of real GDP (percent)

f. Sub-Saharan Africa

Growth of real GDP (percent)

Note: * = estimate.
Source: World Bank estimates.

achieved and will contribute to slowing throughout the region.

- In *South Asia,* despite the moderation of the Chinese and OECD economies, growth is expected to accelerate in 2005, reflecting the enduring impacts of structural reforms, market opening, and stronger domestic demand as the dampening impact of last year's poor crop fades. As agricultural production and related incomes return to trend growth rates in 2006, GDP growth is projected to moderate somewhat.

- Output in *Europe and Central Asia* is forecast to remain strong, with still-high oil prices supporting demand in Russia and the exports of its trading partners. Central and Eastern European countries will continue to benefit from rapid investment growth following the EU accession of some of their members. However, policymakers need to prepare for the next downturn by pursuing fiscal consolidation to reduce worryingly high government and, in some cases, current account deficits.

- Growth in the *Middle East and North Africa* region is expected to remain robust, but well below the highs observed in 2003, which were boosted by sharp increases in oil production. All countries, but especially those of the Maghreb, should benefit from the strengthening export demand emanating from Western Europe; but consumption demand, reflecting still high oil incomes, will continue to be the main source of growth for the region as a whole.

- The return to growth in *Latin America and the Caribbean* is projected to continue, with only Argentina experiencing a significant slowdown as the competitive advantage from its depreciation in 2002 wears off. Elsewhere, growth should remain strong, with Brazil expanding steadily at between 3.7 and 3.9 percent. Because Latin America and the Caribbean is a heavily indebted region, outturns will ultimately depend on the success with which policymakers deal with rising interest rates

and higher payments on debt (see the risks section in this chapter). Here, country-specific conditions and the degree to which fiscal consolidation programs are maintained will play an important role.

- *Sub-Saharan Africa* will also benefit from the revival in Europe, its main trading partner, but many oil-importing countries in Africa remain vulnerable due to high oil prices. Notwithstanding substantially improved performance, growth in the region will continue to lag the rest of the world by a significant margin, implying a further widening of income gaps. Moreover, the terms of trade appear to be turning against this region as non-oil commodity prices are expected to ease. Although additional development aid and debt relief would help, continued efforts to improve fundamentals and the efficiency of public expenditure are also required to speed the pace at which these countries achieve their poverty-reduction objectives.

Commodity Markets

Strong world demand and supply shortages were responsible for commodity prices rebounding sharply during the global recovery (figure 1.3). In dollar terms, metals and minerals

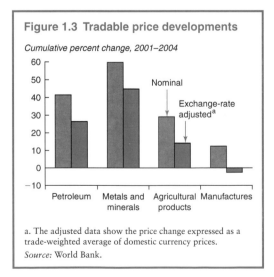

Figure 1.3 Tradable price developments

Cumulative percent change, 2001–2004

a. The adjusted data show the price change expressed as a trade-weighted average of domestic currency prices.
Source: World Bank.

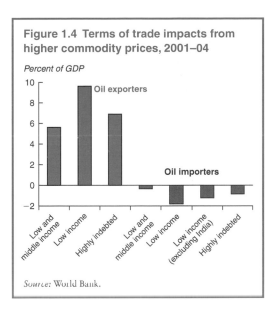

Figure 1.4 Terms of trade impacts from higher commodity prices, 2001–04

Percent of GDP

Source: World Bank.

prices have increased the most since 2001 (up almost 60 percent), but the 40 percent hike in petroleum prices has had the largest economic effect. In domestic currency terms, the impact of these price hikes was less important for many countries because of the 15 percent depreciation[2] of the dollar over the same period.

Higher commodity prices since 2001 have boosted incomes of low- and middle-income countries as a whole by an estimated 1.1 percent of GDP. However, virtually all of the gain accrued to low- and middle-income oil exporters. Most developing country oil importers suffered net terms of trade losses (figure 1.4). The major beneficiaries were the Middle East and North Africa, Europe and Central Asia, and Latin America and the Caribbean Regions—all of which include major oil exporters. In contrast, the net gains from non-oil commodity prices for low-income countries were modest or even negative. This is partly because most of the non-oil commodity price gains were concentrated in metals and minerals prices, which restricted the benefits to a few resource-rich countries. Moreover, many industrializing low-income countries, notably India and Pakistan, are now net commodity importers. The terms-of-trade impact on incomes of oil exporting

developing countries was 5.6 percent of GDP, whereas for oil importers the impact was a loss of 0.3 percent.

For the poorest oil-importing countries, high oil prices have dramatically exacerbated already serious poverty. Many of these countries remain particularly vulnerable to high oil prices. Even before the oil price hikes, a number of these countries were spending more than 5 percent of GDP to cover oil imports. The unweighted average of West-Texas Intermediate, Brent, and Dubai crude oils is estimated to have been $39 in 2004.[3] At this level, it is estimated that as many as seven countries will have oil-import bills in excess of 10 percent of GDP; these countries would be forced to make substantial cuts in spending elsewhere in their economies to compensate for the additional burden (figure 1.5). Indeed, for the poorest countries the net additional burden in 2004 is expected to consume 75 percent of the World Bank funding they receive for all development programs, and

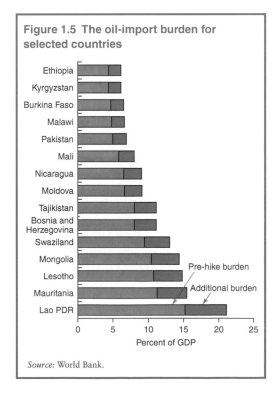

Figure 1.5 The oil-import burden for selected countries

Percent of GDP

Source: World Bank.

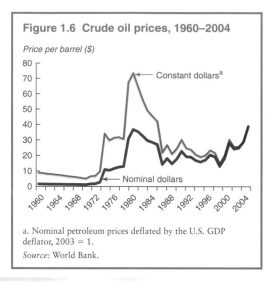

Figure 1.6 Crude oil prices, 1960–2004

Price per barrel ($)

a. Nominal petroleum prices deflated by the U.S. GDP deflator, 2003 = 1.

Source: World Bank.

localized disruptions in production (figure 1.6). Indeed, OPEC excess capacity is estimated to have fallen from 4.6 million barrels per day in 2001 to only 1.4 million barrels per day in 2004. Moreover, oil prices remain well below past peaks. Corrected for inflation and expressed in 2003 dollars, oil prices averaged more than $72 in 1980, and actually reached more than $100 in November of the previous year. Viewed from this perspective, further hikes would not be unprecedented.

World Trade

World trade growth averaged 10.2 percent in 2004, reflecting rapid increases in industrial production and investment activity (figure 1.7). The expansion in trade volumes in 2004 is reminiscent of the increase observed in 2000 and mirrors the rapid recovery in industrial production that began to take shape in the second half of 2003 and continued into 2004. More than 20 percent of the increase in world merchandise trade volumes was represented by China, whose imports increased by 32 percent—reflecting both the positive impact of its accession to the WTO and unsustainable rates of investment and consumption demand.

12 percent of all the bilateral aid they receive. To keep development projects on track, high-income countries will need to increase commitments substantially—at least as long as high oil prices continue.

Although a substantial rise in oil prices is not the most likely scenario, given new sources of supply and reduced oil intensities in the world economy, there remains considerable scope for higher oil prices, particularly given the current sensitivity of oil markets to

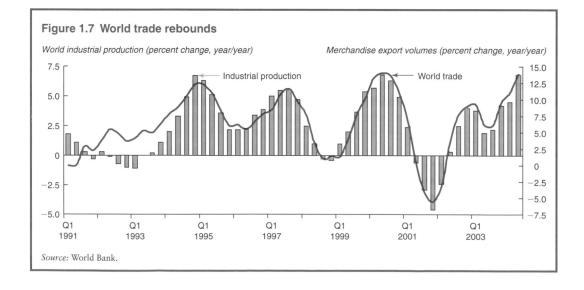

Figure 1.7 World trade rebounds

World industrial production (percent change, year/year)　　　　Merchandise export volumes (percent change, year/year)

Source: World Bank.

Trade in raw materials and investment goods was particularly strong. As discussed above, robust demand for raw materials was an important factor underlying the trade expansion in a number of developing countries. In particular, oil, steel, and minerals trade was strongly influenced by the rapid increase in Chinese manufacturing and construction sectors. Similarly, fast-growing global investment expenditures were particularly important in spurring export demand in countries such as Germany and Japan that specialize in the fabrication of machinery and other physical capital.

As a whole, developing countries have grown their share in world markets by about 19 percent (figure 1.8), up from 19 to 23 percent since 2000. Much of this rise is attributed to China, which has seen its share in world exports double from 2.9 to 5.8 percent between 2000 and 2004. Excluding China, the improvement in the export share of low- and middle-income countries has been more modest (from 16 to 17 percent), although developing countries in the South Asia and Europe and Central Asia regions have increased their market shares considerably. Other regions either maintained their market share (the rest of the Eastern Asia and Pacific and the Middle

East and North Africa) or lost market share (Sub-Saharan Africa and Latin America and the Caribbean).

Within regions the performance of specific countries continues to be dictated, in part, by domestic factors. So notwithstanding very strong Chinese import demand, exports in the rest of East Asia failed to increase as quickly, partly because political instability held back industrial and investment activity in the Philippines and Indonesia. In Latin American and the Caribbean, export volumes in Brazil and Argentina grew briskly under the continued influence of currency devaluations 2 years ago, while strong world demand for metals and minerals gave special impetus to Chilean exports.

Slower activity throughout the global economy should translate into less rapid trade expansion in 2005 and 2006. Trade in goods and nonfactor services is forecast to expand by about 8.5 percent in 2005, down from an estimated 10 percent in 2004. Much of the deceleration is conditional on the success of efforts to dampen the pace of activity in China, which should be reflected in slower import growth in China and slower exports among its trading partners. Looking to other regions, the easing of activity in the United States, coupled with broadly stable growth in Europe, is expected to result in a somewhat more pronounced deceleration of trade volumes in Latin America as compared with Africa, the Middle East, and Eastern European areas.

Major imbalances in the world trading environment persisted during 2004 and will likely continue to play a large role in 2005–06 (figure 1.9). Notwithstanding the sharp acceleration in world import volumes, the U.S. current account deficit reached 5.7 percent of GDP in the second quarter of 2004, as American consumption and investment volumes exceeded domestic production by a wide margin (higher oil prices represented 0.6 percentage points of the 1.4 percentage point deterioration in the current account since the first quarter of 2002). The expansion in the trade deficit since the mid-1990s has been the main

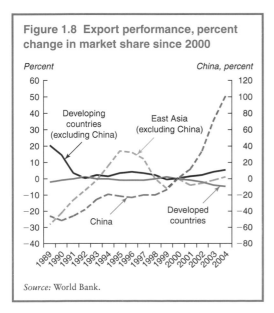

Figure 1.8 Export performance, percent change in market share since 2000

Source: World Bank.

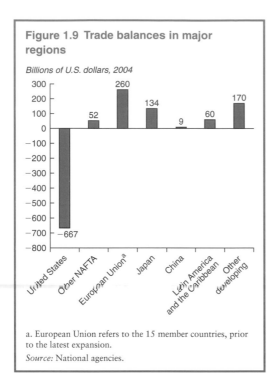

Figure 1.9 Trade balances in major regions

Billions of U.S. dollars, 2004

a. European Union refers to the 15 member countries, prior to the latest expansion.

Source: National agencies.

factor behind the rise in the U.S. current account deficit—itself a major factor behind the 15 percent real effective depreciation of the currency since February 2002. Barring a substantial increase in domestic savings by, for example, a tightening of fiscal policy, downward pressure on the U.S. dollar is likely to resume as U.S. foreign borrowing requirements remain high, and the already large amounts of external debt continue to accumulate (see, for example, Bergsten and Williamson 2004).

The U.S. trade deficit is largely a homegrown problem. While bilateral trade deficits with specific countries are large, notably with respect to China, the fact that these countries have only small overall surpluses supports the view that the deficit with the United States is more a reflection of U.S. trade patterns than an indication of unfair trading practices. For example, China's large bilateral surplus with the United States (but very small global surplus) reflects its specialization in the production of final consumption goods (sold to the United States) based on intermediate and primary

imports from other developing countries with whom China has a cumulatively large trade deficit (Lau 2003).[4]

Failure to address the twin U.S. deficits could have significant impacts on developing countries, especially if that failure leads to an increase in protectionist behavior. This is especially relevant because the substantial improvements in living standards, wages, and incomes in many upper-lower and middle-income countries have been the result of expanding their world market share in manufactures. An increase in protectionism could halt these countries' progress and deny other poor countries the same avenue to development. Moreover, a retreat from recent efforts to reduce trade barriers or a failure to make further progress—especially concerning agricultural subsidies—could have substantial negative consequences on many of the world's poorest countries.

International Finance

Over the past several years, favorable global conditions, strong growth, rapidly expanding trade, and domestic reforms (including lower fiscal deficits and inflation) have allowed developing countries to substantially improve their financial positions (figure 1.10).

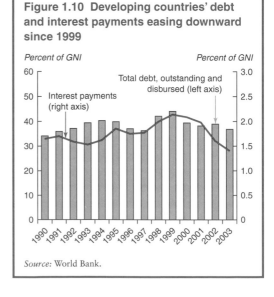

Figure 1.10 Developing countries' debt and interest payments easing downward since 1999

Percent of GNI   *Percent of GNI*

Source: World Bank.

On average, their debt to GNI ratio has fallen from 44 to 37 percent since its peak in 1999. This progress, plus low interest rates and strong growth, has substantially lowered the debt-servicing burden for most countries. While the situation of the most heavily in-debted countries remains serious, they have made the greatest gains—debt to GDP ratios for these countries are down from 161 to 86 percent since 1994—partly because of debt-relief programs instituted over this period.

These favorable conditions have also allowed many countries to strengthen their ex-ternal position. Most countries have succeeded in improving their structural positions so that, even in the face of higher oil prices or a more moderate pace for growth, their current ac-count positions should not deteriorate to the point where financing becomes problematic. As a whole, the current account position of the major groups of developing countries is close to balance or in surplus (table 1.2).

Developing countries have become major sources of international capital. Since 2000, the central banks of some of the largest developing countries have increased their foreign reserves by more than 80 percent. Taken as a group, the re-serves of Brazil, China, India, Mexico, Thailand, and Turkey now represent over 45 percent of de-veloping country reserves. Indeed, following

Table 1.2 Current account balances

Percent of GDP in 2004

East Asia and Pacific	1.5
South Asia	−0.5
Middle East and North Africa	14.4
Sub-Saharan Africa	1.3
Europe and Central Asia	0.1
Latin America and the Caribbean	0.7
High-income countries	−0.8

Source: World Bank estimates.

private investors' retreat from equity and bond investments in U.S. dollar-denominated assets,[5] the central banks of these countries have become one of the most important sources of financing for the large U.S. current account deficit, absorb-ing 51 percent of the overall increase in foreign officially-held U.S. treasury bills between March 2000 and January 2003. While this has allowed these countries to increase their reserves by a sub-stantial margin, it has been achieved at the ex-pense of increasing their exposure to the U.S. dol-lar (figure 1.11). Among these countries, the share of U.S. treasury bills in their official re-serves has increased by as much as 20 percentage points and equals almost 70 percent in the case of Mexico, and 58 percent in China. Should these countries decide to rebalance their reserve port-folio by slowing the pace at which they accumu-late dollar-denominated reserves, either

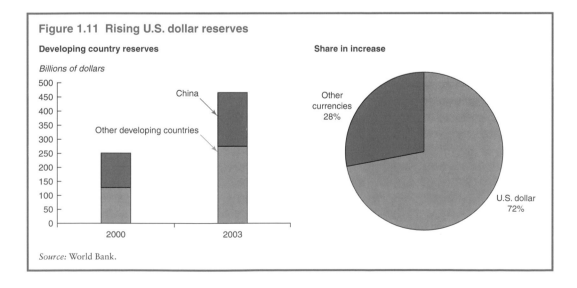

Figure 1.11 Rising U.S. dollar reserves

Developing country reserves

Share in increase

Source: World Bank.

downward pressures on the dollar will accentu- ate, or interest rates will have to rise in order to attract sufficient private capital inflow.

Notwithstanding robust aggregate perfor- mance, many countries have been less successful in reaping the benefits of the last few years of strong economic conditions, and their high current account deficits could im- peril their stability—especially in the context of slower growth in trade and world economic activity. More than 50 developing countries have current account deficits that exceed 5 percent of GDP. As a result, even the moder- ate hikes in interest rates, deterioration in terms of trade, and the slower export demand projected in the baseline will likely require these countries to undergo significant cuts to imports and domestic consumption in order to maintain external stability. If trade growth were to slow more than currently predicted, or if terms of trade were to deteriorate more be- cause of an additional hike in oil prices, the re- quired adjustment could be severe.

Risks and Policy Priorities

Forceful steps are required to reduce the twin deficits in the United States. As the preceding discussion has indicated, over the past few years, private sector equity and di- rect investment financing of the very large U.S. current account deficit has dried up,[6] having been replaced to a large extent by increased purchases of U.S. bonds by foreign central banks, notably those of developing countries. While these countries' build up of reserves has helped improve their external financial posi- tion, the stock of U.S. dollars that they now hold is very high and represents a dispropor- tionate share of their assets. It is not clear that they can or should increase these stocks fur- ther by continuing to absorb the lion's share of net new U.S. treasury bills (6 developing coun- tries absorbed more than half of net new issues since 2000).[7] Assuming their appetite for trea- suries wanes, downward pressure on the U.S. dollar is likely to re-emerge, and yields will

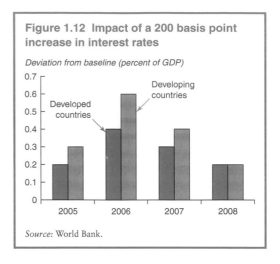

Figure 1.12 Impact of a 200 basis point increase in interest rates

Deviation from baseline (percent of GDP)

Source: World Bank.

probably have to rise in order to motivate private investors to re-enter the market.[8]

Simulations suggest that a 200 basis point in- crease in long-term interest rates could reduce world GDP over the short- to medium-term by about 0.5 percent per annum;[9] the impact would be somewhat stronger for developing countries, because higher rates will raise debt servicing burdens, which require additional cuts to spending and demand (figure 1.12). Over the longer term, if the twin deficits in the United States are not addressed (a tightening of fiscal policy would reduce both deficits by increasing U.S. savings[10]), the problem is likely to intensify. Permanently higher long-term interest rates would render a wide range of investment pro- jects uneconomic and slow the pace of potential output for a considerable time[11]— leading, per- haps, to a period of stagflation similar to that observed during the 1970–80s.

While higher U.S. interest rates might maintain investor interest in the dollar, they would have serious disruptive impacts on countries with large U.S. dollar debts. For countries such as Brazil, Indonesia, the Philip- pines, Poland, and Turkey, a 200 basis point increase in dollar interest rates would signifi- cantly increase debt-servicing charges. In- creased outflows could provoke large deprecia- tions in their currencies (as much as 9 percent), which would only increase the domestic burden of their external debt and generate further downward pressure on their currencies. Maintaining stability would, in all likelihood, require a substantial reduction in imports, consumption, and investment, which would result in slower growth and impede increases in poverty reduction.

The risk of such outcomes makes redressing imbalances all the more pressing. Among developed countries, steps need to be taken to reduce the U.S. government deficit, which would lower overall borrowing requirements and investor's concerns over the long-term financing of the debt. In Europe and other OECD countries, more resolute steps to redress government deficits and to create the fiscal room necessary to deal with the fiscal consequences of aging will be necessary if long-term interest rates are to remain low. For developing countries, a gradual appreciation of some currencies relative to the dollar could help by permitting a further depreciation of the dollar. However, in the absence of fiscal tightening in the United States, such measures are unlikely to have a significant impact. Fiscal consolidation is also required in many developing countries. Recent steps to lower existing government deficits move in the right direction and need to be pursued—as do efforts to reduce trade barriers so that export opportunities can increase. While these actions may well imply hardship and impose real political costs, the human and political consequences of entering into a period of higher interest rates without external and internal finances on a firm footing would be even more dramatic. Finally, funding for initiatives to relieve the debt burden of the poorest countries needs to be increased.

Should oil prices rise even further, the economies of low-income countries are likely to be among the hardest hit. Oil prices are assumed to moderate in the base case, falling from $39 per barrel (for the average of West-Texas Intermediate, Brent, and Dubai oils)[12] in 2004 to $32 in 2006. However, given supply and geopolitical conditions, there is a real risk that prices will either remain at current

levels ($46.8 in October 2004 for this average—$49.5 for Brent) or rise even further. Simulations suggest that were events to temporarily disrupt supply by about 1 million barrels per day, oil prices could be expected to increase by about $10 a barrel. In macroeconomic terms, such an increase would slow economic growth by about 0.5 percentage points in the following year.[13] However, the resulting terms of trade shock would be larger in many poorer countries (−2.4 percent of GDP for highly indebted poor oil-importing countries versus −0.2 percent of GDP for high-income countries) because of the relatively high share that energy represents in their imports. And such economies tend to be more sensitive to a given terms of trade shock because of their limited ability to attract capital flows that would offset any resulting increases in their trade deficits. In contrast to high-income countries, which can increase their external borrowing to offset the real-side impact of higher oil prices, low-income countries are obliged to absorb most of the shock immediately. As a result, they undergo a depreciation and substantial reductions in consumption and investment spending—adjustment mechanisms that ultimately reduce spending on imports by almost the entire amount of the increased oil bill (figure 1.13). Their inability to defer adjustment (like high-income countries do) implies significant costs, both to individuals who see their consumption possibilities reduced and to the economy, as lower levels of investment feed through to reduce the capital stock and diminish productive capacity.

Finally, a failure of current efforts to slow the unsustainable pace of growth in China by engineering a soft landing could result in major disruptions. The Chinese authorities have put into place a number of specific—mainly command and control—measures, that restrict additional investment and lending to the construction and heavy production sectors. In the World Bank's forecast, this is projected to succeed in slowing overall growth

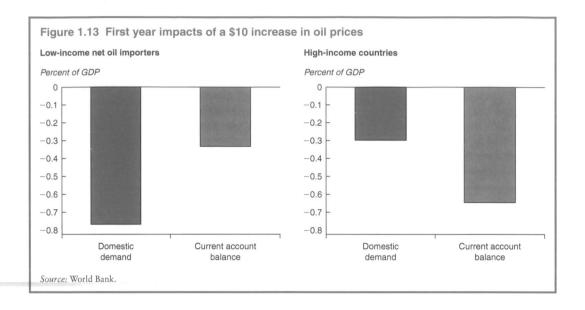

Figure 1.13 First year impacts of a $10 increase in oil prices

Source: World Bank.

to some 7.1 percent in 2006, down from an estimated 8.8 percent this year.

So far, these steps have slowed import demand in a number of sectors, notably metals and ores,[14] while credit restrictions have dramatically reduced the pace of money creation. In contrast, private consumption growth shows no sign of easing, and inflation has picked up rapidly. For the moment increased costs have not found their way into wages, but such a possibility cannot be ruled out. Should overheating contribute to further increases in inflation, a stronger policy response may be required. Moreover, investment levels remain very high, leaving open the possibility of a very rapid correction, especially if bad loans in the banking sector reveal themselves to be a serious problem. Either eventuality could provoke a more abrupt slowdown than forecast.

Long-Term Growth, Structural Change, and Poverty

This part of the report, as in years past, presents a long-term growth scenario for the global economy and its implications for meeting one of the MDGs: the halving of the

proportion of the population living on $1 or less a day by 2015 (compared to 1990 levels). The strong economic growth in developing countries over the last 2 to 3 years, which is expected to continue through 2006, albeit at a somewhat slower pace, is based on solid fundamentals that are likely to carry forward and contribute to long-term economic prospects. In our base scenario this leads to an annual growth of some 3.5 percent in per capita GDP between 2006 and 2015, and contributes to achieving the MDGs. The poverty MDG will be met on a global basis, but a large number of countries will not meet the goal, particularly those in Sub-Saharan Africa. And though growth is necessary to make progress toward achieving the MDGs, in most countries, growth is insufficient without more targeted policies.

At least four factors are responsible for the recent and prospective improvement in growth prospects. As outlined in the first section of this chapter, among the solid fundamental changes in developing countries is an improvement in macroeconomic conditions (e.g., inflation and indebtedness). The recent *World Development Report* stresses the importance of the investment climate, which has improved in many countries and has led to an acceleration in growth. A third factor, explored in more detail below, includes significant structural changes—that is, economic diversification and a move away from reliance on agriculture, and integration with the global economy; both of these structural changes involve increased urbanization. A fourth factor, pursued in greater detail in chapter 6, is the reduction in trade barriers.

The special focus of the long-term scenario in this report is on structural changes, particularly as they affect employment. Rapid growth will, in and of itself, lead to structural changes; that is, a relative decline in agriculture and a rise in the demand for services. Countries need to think ahead, allocate scarce public investment in a rational manner, and promote education to better position their work force for a changing environment. While structural changes are likely to be important, many developing countries face an equal challenge in the sheer growth of the labor force. Labor force growth rates are likely to decline over the next decade, but in many regions they will average between 1.5 to 2.5 percent per annum. For the poor, both growth and structural change are likely to be beneficial. Growth, to the extent that it lifts all incomes, will inevitably lead to a fall in poverty. Structural change can accelerate the process of poverty reduction. A decline in the rural population could ease wage pressures. A rising urban population provides easier access to essential health and education services and can lead to a rise in transfers to rural areas.

The focus on structural change also links to the broader theme of the report—the shape and impacts of regional trade agreements (RTAs). The RTAs will undoubtedly lead to additional structural shifts, and with associated transitional costs. How do RTAs compare with growth-induced structural shifts? Do RTAs produce structural shifts that are broadly consistent with those induced by a truly open global economy (which would emerge from a multilateral agreement)? And, if not, would the vested interests protected by an RTA impede progress toward a globally more beneficial agreement? These questions will be addressed in chapter 6. The conclusion from this chapter is that the challenge for most developing countries will be the creation of jobs for a rising work force, rather than how to deal with employment shifts across economic activities.

Long-term growth scenario

The global economy is currently rebounding from the downturn suffered in 2001 and 2002. Not all regions are benefiting equally from the rebound—Japan and the United States are leading the way among industrial economies—but there is fairly solid progress in all the main developing regions on an aggregate basis. This year, 2004, is likely to be the peak in the current upward cycle, with economies drifting toward long-term trend growth in 2005 and beyond. Table 1.3 reflects a plausible long-term scenario for the high-income countries and the World Bank's six aggregate developing regions (see box 1.1 for details concerning aggregation). The scenario reflects current views on potential trend growth over the 2006–15 decade. Better policies, an acceleration in investment, and other factors could improve the prospects, particularly for the slower growing regions. There is still a considerable gap in the productivity levels between developing and industrial economies, and a number of developing countries—particularly in Asia—have demonstrated, over the last 20 to 30 years, a sustained ability for rapid growth.

The focus of this forecast section this year is on anticipated structural changes. These have many dimensions—demographic, rural versus urban, sectoral, employment shifts, openness, and income distribution, among others. While most of these shifts have long-term positive impacts, they can also be associated with short-term transitional costs. Public policies can limit the costs of transition, but they can also be significantly reduced—at least in terms of duration—in a fast growing economy where job growth is robust.

Box 1.1   The aggregation paradox

The per capita growth rate for the world reflects the so-called aggregation paradox. The long-term per capita growth rates for high-income and developing countries are, respectively, 2.4 and 3.5 percent per annum, but the global growth rate is only 2.1 percent and is not the average of the growth rates (weighted or un-weighted). The following table highlights the aggregation paradox. The paradox is explained by the relatively high weight of high-income countries GDP in the world total, but their low weight in world population.

	High-income	Develop-ing	World
Population (million)			
2006	970	5,340	6,320
2015	990	5,900	6,900
Growth rate[a]	0.3	1.1	1.0
GDP ($billion)			
2006	31,200	8,200	39,400
2015	39,500	12,300	51,800
Growth rate[a]	2.7	4.6	3.1
GDP per capita ($)			
2006	32,090	1,530	6,240
2015	39,700	2,080	7,510
Growth rate[a]	2.4	3.5	2.1

a. Growth rates are percent per annum.

Structural Changes over Two Decades

Looking back on the last 20 years of development, many developing regions have already witnessed significant structural shifts. Perhaps foremost is the decline of agriculture as a source of income and employment. In East Asia and the Pacific, agricultural value added has declined from a 28 percent share in 1982 to only 15 percent in 2002, and manufacturing, other industrial, and services have risen (see figure 1.14). Services, according to these figures, still represented less than 40 percent of GDP in 2002, well below the nearly 65 percent share in the high-income countries of East Asia. Thus there is still significant scope for further structural shifts.

The value added shares also belie the relative employment share in agriculture, which tends to be much higher. Take, for example, Thailand, where agriculture's share of value added is below 10 percent, but still employs around 50 percent of the total labor force. In the high-income countries, the relevant shares are around 2 percent of value added and less than 4 percent of employment.[15] Higher agricultural productivity and relative wage differentials will continue to drive an exodus from agriculture into other sectors. And the change can come rapidly. In the Republic of Korea, the percent of employment in agriculture dropped from 32 percent in 1982 to 10 percent in 2001. The agricultural transformation is present in some of the other developing regions as well; for example, in South Asia the percent of employment in agriculture dropped from 40 percent in 1982 down to 27.2 percent in 2002, and in Latin America and the Caribbean, the percent of employment in agriculture dropped from 14.4 percent down to 10.6 percent over the same two-decade period. There has been no significant shift in either the Middle East and North Africa or Sub-Saharan Africa regions. At the same time, neither of those two regions witnessed much economic growth, with only 0.4 percent per capita growth per annum in the former, and a loss of 0.3 percent per annum in the latter.

In all regions, save East Asia, one can see a climb in the share of services. This is not surprising because services are assumed to be income elastic and a relative rise in the consumption share of services is understood. This effect is reinforced by the relatively high rate of productivity growth in manufacturing. All else being equal, this reduces the price of manufactures relative to services and hence enhances the value share of services. Perhaps what is more surprising is the variation across regions.

Table 1.3 Long-term prospects. Forecast growth of world GDP per capita

Real GDP per capita, annual average percentage change

	1980s	1990s	2000–06	2006–15
World total	1.3	1.1	1.6	2.1
High-income countries	2.5	1.8	1.7	2.4
OECD	2.5	1.7	1.7	2.3
United States	2.2	1.9	1.8	2.5
Japan	3.5	1.1	1.7	1.9
European Union	2.1	1.8	1.5	2.3
Non-OECD countries	3.5	4.1	1.6	3.5
Developing countries	0.6	1.5	3.4	3.5
East Asia and the Pacific	5.8	6.3	6.0	5.3
Europe and Central Asia	1.0	−1.8	5.2	3.5
Latin America & the Caribbean	−0.9	1.5	0.8	2.4
Middle East North Africa	−1.6	1.1	2.4	2.6
South Asia	3.3	3.2	4.2	4.1
Sub-Saharan Africa	−1.2	−0.5	1.2	1.6

Note: Aggregations are moving averages, reweighted annually after calculations of growth in constant prices.
Source: World Bank.

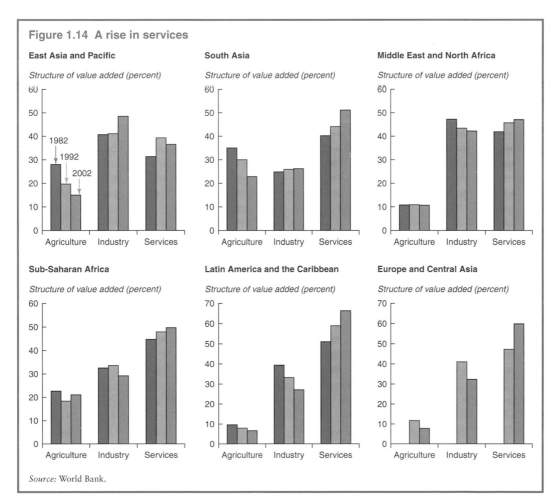

Figure 1.14 A rise in services

East Asia and Pacific

Structure of value added (percent)

1982, 1992, 2002

South Asia

Structure of value added (percent)

Middle East and North Africa

Structure of value added (percent)

Sub-Saharan Africa

Structure of value added (percent)

Latin America and the Caribbean

Structure of value added (percent)

Europe and Central Asia

Structure of value added (percent)

Source: World Bank.

In the high growth regions—East Asia and South Asia—there are two contrasting patterns. In South Asia the employment in agriculture shifted mostly to services, with a small increase in industrial output. In East Asia, employment in agriculture shifted more evenly between industry and services. And there appears to have been a structural break in the 1990s with an acceleration of industrial output. This is consistent with the sharp rise in the trade to GDP ratio doubling from 36 percent in 1982 to 72 percent in 2002, and with East Asia as a hub of assembly and manufacturing activities (see figure 1.15). There are, of course, exceptions in each region. The Philippines, for example, has a sharp rise in services and a decline in manufacturing—perhaps as a result of its regional comparative advantage in back office operations, call centers, and other services requiring specialized language skills. In South Asia, India's services dominate, but growth is much lower in Bangladesh and Pakistan, where textile and clothing exporters may be taking advantage of their relatively generous quotas to the main importing markets.

Three of the other regions—Latin America and the Caribbean, the Middle East and North Africa, and Sub-Saharan Africa—show less growth overall, but are also more dependent on natural resource production, and those relative prices have been declining over most of the period. Natural resources appear under industrial production, so even if volume growth has been positive, with declining relative prices the natural resources share in output could be declining. And apart from Latin America and the Caribbean, these regions have also not really benefited from global production sharing in the more integrated global economy. The Middle East and North Africa Region has barely seen any shift in its trade to GDP ratio. For both Sub-Saharan Africa and Latin America and the Caribbean, however, the ratio has increased markedly, particularly in the 1990s—from 50 percent to 69 percent for Sub-Saharan Africa, and from 27 to 47 percent for Latin America and the Caribbean. The more recent rise in Latin America can be partly explained by the implementation of a raft of regional agreements, including NAFTA and MERCOSUR. At the same time Latin America's degree of openness is lower than that of East Asia, and in general it has been less coopted into global production networks.

The transformation in the economies of Europe and Central Asia over the last 15 years is a result of an abrupt structural shift. The dominance of industry as part of an economic strategy of planned economies was eliminated. Services in the transition economies quickly filled the gap, which led to significant dislocation for a period, but is now forming the basis of more rational and sustained growth.

Looking ahead it is clear that there is the potential for significant change. While the rate of urbanization has been persistent over the last two decades, there is a long way to go, particularly in Asia and Africa, before attaining the 80 percent level of the industrial countries (figure 1.16). The income gap is also huge, even if incomes are measured in purchasing power parity (PPP) terms. In East Asia, per capita incomes averaged just over $1,000 (1995 dollars) in 2002, compared with nearly $31,000 in the industrial countries— roughly a 30 to 1 differential. Even assuming

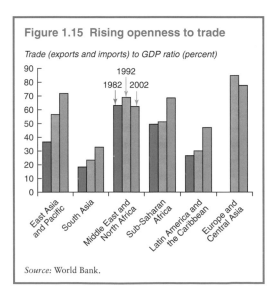

Figure 1.15 Rising openness to trade

Trade (exports and imports) to GDP ratio (percent)

1982 1992 2002

Source: World Bank.

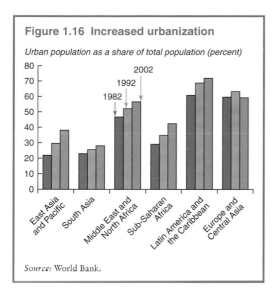

Figure 1.16 Increased urbanization

Urban population as a share of total population (percent)

Source: World Bank.

a PPP exchange rate of 5 would still lead to a significant 6 to 1 ratio in per capita incomes. In Latin America, the richest developing region with a per capita average income of $3,700, would have a ratio similar to East Asia using a PPP exchange rate of around 2.

Structural Change in the Future

Table 1.3 presents the long-term growth rates. This section focuses on some of the consequences of growth and other underlying assumptions of the long-term scenario on structural changes, particularly regarding labor shifts—both in volume terms and across sectors.[16]

In the aggregate, and assuming no change in labor force participation rates, labor supply growth will slow down sharply in most regions after 2010—with the exception of the Middle East and North Africa and Sub-Saharan Africa regions (figure 1.17).[17] In Western and Eastern Europe, Russia, and Japan, the labor supply would most likely shrink (even before 2010), putting additional pressure on underfinanced pension schemes. Additionally, it is the regions with the highest labor force growth rates that also tend to have the lowest per capita growth rates, so these regions are on a knife-edge in terms of their capacity to absorb high rates of new workers. These same regions typically have relatively low labor force participation rates, particularly of females; thus increases in

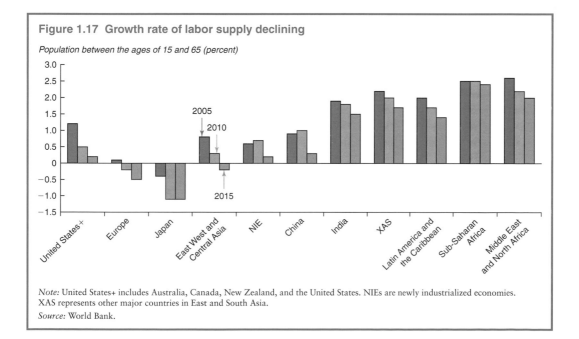

Figure 1.17 Growth rate of labor supply declining

Population between the ages of 15 and 65 (percent)

Note: United States+ includes Australia, Canada, New Zealand, and the United States. NIEs are newly industrialized economies. XAS represents other major countries in East and South Asia.
Source: World Bank.

Table 1.4 Labor market structure, 2005–15

	Growth between 2005–15: percent per annum				Growth decomposition		
	Agric	Manuf	Services	Total	Structure	Expansion	Total
Australia, Canada & New Zealand	−0.7	−0.8	0.7	0.4	3.45	3.90	6.88
United States	−1.1	−0.6	0.8	0.5	2.95	5.62	8.34
Japan	−3.0	−2.2	−0.6	−1.0	3.62	9.35	8.70
Korea and Taiwan	−1.9	−0.6	1.0	0.5	4.18	5.65	9.17
Hong Kong (China) and Singapore	0.0	−0.5	1.0	0.7	4.80	7.28	11.65
EU with EFTA	−2.6	−1.5	0.2	−0.2	4.92	2.28	3.12
Brazil	0.8	0.5	1.4	1.2	3.52	13.09	16.28
China	0.5	0.4	1.3	0.8	5.12	8.44	12.02
India	0.1	1.6	2.4	1.7	9.27	19.89	28.02
Indonesia	1.1	1.8	1.6	1.5	8.32	17.18	22.73
Mexico	−0.2	1.6	2.5	2.0	7.00	22.78	28.84
Russia	−1.0	−1.1	0.0	−0.4	4.97	4.35	2.43
SACU	−0.7	−0.2	0.9	0.6	3.82	6.87	10.36
Vietnam	1.7	1.9	2.0	2.0	5.69	22.23	26.20
Rest of East Asia	0.7	1.2	2.1	1.7	4.72	19.36	23.09
Rest of South Asia	1.8	1.3	2.7	2.4	4.60	27.22	31.38
EU accession countries	−0.8	−1.1	0.2	−0.2	6.51	2.41	4.67
Rest of ECA	−0.3	0.3	1.1	0.8	6.15	8.88	14.43
Middle East	2.3	1.6	2.5	2.3	5.26	26.43	30.79
North Africa	0.8	2.0	2.5	2.0	7.27	23.74	29.83
Rest of Sub-Saharan Africa	2.0	2.2	3.0	2.6	4.50	30.19	34.08
Rest of LAC	2.1	0.9	2.2	1.8	5.36	20.74	25.41
Rest of the world	0.8	1.2	2.1	1.7	4.15	19.45	23.12

Source: World Bank simulations.

participation rates will lead to additional labor market weakness.

With high-income demand elasticity for services and relatively higher labor productivity in manufacturing, labor demand growth will tend to be higher in services than in manufacturing and/or agriculture (see table in endnote 17). This effect is quite pronounced in the industrial countries, where labor demand growth between 2005 and 2015 will be negative, on average, in agriculture and manufacturing in all high-income regions, with all of the net growth occurring in services (with the exception of Japan, where labor force growth could potentially decline by 1 percent per annum on average). The shift toward services also occurs in developing countries, but with continued high growth in manufacturing and less growth in agriculture.

Table 1.4 also shows a summary measure of the structural changes. It decomposes the total change in the structure of the labor force into two components. The first is the "structural" component, which measures the quantity of labor force movement across sectors, assuming no change in the volume of labor. The second is an "expansion" component, measuring the overall growth in the labor force. In the case of India, for example, the numbers suggest that the labor force will grow by about 20 percent between 2005 and 2015, or about 1.8 percent per annum. And in each year, about 0.9 percent of the initial labor force will move across sectors. Thus the total annual movement of 2.5 percent per annum is composed roughly of 2/3 expansion and 1/3 by intersectoral movements. It should be clear from the decomposition that for most of the developing regions, there will be more labor movement from the expansion of the labor force than from structural change, with the notable exceptions of Russia and the other countries in Europe and Central Asia—and, perhaps somewhat more surprisingly, China. For the industrial regions with low or declining labor growth, clearly the structural shifts will be relatively the same order of magnitude as the expansion component. But the shifts are relatively small on an annual basis, perhaps 0.3 to 0.5 percent of the labor force.

Chapter 6 of this report will re-address one issue related to structural shifts in the context of RTAs. Do RTAs lead to structural changes that are inconsistent with the structural changes from a broad multilateral agreement? For example, a country signing an RTA may have a local comparative advantage in a given sector, but not a global comparative advantage. In this case, would the country need to undergo two potentially costly adjustments, should a multilateral agreement be signed subsequent to an RTA? And would the vested interests that benefit from the RTA hamper the ability to achieve a broader multilateral agreement,

with positive aggregate benefits, but hurt the sectors that thrived under the preferential arrangement?

Poverty Forecast

Developing country economic performance has been strong since 2002, and this is projected to continue over the next two years and beyond (tables 1.1 and 1.3). This pattern of high growth would in all likelihood lead to a halving of the number of poor (i.e., the percentage of poor living on $1 or less a day) in developing countries between 1990 and 2015 (table 1.5)—one of the key MDGs. At the global level, the target to be achieved in 2015 is around 14 percent (one-half of 27.9), and the forecast is for a headcount index of 10.2 percent. This translates into a forecast of

Table 1.5 Regional breakdown of poverty in developing countries

	Number of people living on less than $1 per day (millions)					
	GEP2004			GEP2005		
Region	1990	2000	2015	1990	2001	2015
East Asia and Pacific	470	261	44	472	271	19
China	361	204	41	375	212	16
Rest of East Asia and Pacific	110	57	3	97	60	2
Europe and Central Asia	6	20	6	2	17	2
Latin America and the Caribbean	48	56	46	49	50	43
Middle East and North Africa	5	8	4	6	7	4
South Asia	467	432	268	462	431	216
Sub-Saharan Africa	241	323	366	227	313	340
Total	1,237	1,100	734	1,218	1,089	622
Excluding China	877	896	692	844	877	606

	$1 per day head count index (percent)					
	GEP2004			GEP2005		
Region	1990	2000	2015	1990	2001	2015
East Asia and Pacific	29.4	14.5	2.3	29.6	14.9	0.9
China	31.5	16.1	3.0	33.0	16.6	1.2
Rest of East Asia and Pacific	24.1	10.6	0.5	21.1	10.8	0.4
Europe and Central Asia	1.4	4.2	1.3	0.5	3.6	0.4
Latin America and the Caribbean	11.0	10.8	7.6	11.3	9.5	6.9
Middle East and North Africa	2.1	2.8	1.2	2.3	2.4	0.9
South Asia	41.5	31.9	16.4	41.3	31.3	12.8
Sub-Saharan Africa	47.4	49.0	42.3	44.6	46.4	38.4
Total	28.3	21.6	12.5	27.9	21.1	10.2
Excluding China	27.2	23.3	15.4	26.1	22.5	12.9

Table 1.5 Regional breakdown of poverty in developing countries (continued)

	Number of people living on less than $2 per day (millions)					
	GEP2004			GEP2005		
Region	1990	2000	2015	1990	2001	2015
East Asia and Pacific	1,094	873	354	1,116	864	230
China	800	600	256	825	594	134
Rest of East Asia and Pacific	295	273	98	292	271	95
Europe and Central Asia	31	101	48	23	93	25
Latin America and the Caribbean	121	136	124	125	128	122
Middle East and North Africa	50	72	38	51	70	46
South Asia	971	1,052	968	958	1,064	912
Sub-Saharan Africa	386	504	612	382	516	612
Total	2,653	2,737	2,144	2,654	2,735	1,946
Excluding China	1,854	2,138	1,888	1,829	2,142	1,812

	$2 per day head count index (percent)					
	GEP2004			GEP2005		
Region	1990	2000	2015	1990	2001	2015
East Asia and Pacific	68.5	48.3	18.2	69.9	47.4	11.3
China	69.9	47.3	18.4	72.6	46.7	9.7
Rest of East Asia and Pacific	64.9	50.8	17.6	63.2	49.2	14.7
Europe and Central Asia	6.8	21.3	10.3	4.9	19.7	5.2
Latin America and the Caribbean	27.6	26.3	20.5	28.4	24.5	19.6
Middle East and North Africa	21.0	24.4	10.2	21.4	23.2	11.9
South Asia	86.3	77.7	59.2	85.5	77.2	54.2
Sub-Saharan Africa	76.0	76.5	70.7	75.0	76.6	69.2
Total	60.8	53.6	36.4	60.8	52.9	32.0
Excluding China	57.5	55.7	42.0	56.6	54.9	38.6

Source: World Bank.

622 million persons living $1 or less a day in 2015, compared with 1.2 billion in 1990 and an estimated 1.1 billion in 2001.[18] With respect to the somewhat higher poverty line of $2 a day, the headcount should improve to 32 percent in 2015—not quite a halving of the estimated 61 percent headcount index in 1990—and corresponding to almost 2 billion poor.

However, progress is highly uneven across and within countries. The global target will largely be achieved because of the significant progress on poverty reduction in China and India. Sub-Saharan Africa lags far behind, and though poverty rates are much lower in some of the other regions, for example Latin America and the Caribbean, progress over the last

15 years has been insufficient to be on track to achieve the income poverty target in 2015 without more rapid growth or policies that are better targeted to the poor. Within regions, progress has also been uneven. Despite the huge overall reduction in East Asia, several countries, for example, Cambodia, Lao PDR, and Papua New Guinea, are off track to meet the goal. In Sub-Saharan Africa, there are only eight countries—representing 15 percent of the subcontinent's population—that will potentially make significant progress toward achieving the income poverty target. Within countries, such as China, there are large pockets of poor people, and reducing poverty in these pockets is difficult because they are often concentrated in remote, hard-to-reach locations. Links to the

national and/or global economy are weak, and provision of public services—education, health, water and sanitation—is difficult and expensive.

This year's poverty forecast, as in years past, reflects changes in two key dimensions. First, new country surveys lead to a re-evaluation of the level of poverty in 1990 and in the most recent base year, 2001. At the global level, the $1/day headcount index for 1990 has been shaved slightly from 28.3 percent in last year's report, to 27.9 percent in this year's report. There is also a very modest decline in the estimated level of poverty for 2001. The new surveys also force a re-evaluation of the link between income growth and poverty reduction. Using the latest survey information and last year's economic forecast, the forecasted decline in poverty is somewhat more rapid, with the headcount index declining to 10.4 percent (from 21.1 percent in 2001), instead of 12.5 percent (from 21.6 percent in 2000).[19] The second key dimension is the change in the long-term economic forecast. The changes overall are relatively modest. However, the somewhat improved performance anticipated between 2003 and 2006 generates better average growth for the forecast period 2001–15 and drops the headcount index for 2015 from 10.4 percent to 10.2 percent.

While progress on income poverty in parts of the world, particularly East and South Asia, has been spectacular if not historic, there is no room for complacency. As mentioned earlier, there are significant pockets of poverty even within the more successful countries. Moreover, there are other dimensions of poverty in which progress has been more limited, and almost all developing countries are off track. In East Asia, for example, the region scores relatively well for achieving 100 percent primary school completion rates, with China and Vietnam already having achieved the target and the Philippines on track.[20] But Thailand and Indonesia are off track, as are some of the poorer countries in the region. For the child mortality MDG, the situation is more worrying. Four

countries are on track to achieve the target—Indonesia, Lao PDR, Malaysia, and the Philippines. All other countries are off track, and two—Cambodia and Papua New Guinea—are seriously off track. The situation is also dire for births attended (linked to maternal mortality) and access to safe water. These examples also illustrate that the other MDG targets are less directly correlated to income levels.[21] For example, Lao PDR and Indonesia are on track for the child mortality target, but Thailand is not.

Concluding Remarks

The rapid growth of developing economies, mostly concentrated in East and South Asia, has produced a spectacular, if not historic, fall in poverty that will enable the achievement of the poverty MDG on a global basis, although many countries will be seriously off-target. The rapid growth has been associated with large structural shifts—greater openness, more urbanized populations, and a sharp fall in agricultural employment. These trends will persist in the future as growth rates remain high, and incomes and productivity levels in developing countries are still well below industrial country averages—even taking into account PPP adjustments. As an example of potential structural shifts, take China's level of urbanization. Its rural population may not approach the 20 percent level of industrial countries, but a 50 percent share in 2015 could lead to a cumulative migration in the range of 140 to 175 million persons between 2005 and 2015. Such large shifts will require considerable public and private resources and their efficient allocation. Chapter 6 addresses a complementary issue—structural changes induced by changes in trade policies, notably the impacts of preferential trade agreements.

Notes

1. The investment to GDP ratio in the United States is currently 21 percent, close to its peak of 21.5 percent during the Internet bubble, and well above historical peaks of less than 18 percent.

2. The weighted average of the dollar's fluctuations relative to world currencies.

3. West-Texas Intermediate was much higher in October 2004 ($56). The overall average was depressed by the price of other oil (notably from Dubai), which was lower because producers increased the supply of lower quality oil.

4. Lau (2003) estimates that because of the re-export nature of its trade, the domestic value-added content of Chinese exports may be as little as 20 percent.

5. Net equity and foreign direct inflows of foreign private investors declined by 73 percent between 2001 and 2003. At the same time, net outflows by American private investors increased by 10 percent. As a result, total flows have reversed, from a significant inflow of $35 billion in 2001 to a $195 billion outflow in 2003. Since then, these trends have continued, with total outflows representing $267 billion in the second quarter of 2004.

6. See endnote 5.

7. Calculated as the change in U.S. t-bills held by the central banks of these countries divided by the net increase in t-bills held by official lenders (see http://www.treas.gov/tic/mfhhis01.txt).

8. Mussa (2004) suggests that a further 20 percent depreciation might be required to bring the U.S. economy into external balance.

9. These results are consistent with those published by the OECD for developing countries (see Dalsgaard and others 2001).

10. Even after Ricardian equivalence-based changes to private saving. Nevertheless, Brooks and others (2003) show that, taken alone, neither a 2 percentage point cut in fiscal spending, nor a 10 percent effective depreciation would be sufficient to restore external balance in the United States. They argue that a combination of depreciation, stronger world demand, and a larger fiscal contraction would be required.

11. Under higher interest rates, the desired stock of capital declines, which requires a prolonged period of slower growth before the economy adjusts to the new lower levels of output and capital.

12. In October 2004, this average price was $46.8 comprised of $53 for West-Texas Intermediate, $49.5 for Brent, and $37.7 for Dubai oil.

13. Dalsgaard and others (2001) estimate similar impacts for OECD countries.

14. Growth in steel demand fell 36 percent during the 3-month period ending in July, while copper imports were flat.

15. World Bank 2003b.

16. Unlike the previous section, which focused on the structure of value added, this section focuses on labor. The focus on labor provides a better perspective on the poverty dimension of structural shift. The historical analysis focused on output because of the greater availability and reliability of the data. Historical data on employment patterns has many gaps, and the data that does exist is often not compatible across countries.

17. The baseline scenario and the induced structural changes are predicated on a number of assumptions. First, growth in the labor supply is equated with growth of the working age population. For all regions, this implies a slowing of labor force growth, albeit with high growth in some developing regions. At the same time, the labor force is assumed to be flexible and thus will reinforce anticipated structural shifts. Second, savings are similarly influenced by demographics. In many developing countries this will translate into a slight acceleration in savings as the ratio of youth to workers declines, and a decline in industrial countries as the ratio of elderly to workers rise (explored in more detail in World Bank 2003a). Investment growth will largely be driven by domestic savings, as it has in the past; however, with modest increases in net capital flows toward developing countries, with the exception of East Asia, which has been a major source of international capital over the last five years.

Third are the assumptions regarding productivity growth; based on previously observed trends, these are divided into three broad economic sectors. In agriculture, it is assumed that the past growth of roughly 2.5 percent per annum is maintained through 2015 (see, for example, Martin and Devashish 1999). Maintaining this high rate of agricultural productivity will require continued and perhaps increasing investment in agricultural research and extension, combined with rising investment in agricultural infrastructure, particularly for water resource management. This rate of productivity growth in agriculture is consistent with a modest secular decline in agricultural prices, relative to the general price trend, as observed in the past. The other two broad sectors are manufacturing and services. Again, based on past trends, it is assumed that productivity growth in manufacturing will be higher than in services. This has two impacts: (1) it reduces the price of manufactures relative to services, all else being equal, and thus enhances the share of services in value terms; and (2) for the same level of output, it reduces the

Income elasticities in the Linkage model

	Ag. and food	Energy	Industrial goods	Services
United States	0.01	0.58	0.78	1.14
Japan	0.04	0.64	0.68	1.24
Europe	0.08	0.72	0.71	1.29
Rest of high-income	0.16	0.86	0.80	1.26
Low-income	0.52	1.40	1.08	1.41

demand for employment in the manufacturing sectors, and thus allows for a shift of labor toward services.

Fourth are the demand assumptions—the other side of the coin regarding structural changes. High-income countries have already witnessed a large decline in the demand for agriculture and food relative to income. Demand for services has increased relative to income and the demand for other goods. And there is no reason for these trends not to continue in the future. Thus the forward-looking scenarios assume that income elasticities over the next 10 years will largely reflect their current levels, though highly differentiated across commodities and regions (see table).

18. The absolute number of poor won't necessarily be halved due to population growth.

19. A more subtle change in the methodology has also been incorporated in this year's poverty forecast. The poverty forecast is based on the growth of the survey-based per capita consumption, assuming distribution neutrality (with some exceptions). However, it has been observed in the past that survey-based consumption growth deviates from consumption growth as measured in the national accounts. A conversion factor has been used to adjust for this deviation, which for most countries implied an elasticity of 0.9. In other words, if national income consumption grows at 10 percent, the assumed growth in survey-based consumption is 9 percent. More recent econometric evidence suggests that the long-run elasticity is 1, but that there are short-term deviations from the long-run elasticity. Because of the robustness of the long-run relationship, the new forecast assumes an elasticity of 1. Thus, all else being equal, this year's forecast will be lower than in the past because of higher implied consumption growth.

20. See World Bank 2004.

21. The World Bank, in its effort to improve its ability to monitor and forecast the other dimensions of the Millennium Development Goals, is developing and testing a new tool to forecast some of the MDGs. The tool will link economic growth with expenditures on health, education, and infrastructure. It will also capture some of the complementarities across targets, for example the degree to which improvements in access to safe water can improve health outcomes. A pilot study is currently being undertaken for Ethiopia and first results will be described in the *Global Monitoring Report 2005*.

References

Bergsten, Fred C. and John Williamson, eds. 2004. Dollar Adjustment: How far? Against What? In Special Report, No. 17, Institute for International Economics, Washington DC.

Brook, Anne-Marie, Franck Sédillot, and Patrice Ollivaud. 2004. Channels For Narrowing The US Current Account Deficit And Implications For Other Economies. OECD Economics Department Working Papers, No. 390, OECD, Paris.

Dalsgaard, Thomas, Christophe André, and Pete Richardson. 2001. Standard Shocks In The OECD Interlink Model OECD Economics Department Working Papers, No. 306, OECD, Paris.

Lau, Larence. 2003. Is China Playing by the Rules? Free Trade, Fair Trade, and WTO Compliance. Testimony at a Hearing of the Congressional Executive Commission on China, Washington, DC.

Martin, Will, and Devashish Mitra 1999. Productivity Growth and Convergence in Agriculture and Manufacturing. Working Papers, No. 2171, World Bank, Washington, DC.

Mussa, Michael. 2004. Exchange Rate Adjustments Needed to Reduce Global Payments Imbalances. Special Report, No 17, Institute for International Economics, Washington DC.

World Bank. 2003a. *Global Economic Prospects: Investing to Unlock Global Opportunities*. Washington, DC: World Bank.

———. 2003b. *World Development Indicators*. Washington, DC: World Bank.

———. 2004. *Global Monitoring Report*. Washington, DC: World Bank.

2

Regional Trade and Preferential Trading Agreements: A Global Perspective

In the last four decades, developing countries have burst onto the global marketplace. Their share of global trade increased from about one-fifth in 1960 to about one-third in 2004—at a time when global trade as whole was increasing to unprecedented levels. In every region, exports have outpaced the growth of output and increased as a share of GDP. Three rounds of multilateral trade negotiations combined with structural economic reforms undertaken throughout the world ushered in the sustained reduction in border protection that made this growth possible. The World Trade Organization (WTO), formed in 1994, consolidated an evolving system of rules based on nondiscrimination among trading partners—a cornerstone of the multilateral system.

Today a second trend in the trading system is rapidly gaining momentum and establishing a very different set of rules. This new trend is the proliferation of regional and bilateral trade agreements (RTAs)—agreements among a group of countries that reduce barriers to trade on a reciprocal and preferential basis for those in the group. The number of these agreements has more than quadrupled since 1990, rising to around 230 by late 2004.[1] Trade between RTA partners now makes up nearly 40 percent of total global trade, and new agreements increasingly address issues beyond trade. The value of preferences has steadily fallen, however, as most countries have been reducing tariffs across the board to all

partners on a most favored nation, or nondiscriminatory (MFN) basis, at the same time as they have been eliminating barriers preferentially through RTAs. In fact, roughly 66 percent of the decline in average tariffs in developing countries during the last two decades has come from unilateral reductions, as distinct from 25 percent coming out of the Uruguay Round and around 10 percent from RTAs. Moreover, product exclusions and restrictive rules of origin further limit the trade-expanding effects of preferences. Nonetheless, the result of this proliferation is an increasingly complex global trading system where different countries' access to a given market are often governed by very different sets of rules.

This chapter charts the rise of RTAs, examines the different motivations countries have for pursuing RTAs, and draws attention to the complexity they generate. It then describes the evolution of regional trading patterns and shows how the major developing regions differed strikingly in their timing of integration, their pace of export growth, their policies toward import competition and foreign investment, and the impact of regional trading arrangements. It concludes that those regions that aspired to trade most with the global economy became the most regionally integrated as well. Further, regional trade tends to precede preferential trade agreements rather than the other way around.

Box 2.1   RTAs and types of trade liberalization

Following WTO convention, the term *regional trade agreement* encompasses both reciprocal bilateral free trade or customs areas and multicountry (plurilateral) agreements. Regional and bilateral trade agreements provide for one type of trade liberalization, and they must be seen in a broader context of alternative methods of liberalization. Members of RTAs liberalize trade on a *reciprocal and preferential* basis. While programs such as the U.S. African Growth and Opportunity Act (AGOA) and the EU's Everything But Arms (EBA) also liberalize trade preferentially (i.e., different trade partners receive different treatment), the United States and EU extend these preferences *unilaterally* rather than reciprocally. In contrast to both of these types of preferential liberalization, countries often lower trade barriers in a *nondiscriminatory* fashion for all trade partners. They might do so *multilaterally*—through GATT/WTO negotiating rounds—or *autonomously,* as in the case of Pakistan in the late 1990s. The matrix below illustrates this taxonomy of liberalization methods.

RTAs are commonly divided into several basic categories, according the degree of economic integration they provide. The canonical taxonomy of RTAs contains the following four levels of integration:

1. In a *Free Trade Area*, members eliminate barriers to trade in goods (and increasingly services) among members, but each member is free to maintain

different MFN barriers on nonmembers. This latter characteristic requires members to develop rules of origin to prevent imports from third countries from being transshipped through the member country with the lowest tariffs.

2. A *Customs Union* moves beyond a free trade area by establishing a common external tariff on all trade between members and nonmembers. Customs unions typically contain mechanisms to redistribute tariff revenue among members.

3. A *Common Market* deepens a customs union by providing for the free flow of factors of production (labor and capital) in addition to the free flow of outputs.

4. In an *Economic and Monetary Union,* members share a common currency and macroeconomic policies.

The international experience with RTAs is much richer than this simple taxonomy suggests. NAFTA andother more recent agreements establishing free trade areas contain provisions governing domestic labor standards and other regulatory issues, which one traditionally associated with agreements for deeper integration. On the other hand, many free trade agreements exclude important categories of goods (notably agriculture) from trade liberalization. In some cases customs unions still levy tariffs on trade between members.

Scope of beneficiaries	Method of implementation	
	Reciprocal	Unilateral
Preferential: selected countries	NAFTA, EU, COMESA, EPAs, and other RTAs	GSP, AGOA, EBA, Cotonou
Nondiscriminatory (MFN): all countries	GATT/WTO multilateral agreements	Autonomous liberalization

Source: World Bank staff.

The Proliferation of Regional Preference Systems

More agreements are being signed. Since 1990, the number of RTAs in force rose from 50 to nearly 230 (figure 2.1). The WTO estimates that another 60 agreements are in various stages of negotiation. The boom in RTAs reflects changes in certain countries' trade policy objectives, the changing perceptions of the multilateral liberalization

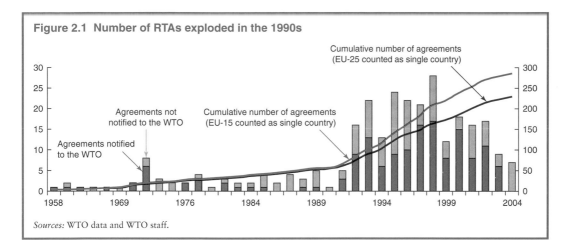

Figure 2.1 Number of RTAs exploded in the 1990s

Sources: WTO data and WTO staff.

process, and the reintegration into the global economy of countries in transition from socialism. This last category accounts for many of the new agreements signed in the early 1990s, when countries in Eastern Europe and the former Soviet Union negotiated RTAs with Western Europe [both the EU and the European Free Trade Association (EFTA)] and with each other.

Some of the RTAs included in figure 2.1 have never been reported to the WTO, for any of several reasons. One reason is that the WTO does not enforce notification (the same is true of notification requirements in other WTO agreements). Another is that several countries that have yet to join the WTO have been quite active in forming RTAs. Russia, for example, is in the process of joining the WTO and has signed bilateral free trade agreements (FTAs) with other members of the Commonwealth of Independent States (CIS). It is also

pursuing two regional arrangements that are designated to become customs unions: the Euroasian Economic Community and the Single Economic Space. Because a consistent data source covering all RTAs is lacking, data are based on the information contained in the WTO database, supplemented by data from the major unreported agreements.

Most countries are participating

Nearly all countries belong to at least one RTA,[2] and some are party to numerous agreements (table 2.1). On average, each country belongs to six RTAs, though there is considerable variation across regions and levels of development. East Asian countries sign fewer agreements than countries in other regions. Northern countries have participated to the greatest extent, each signing, on average, 13 agreements. A substantial

Box 2.2   Reporting RTAs to the WTO

RTAs represent a fundamental departure from the core WTO principle of nondiscrimination. Nonetheless, the WTO affords its members a large degree of flexibility in entering new RTAs. Within the WTO mandate, countries may join agreements by meeting the requirements of the General Agreement on Tariffs and Trade (GATT) Article XXIV

covering the formation of customs unions and free trade areas in merchandise trade; the General Agreement on Trade in Services (GATS) Article V on agreements in services; or the Enabling Clause (the 1979 Decision on Differential and More Favorable Treatment, Reciprocity, and Fuller Participation of

(Box continues on next page)

Box 2.2   *(continued)*

Developing Countries) dealing with trade in goods between developing countries.

Countries are required to notify the WTO secretariat of any RTAs they enter into, and their provisions are subject to review by the WTO. However, the review process in practice ends with the committee's queries of the parties and has not led to a subsequent report to the membership or formal WTO endorsement in any case. Furthermore, even the notification requirement, though a formal rule, has enjoyed only inconsistent compliance. An examination of the WTO RTA database reveals very large gaps between the date agreements are signed and the date they are reported to the WTO. Several agreements with WTO members have yet to be reported to the organization. These include the Greater Arab Free Trade Area, the Aghadir Agreement in the Middle East and North Africa, the India-Nepal and India-Bhutan agreements in South Asia, and several agreements in Africa. Some agreements, such as EU accessions, are reported more than a year in advance, while other agreements are notified six or more years after entry into force. The average gap is 354 days. Excluding agreements notified before signature, the average gap rises to 446. The median delays between entry into force and notification are 135 and 188 days, respectively.

Sources: World Bank and WTO staff.

Table 2.1 Most countries belong to more than one RTA

	East Asia and Pacific	Europe and Central Asia	Latin America and the Caribbean	Middle East and North Africa	South Asia	Sub-Saharan Africa	North	Total
Number of countries	32	36	39	21	8	48	25	209
North-South bilateral								
Countries belonging to at least one RTA	4	12	6	10	0	2	10	44
Average number of RTAs per country	2	1	2	1		1	4	2
Maximum number of RTAs per country	4	4	4	3	0	1	24	24
All others								
Countries belonging to at least one RTA	24	22	33	20	8	47	10	164
Average number of RTAs per country	2	6	8	5	4	4	8	5
Maximum number of RTAs per country	3	12	17	12	9	9	15	17
Total								
Countries belonging to at least one RTA	26	26	35	20	8	48	11	174
Average number of RTAs per country	2	6	8	5	4	4	11	5
Maximum number of RTAs per country	7	12	19	13	9	9	29	29

Note: Bilateral agreements are defined as an RTA with two members. North is OECD 24 plus Lichtenstein, and South is all other countries.
Source: Published WTO data, World Bank staff.

---

number of developing countries (45) have signed bilateral preferential agreements with a Northern partner. However, this activity is not spread evenly across regions. Most activity has been in Eastern Europe, Northern Africa, and Latin America. There are no countries in South Asia that have signed a bilateral agreement with a Northern partner. The enlargement of the EU in May 2004 led to a fall in the number of North-South RTAs in Europe.

Since 2000, several major new trends have emerged in the pattern of regional trade agreements. One unifying characteristic is that these take RTAs well beyond agreements between adjacent countries. For example,

- The EU's move toward bilateral market access FTAs and Economic Partnership Agreements (EPAs) with the ACP countries;
- The shift in the U.S. position toward bilateral preferential agreements; and
- The effort of a handful of developing countries to open markets through RTAs.

We turn now to a more in-depth investigation of these trends.

EU Preferential Trade Arrangements

During the 1990s, the EU was an active sponsor of bilateral arrangements with individual countries and groups of countries and was the major player in the RTA game. Prior to the recent accession of 10 new members, the EU had bilateral or regional agreements with 111 countries. Trade agreements became an integral instrument of European foreign policy, particularly in the aftermath of the collapse of the Soviet Union.[3]

Three types of agreements were intended to stabilize the region after 1989. *Europe Agreements* were intended to prepare bordering Eastern European countries for eventual accession into the EU. They involved bilateral agreements between each other and with the EU to reduce tariffs, develop uniform rules of origin, EU-consistent regulatory approaches to services, and common treatment of standards as well as transition rules in sectors such as agriculture. These efforts culminated with the full admission of 10 new countries into the EU in 2004—which is why the number of RTAs registered with the WTO fell for the first time ever.

Euro-Mediterranean Agreements were intended to build bilateral trade relations between neighbors, with the objective of forming a NAFTA-like free trade area by 2010. Launched in 1995, the EU and 12 countries have been involved in talks on "association agreements" that would subsume some existing bilateral arrangements. To date, bilateral agreements have been signed with Tunisia

(1995), Israel (1995), Morocco (1996), Jordan (1997), the Palestinian Authority (1997), Algeria (2001), Egypt (2001), and Lebanon (2002). In general, services liberalization provisions are limited to the restatement of WTO GATS commitments with no new liberalization or with preferential access reserved for suppliers based in member countries. Dispute settlement is state-to-state based on ad hoc arbitration.

Partnership and Cooperation Agreements (PCAs) with the Western Balkans, Russia, and the CIS were designed to help promote stability on the border of the EU, and in the case of Russia, expand trade. The EU has been providing technical assistance to these governments to help implement the institutional reforms that are part of the PCAs.

Two new agreements have been added to this list since 2000.

- *Economic Partnership Agreements (EPAs)* are designed to replace the preferential systems embodied in the Cotonou Agreement (the successor to the Lomé Convention), which had received a waiver under the enabling clause from GATT Article XXIV, a waiver that expires in 2007. EPAs are designed to promote trade and development in the ACP 77 countries in a WTO-consistent fashion by establishing agreements between large groups of countries forming customs unions (box 2.3).
- *Free Trade Agreements* with South Africa (which entered into force in 2000), Mexico (2000), and Chile (2003) are designed to open markets and secure trade. Agreements with the Gulf Cooperation Council (GCC) and the Common Market for the South (MERCOSUR) are under active negotiation. These embody free trade provisions for a range of products as well as provisions to liberalize at least some services (Ullrich 2004).

The EU agreements govern services trade in addition to trade in goods. The agreements

Box 2.3 EPAs become the EU's trade and development instrument: An experiment in "North–South–South" integration

EPAs are the most ambitious attempt to harness trade, development resources, and technical-legal assistance to the cause of integration-led development. The objective is to promote development, strengthen regional integration, and ensure compatibility with WTO principles. By negotiating reciprocal liberalization with existing South-South regional groupings and by providing common rules of origin with cumulative provisions, participants hope to prevent the hub-and-spoke effects that plague many bilateral North-South agreements. The EPAs will also encourage liberalization of services, provide for common product standards, and set up the negotiation of investor protections, based on state-to-state ad hoc arbitration of disputes.

After a one-year clarification phase by the African Caribbean and Pacific states (ACP), the first negotiations were launched in October 2003. The EU initiated discussions with the Economic Community of West African States (ECOWAS) plus Mauritania, the Economic and Monetary Community of Central Africa (CEMAC) plus São Tomé, Eastern and Southern Africa (16 countries), the Southern African Development Community (SADC), the Caribbean ACP countries, and the Pacific states (Kiener 2004).

The content for the agreements is currently open for discussion. Reciprocal trade liberalization would be the centerpiece under the terms of the EPA program . . . (Most of the EPA countries already enjoy preferential market access that the EU grants unilaterally under this program.) In addition, the EU has stated that it would like to have services liberalization, investment, competition, government procurement, and trade facilitation covered in the agreements (Falkenberg 2004).

Several issues will determine the ultimate effectiveness of the EPAs in promoting development: the degree of additional MFN liberalization in goods and services markets in both the RTAs and in the EU; the restrictiveness of the rules of origin for goods; and the extent of trade diversion that could occur in the event that there are no concomitant reductions in MFN border protections (see Hinkle and Schiff 2004).

---

with Mexico and Chile provide for specific liberalization commitments in the financial sector over and above those included in GATS, with the Chilean agreement adding telecommunications and maritime services (see Ullrich 2004). The South African agreement alludes to possible services liberalization, but without commitment. The EU agreements differ in important respects from the U.S. agreements in that they are generally less comprehensive, provide less market access in agriculture, and do not provide for investor-state dispute resolution (see chapter 5).

The U.S. embraces bilateralism

Prior to the present administration, the U.S. had generally eschewed reciprocal preferential trade agreements, whether regional or bilateral.

Exceptions included only Canada and Israel in the 1980s and NAFTA in the early 1990s. Indeed, many U.S. trade observers contend that opening NAFTA talks was designed primarily to support multilateral trade negotiations—to spur the Europeans and others into acting on the Uruguay Round. Two years later, the Clinton administration announced its desire to form a Free Trade Area of the Americas (FTAA), and it signed an FTA with Jordan in 2000.

Since the approval of trade promotion authority in 2002, however, the United States has given much greater emphasis to securing bilateral FTAs in tandem with its efforts to achieve multilateral liberalization through the WTO. Since 2002 the United States has signed bilateral accords with Australia, Bahrain, Central America plus the Dominican Republic, Chile,

Morocco, and Singapore. The United States appears to have intensified its pursuit of RTAs since the Cancun WTO Ministerial (September 2003). Negotiations are officially[4] under way with Colombia, Ecuador, Panama, Peru, SACU, and Thailand. Other economies deemed to be in the queue are Bolivia, Egypt, New Zealand, Pakistan, the Philippines, South Korea, Sri Lanka, and Taiwan (China), and Uruguay (Schott 2004). This intensified pace may reflect the intention to prod both the multilateral negotiations and the FTAA, as well as to respond to U.S. businesses that fear being shut out of export markets by a growing number of RTAs in which the United States is not a member.

In the broadest of terms, developing countries seek to provide access to their services markets and guarantees in many nontrade areas in exchange for assured access to U.S. goods markets. Key facets of these agreements include:[5]

- Tariff rates on most nonagricultural products are bound at zero; for example, the U.S.-Chile FTA will bind duties at zero for 85 percent of trade.
- Exclusion or delayed liberalization of sensitive products, commonly including agricultural products such as dairy products, cotton, ethyl alcohol, peanuts and peanut butter, sugar, and tobacco for the United States. Some exclusions are due to be phased out according to lengthy timetables; in the Chile-U.S. FTA, for example, all duties will be phased out in 12 years (USTR 2004).
- Intellectual property rights are conventionally accorded stronger protections than under the WTO's TRIPS agreement, with investor-state suits permitted in the event of disputes.
- Investment protections, with provisions for national treatment and nondiscrimination in pre-establishment provisions for companies based in each others markets (though liberal rules of origin indicate foreign subsidiaries located in member countries qualify for eligibility).
- Services trade are to be open except for those excluded in a negative list; notably excluded are labor service providers, except for the provisional visas held by professionals associated with investing firms.
- Labor and environment issues are included in recent agreements, with signatory countries undertaking commitments to enforce their own environmental and labor laws. Dispute settlement panels are empowered to impose monetary fines rather than using trade sanctions to force compliance (box 2.4.)

Box 2.4   Labor in U.S. FTAs

Until NAFTA, the United States did not attempt to include provisions on labor in trade agreements that it negotiated. As a presidential candidate, Bill Clinton promised to negotiate new side agreements to NAFTA on labor in order to secure sufficient political support for NAFTA. Since then labor issues have featured prominently in Congressional debates on granting the president negotiating authority and the resulting trade agreements.

All recent FTAs negotiated with the United States contain provisions requiring parties to enforce their own labor laws. These are premised on the assumption that each member's existing laws are satisfactory and therefore any trade distortions that might arise are caused by a lack of enforcement. The agreements enumerate five core standards: the right of association; the right to organize and bargain collectively; prohibitions on forced labor; a minimum age for employment of children; and acceptable working conditions. The FTAs establish a procedure for making complaints, encouraging resolution first through consultation and, if this fails, by establishing a panel of experts to hear the dispute.

(Box continues on next page)

Box 2.4 *(continued)*

The labor provisions break new ground in how a dispute settlement panel's decisions are enforced. Rather than using trade remedies (i.e., granting the injured party the right to withhold trade concessions), a panel can impose a monetary fine of up to $15 million per year (adjusted for inflation). Payments of the fines would go into a fund to support appropriate labor initiatives, which may include efforts to improve enforcement of labor laws. This mechanism appears in the agreements that the United States has signed with Australia, Bahrain, Chile, Central America and Dominican Republic, Morocco, and Singapore.

Using fines rather than trade sanctions has several advantages: while trade sanctions penalize both polluting and clean exporters, fines target the polluters; increased trade sanctions hurt all workers in export industries, but fines help restructure plants and maintain employment; and fines build in targeted solutions to the problem rather than present protracted trade disputes.

Sources: Destler and Balint 1999, texts of FTAs on the USTR web site (www.ustr.gov), and Weintraub 2004.

The United States indicated it would not negotiate changes in its antidumping statutes or on its agricultural subsidies, insisting on addressing both through the WTO's multilateral negotiations. In chapter 5, we return to a deeper discussion of provision for services, investment, and intellectual property rights (IPR).

Developing countries actively pursue major markets

The launching of NAFTA spawned a new flurry of interest among developing countries eager to use RTAs to secure market access. Mexico and Chile have been at the forefront of these developments. Mexico, having created a world-class trade negotiating team for NAFTA, turned its attention to Central America and other countries in Latin America. It established arrangements with Costa Rica (1995), Bolivia (1995), Nicaragua (1998), the EU (2000), EFTA (2001), and Japan (2004). After NAFTA was signed, Chile immediately solicited entry into the accord. Rebuffed initially, the country embarked on a wider strategy. Chile established agreements with MERCOSUR (1996), Canada (1997), Peru (1998), Mexico (1999), Central America (2002), the United States and EU (2003), and EFTA (2004). By 2004, Chile had signed free trade agreements that provided over 60 percent of its exports with duty-free access to markets around the world (see Devlin and Estevadeordal 2004).

Many existing regional organizations in Africa also moved aggressively to intensify preferential trade liberalization during the 1990s. For example, the treaty establishing the Common Market for Eastern and Southern Africa (COMESA), which was signed in 1993 to replace the Preferential Trade Area, called for a free trade area by 2000 and a customs union by 2004. The East African Community was formed in the mid-1990s to accelerate economic integration among three COMESA members (Kenya, Tanzania, and Uganda). The SADC Trade Cooperation Protocol was signed in 1996 as part of an effort to reintegrate South Africa into the regional economy after the end of apartheid.

Asian countries have launched similar negotiations since 2001. India has concluded or is negotiating limited arrangements with MERCOSUR and Thailand; MERCOSUR is negotiating with the Andean countries; China has launched bilateral accords with members of the Association of Southeast Asian Nations (ASEAN), to mention a few. In 2004, India, Pakistan, and other South Asian countries announced the South Asian Free Trade Agreement

Table 2.2 RTAs cover many topics besides merchandise trade

	Standards	Transport	Customs Cooperation	Services	Intellectual Property	Investment	Dispute Settlement	Labor	Competition
U.S.									
U.S.-Jordan	No	No	Yes	Yes	Yes	Yes	Yes	Yes	Yes
U.S.-Chile	Yes	No	Yes	Yes	Yes	Yes	Yes	Yes	Yes
U.S.-Singapore	Yes	No	Yes	Yes	Yes	Yes	Yes	Yes	Yes
U.S.-Australia	Yes	No	Yes	Yes	Yes	Yes	Yes	Yes	Yes
U.S.-CAFTA	Yes	No	Yes	Yes	Yes	Yes	Yes	Yes	No
U.S.-Morocco	Yes	No	Yes	Yes	Yes	Yes	Yes	Yes	No
NAFTA	Yes	No	Yes	Yes	Yes	Yes	Yes	Yes	Yes
EU†									
EU-South Africa	No	No	No	No	Yes	No	Yes	No	Yes
EU-Mexico	Yes*	Yes	Yes*	Yes	Yes	Yes	Yes	No	Yes
EU-Chile	Yes*	Yes	Yes	Yes	Yes	Yes	Yes	No	Yes
Euro-Med. Agreements	No	No	No	No	Yes	No	Yes	No	Yes*
South-South									
MERCOSUR	Yes	Yes	Yes	Yes	No	Yes	Yes		Yes
Andean Community	Yes	Yes	Yes	Yes	No	Yes	Yes	Yes	Yes
CARICOM	Yes	Yes	Yes	Yes	No	Yes	Yes	Yes	Yes
AFTA	Yes	Yes	Yes	Yes	No	Yes	No	No	No
SADC		Yes	Yes		Yes	No	Yes		
COMESA	Yes	Yes	Yes	Yes	No	Yes	Yes	Yes	Yes
Other									
Japan-Singapore	Yes	No	Yes	Yes	Yes	Yes	Yes	Yes	Yes
Canada-Chile	No	No	Yes	Yes	No	Yes	Yes	Yes	Yes
Chile-Mexico	Yes		Yes	Yes	Yes	Yes	Yes	Yes	Yes

Source: World Bank staff.
†While EU agreements mention cooperation in most of the subject areas, only those in which specific commitments are undertaken receive a "Yes" rating.
*Implementation steps are to be agreed on at a later date.

(SAFTA), which is intended to encompass all of the countries of the region (see Baysan 2004; Newfarmer 2004).

Many RTAs, diverse provisions

RTAs have increasingly been designed to cover much more than liberalization of tariffs and quotas. New provisions on enforcement of domestic labor and environmental laws have already been mentioned. Table 2.2 gives a flavor of the range of services and intellectual property rights issues that are addressed in current agreements. Many of these issues, which are dealt with in more detail in later chapters, have implications for trade, although the precise mechanisms by which trade is affected are not always well defined.

Many RTAs, many rationales

These recent trends highlight different rationales that drive the quest for preferential

agreements, but in nearly all cases politics is as important as economics. The classic *North-North* agreement, the European Union, had its origin in politics (see Schiff and Winters 2003). The fathers of the European Community, Robert Schumann and Jean Monnet, clearly believed that Franco-German integration through trade and investment would produce a new constellation of common economic interests that would attenuate historic military animosity. As a first step, they felt that placing French and German coal and steel industries under a single authority, the European Coal and Steel Community, would make it impossible for either of these historical enemies to use these resources for military purposes against the other.

Today, for *North-South* agreements, Northern partners often have a complex mix of rationales—rooted in foreign policy, commercial diplomacy, and development policy.

"Trade policy has always been the principal instrument of foreign policy for the European Union" (Sapir 1998). The United States now appears to be using preferential agreements for reasons that are similarly broad. Both the EU and the United States seek trade agreements that go beyond simple tariff removal to include rules governing services, protection of intellectual property, and adherence to health, labor, and environmental standards.

One goal of developing countries seeking an RTA with a large market, such as the EU[6] or the United States, is simply to secure market access. One should note, however, that most developing countries, especially the least developed countries (LDCs), already enjoy considerable access to these markets for most manufactured products (whether through unilateral preference programs or because MFN tariffs are already quite low), and RTAs with these countries often exclude agriculture and other politically sensitive products. Nevertheless, RTAs provide some insurance against future protectionist policies, and by reaching an agreement "preemptively," they seek to avoid being left out of a future agreement.

A second objective is to reinforce internal regulatory reforms through external treaty obligations and visible political commitments. Locking in domestic reforms through a foreign trade agreement with the EU clearly motivated countries making the transition from socialism in the 1990s. Mexico under NAFTA was motivated by a similar objective. Guaranteed market access combined with credible domestic reforms can attract foreign direct investment (see chapter 5).

South-South agreements often reflect a political desire to form or join a broadly based regional initiative, such as ASEAN, COMESA, or MERCOSUR. The drive for economic integration often begins with political objectives. Like France and Germany in the 1950s, the newly established democracies of the Southern Cone formed MERCOSUR in the mid-1980s in the hopes of damping the traditional military hostility between major regional powers—Argentina and Brazil. SADC originated in the 1980s as a coalition opposed to apartheid in South Africa and has more recently turned to creating a free trade area. Some observers note that African customs unions and free trade areas are as active in areas such as conflict resolution as in trade liberalization. Finally, many see relaxed tensions between India and Pakistan as the real payoff from the proposed SAFTA agreement, regardless of what happens to trade barriers in the region. The tentative conclusion of existing studies is that RTAs that expand trade flows appear to have a substantial dampening impact on conflict (box 2.6).

Box 2.5   Trade agreements and the environment

It is important to establish coherent relationships between environmental policies and the trade obligations set out in various RTAs. The following examples illustrate the various ways that environmental issues are handled in these trade agreements.

WTO. Within the WTO, environmental provisions are limited to the adoption of product-related measures as "necessary to protect human, animal or plant life or health," or "relating to the conservation of exhaustible natural resources." Process-related requirements continue to remain outside the scope of the WTO. However, in the absence of agreed-on international standards (e.g., fisheries), the risk of disguised protectionism has prevented further consensus on the way forward. Long-standing disputes between the United States and other countries on tuna fishing and dolphin or turtle protection are cases in point.

NAFTA. The environmental agreement under NAFTA created the Commission for Environmental Cooperation to promote environmental cooperation among the three members. The commission itself does

(Box continues on next page)

Box 2.5 *(continued)*

not set standards in the various countries, though part of its mandate is to help harmonize them upward. If a country persistently fails to enforce environmental laws that have conferred a trade benefit, dispute settlement provisions can be invoked. The commission's role in the disputes is to see that enforcement of existing laws takes place. In addition, it is charged with monitoring the environmental effects of NAFTA. Articles of agreement also dictate that countries will not try to attract investment by relaxing or ignoring domestic health, safety, or environmental regulations. International environmental agreements recognized by the three parties take precedence over national rules.

MERCOSUR. Environmental concerns are currently being dealt with in MERCOSUR by a working group. This group has discussed issues such as the environment, competitiveness, non-tariff barriers to trade, and common systems of environmental information. A draft agreement from this working group provides for upward harmonization of environmental management systems and increased cooperation on shared ecosystems, in addition to mechanisms for social participation. It also includes provisions on instruments for environmental management, including quality standards, environmental impact assessment methods, environmental monitoring and costing, environmental information systems and certification processes, provisions for protecting health and quality of life, and other general

mechanisms for implementing the protocol. The regime is still evolving, and the challenge at hand is to ensure that the promise of the protocol leads to effective regional cooperation and action.

Bilateral agreements. A number of recently concluded bilateral FTAs, including the U.S.–Singapore FTA and the Japan–Singapore Economic Agreement for a New Age Partnership, contain environmental provisions. The U.S.–Singapore FTA establishes an important precedent for dealing with environmental issues by including a chapter specifically on the environment. As discussed in box 2.4 on labor laws, this agreement ensures that countries effectively enforce their environmental laws, and it provides for enforcement mechanisms, including fines.

Even in the absence of such special provisions, however, trade agreements can contribute to a cleaner environment simply by making trade more responsive to market forces. In general, countries that are more open to trade adopt cleaner technologies more quickly, and increases in real income are often associated with greater demand for environmental quality (WTO 1999). Opening up domestic markets also encourages cleaner manufacturing, because protectionist countries tend to shelter pollution-intensive heavy industries. The incentives to over-exploit or deplete resources are more directly related to policies and institutions within the sector than to trade openness per se (World Bank 1999).

Not all political objectives involve war and peace issues; some *South-South* agreements are designed to pool resources for trade negotiations and trade policymaking. Much as the European Union established a common trade policy with a common commissioner in charge of trade (in part to negotiate more forcefully with the United States in the GATT), so too a driving force for MERCOSUR was to establish a common trade policy relative to the multilateral and hemispheric system.

Entering into a regional agreement may also reflect a desire to deal with region-specific issues—such as transit, water, energy, migration,

movement of labor, customs, and standards—that are difficult to broach at the global level. RTAs among CIS countries are arguably an attempt to reconstruct some of the economic linkages that were severed with the disintegration of the Soviet Union and the disorganization caused by the collapse of central planning. Although many of these regional externalities can be handled without a *trade* agreement, RTAs may provide institutions and a framework through which to make progress on these issues (see chapter 4).

The wide variation in RTAs flows from the very different motivations countries have for

Box 2.6   Can RTAs prevent conflict?

Does trade inhibit or increase hostilities between states? Greater contact among traders and consumers across borders may stimulate mutual respect and more harmonious relations, and high levels of trade can create economic interdependence, which, in turn, raises the cost of political disputes and military conflict.

In 1889, Wilfred Pareto suggested that "customs unions and other systems of closer commercial relations [could serve] as means to the improvement of political relations and the maintenance of peace." In 1919, John Maynard Keynes wrote that "a Free Trade Union, comprising the whole of Central, Eastern and South-Eastern Europe, Siberia, Turkey, and (I should hope) the United Kingdom, Egypt and India, might do as much for the peace and prosperity of the world as the League of Nations itself."

RTAs also can provide institutions and a forum for bargaining and negotiation—to address tensions before they erupt in conflict. European integration, ASEAN, and MERCOSUR are often cited as venues for improving political-military relations. Regional trade agreements do not ensure positive political outcomes, however. The U.S. civil war (1861–65) was fought—at least in part—over high protection of northern manufactures and trade restrictions on cotton. Similarly, the Central American soccer war of 1969 emerged out of lingering hostility over trade arrangements that created advantages for El Salvador at the expense of Honduras. And one reason Bangladesh seceded from Pakistan was the common

external tariff structure that deprived it of access to cheaper inputs from the global market and diverted trade to Pakistan (Schiff and Winters 2003).

Mansfield and Pevehouse (2000) attempt to identify empirically the role of RTAs in ameliorating conflict. They find that, on average, the likelihood that a pair of states will see the outbreak of a militarized interstate dispute declines by around 50 percent if both belong to the same RTA. However, only RTAs that expand trade flows appear to have a substantial impact on conflict. When evaluated at the lowest level of trade between partners, it appears that membership in a RTA reduces the chance of dispute by just 15 percent. Other studies have suggested that RTAs that have little impact on trade may actually exacerbate conflict (see Powers 2003). If the gains from trade are not distributed evenly, for example, then the subsequent change in interstate power relations can be a source of increased tension. Also, rising interdependence may be seen as a source of increasing vulnerability, making expansion through military force appear more attractive.

These results, which suggest that RTAs could contribute to a reduced risk of military conflict, should be treated with a high degree of caution, due to problems of causality and omitted factors, such as the broader institutional framework governing relations between particular pairs of countries. In Africa, for example, RTAs that address the management of cross-border resource issues (such as water) are more effective in reducing military conflict than other RTAs.

---

entering into the arrangements. As we will see in subsequent sections, these motivations contribute to greater complexity in rules governing world trade.

Many RTAs can complicate administrative procedures

An important feature of the rise in the number of RTAs is the growing number of overlapping agreements and the so-called "spaghetti bowl" that has emerged from the proliferation of bilateral agreements (figure 2.2). The associated myriad of rules

strains institutions charged with administering trade agreements. A web of differing trade arrangements can tangle administrative procedures—customs procedures, technical standards, rules of origin, and so on—and thereby raises the costs for both enterprises and governments. This complexity undermines work toward greater trade facilitation in developing countries.

Many agreements between country pairs are duplicated by other agreements to which the same two countries are parties. In Sub-Saharan Africa, for example, about one-half of

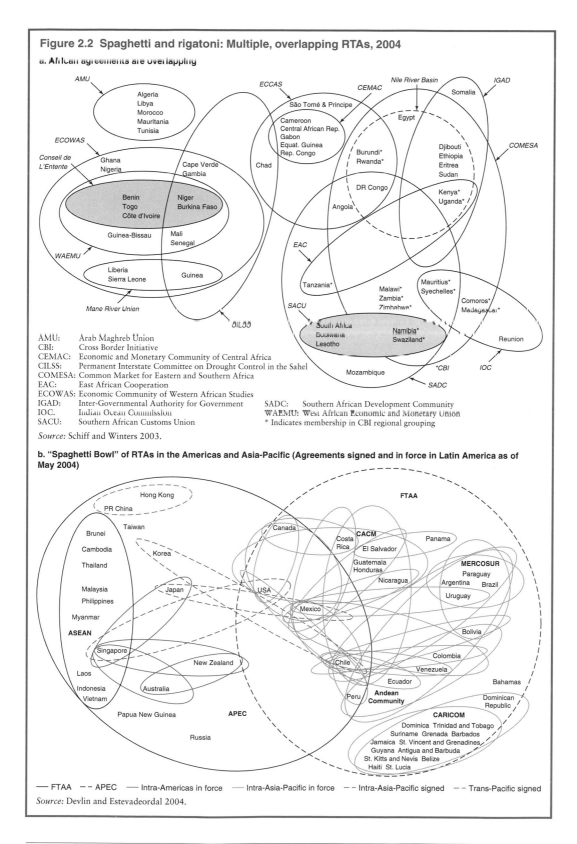

Figure 2.2 Spaghetti and rigatoni: Multiple, overlapping RTAs, 2004

a. African agreements are overlapping

AMU: Arab Maghreb Union
CBI: Cross Border Initiative
CEMAC: Economic and Monetary Community of Central Africa
CILSS: Permanent Interstate Committee on Drought Control in the Sahel
COMESA: Common Market for Eastern and Southern Africa
EAC: East African Cooperation
ECOWAS: Economic Community of Western African Studies
IGAD: Inter-Governmental Authority for Government
IOC: Indian Ocean Commission
SACU: Southern African Customs Union

SADC: Southern African Development Community
WAEMU: West African Economic and Monetary Union
* Indicates membership in CBI regional grouping

Source: Schiff and Winters 2003.

b. "Spaghetti Bowl" of RTAs in the Americas and Asia-Pacific (Agreements signed and in force in Latin America as of May 2004)

— FTAA – – APEC — Intra-Americas in force — Intra-Asia-Pacific in force – – Intra-Asia-Pacific signed – – Trans-Pacific signed

Source: Devlin and Estevadeordal 2004.

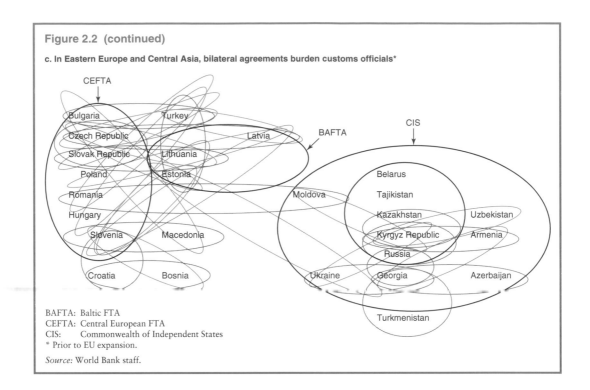

Figure 2.2 (continued)

c. In Eastern Europe and Central Asia, bilateral agreements burden customs officials*

BAFTA: Baltic FTA
CEFTA: Central European FTA
CIS: Commonwealth of Independent States
* Prior to EU expansion.
Source: World Bank staff.

the pairwise trade relationships covered by an RTA are also covered by another agreement. In other regions, overlapping agreements also comprise a substantial share of the total number of agreements. There would be significant benefits, in terms of lower administrative costs and more effective implementation, from a rationalization of the current structure of overlapping agreements.

Uneven terms—hub-and-spoke integration

The substantial number of bilateral agreements involving large northern countries, most of which have been signed since 1990, suggests that a hub-and-spoke structure in world trade is emerging. Of the 109 North-South bilateral agreements, 86 have been created since 1990. In a hub-and-spoke trading system, the largest markets sign individual agreements with a wide range of peripheral countries among which market access remains restricted. Such agreements can marginalize the spokes, where market access conditions are usually less

advantageous than in the hub, which enjoys improved access to all of the spokes. In comparison with a broad preferential trade agreement, a hub-and-spoke approach in theory generates lower gains, which accrue mainly to the hub (Wonnacott 1996). Hubs and spokes are already clearly discernible as the EU and United States extend restrictive rules of origin from one bilateral agreement to another.[7]

Trade within RTAs is rising but preferential trade is less important

Trade between RTA members is growing as the number of agreements increases, and one-third of world trade now takes place between RTA members (figure 2.3). (Here we cover only reciprocal agreements and exclude trade under the Generalized System of Preferences, Cotonou Agreement, and AGOA.) Disregarding intra-EU trade, bilateral flows between RTA members have been growing at a rate similar to the growth rate of agreements themselves, as shown in figure 2.3. This figure

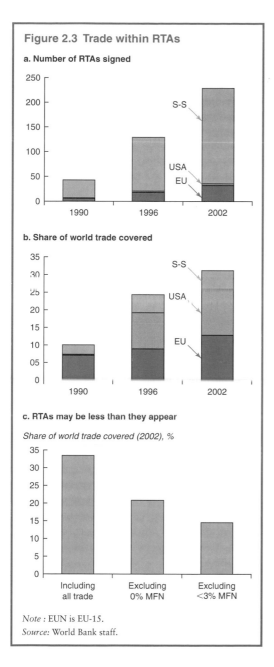

Figure 2.3 Trade within RTAs

a. Number of RTAs signed

b. Share of world trade covered

c. RTAs may be less than they appear

Share of world trade covered (2002), %

Note: EUN is EU-15.
Source: World Bank staff.

Examining total trade flows between RTA partners overstates the amount of trade that takes place on a preferential basis. However, tariff schedules of many RTA members increasingly contain duty-free MFN rates on which no preference can be given. We estimate that the amount of preferential trade among RTA members, after accounting for MFN rates of zero, is much lower at 21 percent of world trade (figure 2.3). Furthermore, it is often more profitable for enterprises to pay a low MFN tariff when there are high costs to satisfy rules of origin or other administrative procedures that a trader must follow to qualify for preferential treatment under an RTA. If we exclude trade covered by facing tariffs of 3 percent or less, we conclude that, at present, the amount of global trade taking place under an economically meaningful tariff preference is around 15 percent. An earlier estimate on a similar, but not directly comparable, basis suggests that in the mid 1990s, trade on a preferential basis amounted to 27 percent of global trade.[8]

While the number of RTAs has been increasing, the importance of preferential trade has been falling, reflecting lower tariff barriers, especially in OECD countries. Since 1996 the number of zero duty lines in the EU tariff schedule has increased from 13 to 21 percent of the total number of tariff lines and from 18 to 32 percent for the United States. In 2002 about 45 percent of the tariff lines in the EU and United States schedules had duties of 3 percent or less. This reflects the impact of multilateral liberalization under the Uruguay and earlier trade rounds. Thus a large and growing proportion of EU and U.S. imports from preferential trade partners is unlikely to actually receive preferential access relative to other countries.

For many developing country agreements, the situation is different because the number of low-duty tariff lines is small. In 2002, 6 percent of Brazilian tariff lines had MFN tariff rates of zero, as did 1 percent of Indian tariff lines. We estimate that 88 percent of trade between

also reveals that the rapid increase in the number of South-South RTAs signed in the past decade has not been matched by much change in trade flows among parties to these agreements. This discrepancy highlights a point made earlier: many new South-South agreements overlap with existing agreements.

Box 2.7   Regional versus multilateral and unilateral liberalization: What's more important?

How does liberalization in RTAs compare to autonomous and multilateral liberalization? The rapid expansion of RTAs has occurred during a period when developing countries were undertaking autonomous liberalization and also fulfilling commitments made during the Uruguay Round of the GATT. An examination of tariff reductions by developing countries finds that neither RTAs nor multilateral negotiations represent the largest driver of liberalization. Autonomous liberalization accounts for the lion's share of trade liberalization since the 1980s. The trade-weighted average MFN tariff rate levied by the 33 largest developing country importers (which collectively account for 90 percent of all developing country imports) was 29.9 percent in the 1980s. By 2003 the average MFN rate had dropped to 11.3 percent. Based on tariff concessions granted during the Uruguay Round, multilateral negotiations account for 5.1 percentage points of the total decline in MFN tariffs, and the remaining 13.5 percentage points resulted from autonomous liberalization. If the RTAs that these 33 countries have signed were fully implemented, the trade-weighted average applied tariff would fall further to 9.3 percent. The

chart below shows how trade liberalization is allocated according to these different sources.

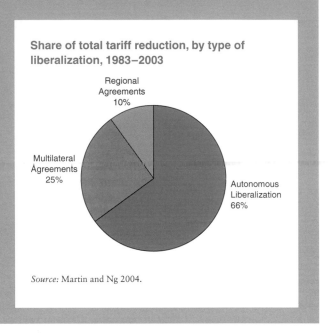

Share of total tariff reduction, by type of liberalization, 1983–2003

Regional Agreements 10%

Multilateral Agreements 25%

Autonomous Liberalization 66%

Source: Martin and Ng 2004.

countries in Latin America is potentially eligible for preferential treatment under an RTA.[9] For the Middle East and North African countries it is 83 percent of the total. The new SAFTA will lead to three-quarters of the trade between members taking place on a preferential basis (assuming all products are included). East Asia is an exception, where, for example, 22 percent of Indonesian and 59 percent of Malaysian tariffs are zero. Thus the amount of trade between East Asian countries receiving tariff preferences is very small. Like OECD countries, however, developing countries have taken great strides to reduce MFN tariffs during the past two decades. Most of this liberalization has come from autonomous reductions and not through trade agreements—either RTAs or multilateral trade negotiations (see box 2.7).

Trends in Trade and Growth by Region

These agreements were superimposed in a context of deep changes in global trading patterns.[10] The postwar period has seen major global shocks and changes in the economic environment, including oil crises in the 1970s and financial crises in the 1980s and 1990s. In the past 20 years there have also been major changes in policy regimes. Socialist countries across the world restructured their economic systems and started the process of reorienting their trade to the world economy. In the former Soviet Union, this meant collapse and reconstruction; in East Asia it meant progressive, sustained, and profound institutional change. Latin America went through its own, if less dramatic, transition from import-substitution industrialization to a strategy of outward-oriented growth. Apartheid in South Africa, political strife in various parts of the continent, and the struggle against HIV/AIDS delayed the establishment of stable policies and depressed growth throughout Africa. It has been a period of major transitions.

The growth performance of developing countries in the past 20 years reflects this varied experience (figure 2.4). Only the East

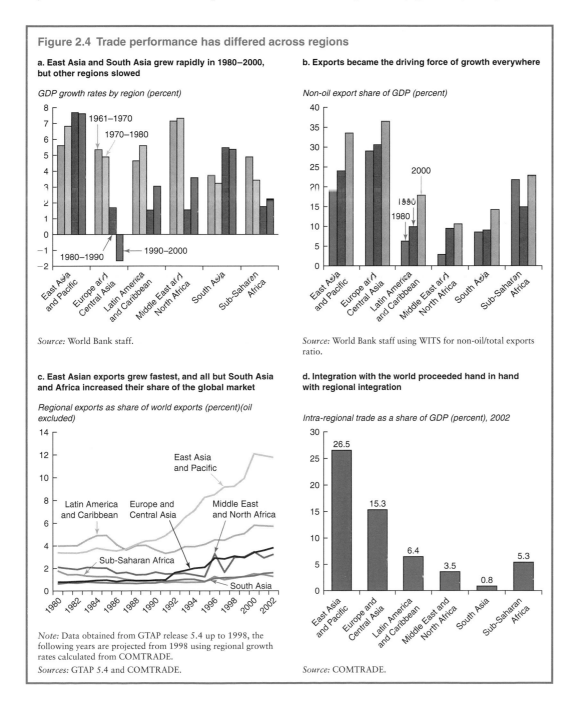

Figure 2.4 Trade performance has differed across regions

a. East Asia and South Asia grew rapidly in 1980–2000, but other regions slowed

GDP growth rates by region (percent)

1961–1970
1970–1980
1980–1990
1990–2000

Source: World Bank staff.

b. Exports became the driving force of growth everywhere

Non-oil export share of GDP (percent)

1980
1990
2000

Source: World Bank staff using WITS for non-oil/total exports ratio.

c. East Asian exports grew fastest, and all but South Asia and Africa increased their share of the global market

Regional exports as share of world exports (percent)(oil excluded)

East Asia and Pacific
Latin America and Caribbean
Europe and Central Asia
Middle East and North Africa
Sub-Saharan Africa
South Asia

Note: Data obtained from GTAP release 5.4 up to 1998, the following years are projected from 1998 using regional growth rates calculated from COMTRADE.
Sources: GTAP 5.4 and COMTRADE.

d. Integration with the world proceeded hand in hand with regional integration

Intra-regional trade as a share of GDP (percent), 2002

East Asia and Pacific — 26.5
Europe and Central Asia — 15.3
Latin America and Caribbean — 6.4
Middle East and North Africa — 3.5
South Asia — 0.8
Sub-Saharan Africa — 5.3

Source: COMTRADE.

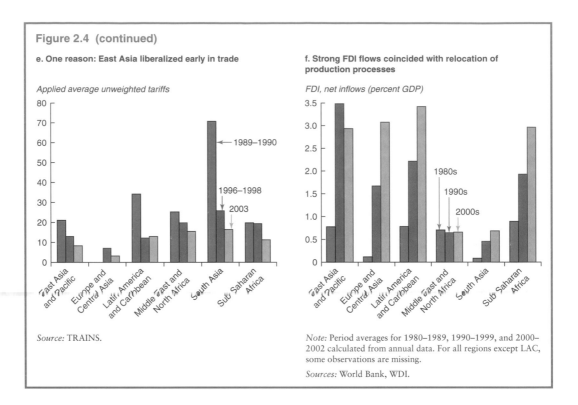

Figure 2.4 (continued)

e. One reason: East Asia liberalized early in trade

Applied average unweighted tariffs

(Bars labeled: 1989–1990, 1996–1998, 2003 for regions: East Asia and Pacific, Europe and Central Asia, Latin America and Caribbean, Middle East and North Africa, South Asia, Sub-Saharan Africa)

Source: TRAINS.

f. Strong FDI flows coincided with relocation of production processes

FDI, net inflows (percent GDP)

(Bars labeled: 1980s, 1990s, 2000s for regions: East Asia and Pacific, Europe and Central Asia, Latin America and Caribbean, Middle East and North Africa, South Asia, Sub-Saharan Africa)

Note: Period averages for 1980–1989, 1990–1999, and 2000–2002 calculated from annual data. For all regions except LAC, some observations are missing.

Sources: World Bank, WDI.

Asia and Pacific and South Asia regions experienced higher GDP growth rates in the 1980–2000 period than during 1960–1980. The other four regions fared worse in the last two decades, with GDP growth rates that were one-half to two-thirds smaller than between 1960 and 1980.

Nonetheless, trade grew. The share of trade in GDP grew in all regions in the 1990s. East Asian exports grew faster than the other regions, and the region increased its share of total world exports throughout the 1980s and 1990s. Latin American exports also grew consistently as a share of the world market during the 1990s, but not as steeply as for East Asia. In South Asia, however, although GDP growth increased in the 1980–2000 period and the export share of GDP rose in the latter part of that period, the trade growth is from a much smaller base. South Asia still has the lowest trade shares of any region. Sub-Saharan Africa has also had disappointing growth

performance. These trends reflect different initial conditions and external shocks, changes in development strategies, and policies toward trade liberalization.

East Asia generally followed a strategy of export-led growth, through elimination of anti-export bias and sustained nondiscriminatory (MFN) liberalization. This trend was most dramatic in China, where border barriers at the start of the decade were prohibitive for most tariff lines, and by the end of the decade averaged less than 12 percent, with a plan to go to less than 10 percent by 2004. But virtually all countries were liberalizing. Average tariffs for the region as a whole fell from about 23 percent in 1989–90 to 8 percent in 2003.

In Europe and Central Asia the disintegration of the Soviet Union after 1990 caused the collapse of growth and required profound restructuring of the region's economies and a redirection of its trade. Roughly half of the region was drawn to the magnet of the EU's large and stable market. The EU responded with technical assistance and a political willingness to admit its Eastern European neighbors as full members. The combination of a political framework, trade, investment, and technical assistance led to an unprecedented pace of reforms and economic integration that culminated with 10 states joining the EU on May 1, 2004. With their eyes turned toward markets in the EU, the Central European and Baltic countries achieved more extensive integration and higher trade and FDI flows, which is evident in the rapid export growth of the region as a whole.

The CIS has moved much more slowly in its process of reform and reorientation, particularly in Central Asia and the Caucasus. Under the CIS-7 initiative, trade regimes have been generally liberalized, but have been limited by regional trade and transit barriers.

Latin America reversed its trade policy stance, and during the 1990s average tariffs in the region declined from over 30 percent to 12 percent. The region's share of the world markets increased and net inflows of foreign direct investment (FDI) as a percent of GDP steadily climbed, reaching 5 percent of GDP in 1999—higher than East Asia. Overall, FDI net inflows in the latter half of the decade more than doubled from an average of 1.4 percent of GDP in the first half to an average of 3.6 percent in the second half.

In the Middle East, policy and economic barriers, together with a reliance on oil for several countries, prevented rapid growth in trade. High tariff rates, restrictions on services entry, and controls on agriculture interacted with poor investment climates to impede trade and keep transactions costs high. A large state-led sector also shaped a noncompetitive industrial policy that discouraged trade. Average tariff rates were almost 30 percent in the late 1990s, mirroring the import substitution policies early in Latin America and more recently in India. Flows of foreign direct investment as a percent of GDP have recovered

in the last decade, but still remain quite low at less than one percent.

South Asian countries other than Sri Lanka neither liberalized trade rules nor the rules governing inflows of foreign direct investment until the 1990s. Removal of the most egregious forms of anti-export bias and gradual domestic reforms, together with textile preferences, produced a rapid expansion in garment/textile exports, and led to high growth rates for exports in the 1990–2000 period and an increasing share of exports in GDP. Since growth was from a low base, South Asian exports as a share of world trade have remained low throughout the 1980–2000 period. South Asia maintained the highest levels of average applied tariffs, even compared to the import-substitution industrialization period of other regions. However, this is changing. Nepal launched trade liberalization in the early 1990s. Sri Lanka and then Pakistan in 1997 began to reduce their border barriers and increase their trade with the world economy. India began to reduce border protection from very high levels in the early 1990s and has continued doing so; in early 2004, India announced tariff cuts of roughly one-third, reducing the average tariff rate to about 22 percent. Bangladeshi border protections are still among the highest in the world, but they too announced reductions in 2004.[11] The region remains only minimally integrated in world capital markets. Net inflows of FDI, although higher than in the early 1980s, are less than 0.8 percent of GDP—the lowest of all the regions.

As with the Middle East and North Africa and South Asia regions, Sub-Saharan Africa remains weakly integrated into the global market. Although exports as a share of GDP in Sub-Saharan Africa increased in 2000, exports as a share of world exports have remained flat throughout the last decade and are lower than in the early 1980s. GDP growth has also been worse than in the earlier decades. Many countries in Sub-Saharan Africa are dependent on only a handful of commodities with highly volatile prices; most face very high transport costs and have weak institutions to facilitate trade. These countries have also experienced a number of armed conflicts throughout the previous decades and are plagued by endemic diseases such as malaria and HIV/AIDS, which have major impacts on their economies and societies. All these factors hobble trade performance.

Changing Export Composition and the Rise of Global Production Networks

The differential in trade and growth performance reflects the fact that certain regions have been better placed—in part through the policies they adopted—to take advantage of new technologies and changes in the nature of world trade. Not only has the volume of international trade expanded in the postwar period, but also its structure has changed in three fundamental ways. First, exports of manufactured products from developing countries, and trade in manufactures among them, have become increasingly important for all regions. Second, trade integration has allowed developing countries to specialize (most evident in the emergence of production chains), with trade in intermediates becoming more important. This trend is also evident in the role that new products play in production. Finally, foreign direct investment is playing an ever-increasing role in the integration process. These developments have facilitated the integration of countries that have adopted relatively open trade policies, and have increased the disadvantages facing countries that have segmented themselves from global markets.

Specialization in manufactures

Manufactured products as a share of exports increased strongly between 1981 and 2001 for all regions (figure 2.5). Countries in East Asia and later, Latin America and Eastern and Central Europe, have followed open development strategies that have led to increasing exports, especially of manufactures. The share of manufacturing in exports from East Asia, for example, increased from about 52 percent in 1981 to 88 percent in 2001, while the share in Latin America tripled from about 20 percent to 60 percent.

Trade has allowed manufacturers to exploit economies of scale, specialization, and scope. This is reflected in the growing share of parts and components in total exports. In the three more open regions—East Asia and Pacific, Europe and Central Asia, and Latin America and the Caribbean—parts and components trade has surged. This international segmentation of production—"production chains" in which intermediate inputs are traded and transformed into more processed intermediate inputs, which are then moved across borders to the next stage in production—has been a major factor driving the surges in intra-regional trade in those areas.

One indicator of specialization is the import content of exports. To measure the role of imported intermediates in trade, we calculated an index of vertical specialization, which measures the share of the value added of an export accounted for by imported intermediate inputs, either directly as imported inputs in the exporting sector or indirectly through the use of imported inputs in the domestic production of intermediate goods used by the exporting sector.[12] Vertical specialization is most important in East Asia, and least important in South Asia and Sub-Saharan Africa (figure 2.5c).

The evolution of production chains and finer division of the production processes across countries, including developing countries, allows producers to exploit potential efficiency gains from: (1) local increasing returns to scale in the production of intermediate inputs, (2) regional differences in factor costs for different parts of the production process, (3) increased competition from a wider market, and (4) technology transfer

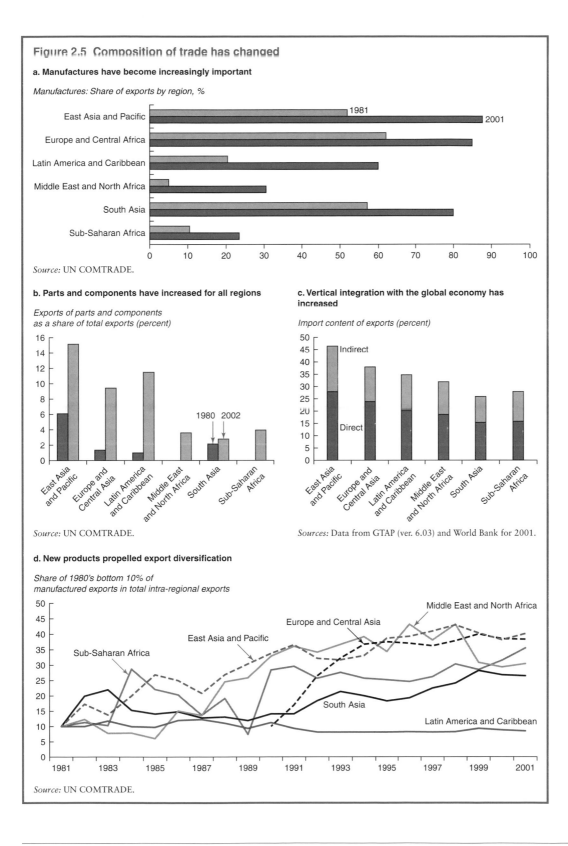

Figure 2.5 Composition of trade has changed

a. Manufactures have become increasingly important

Manufactures: Share of exports by region, %

Source: UN COMTRADE.

b. Parts and components have increased for all regions

*Exports of parts and components
as a share of total exports (percent)*

Source: UN COMTRADE.

c. Vertical integration with the global economy has increased

Import content of exports (percent)

Sources: Data from GTAP (ver. 6.03) and World Bank for 2001.

d. New products propelled export diversification

*Share of 1980's bottom 10% of
manufactured exports in total intra-regional exports*

Source: UN COMTRADE.

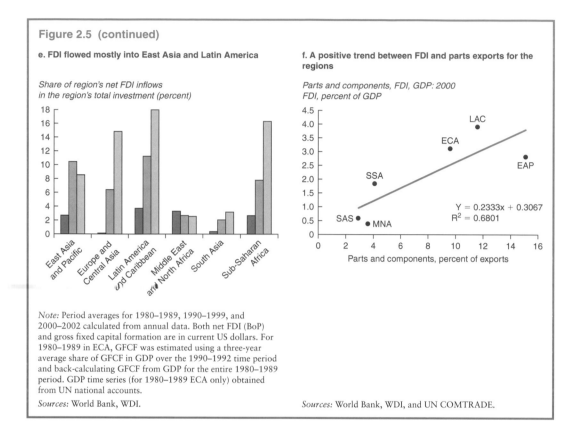

Figure 2.5 (continued)

e. FDI flowed mostly into East Asia and Latin America

Share of region's net FDI inflows
in the region's total investment (percent)

f. A positive trend between FDI and parts exports for the regions

Parts and components, FDI, GDP: 2000
FDI, percent of GDP

$Y = 0.2333x + 0.3067$
$R^2 = 0.6801$

Parts and components, percent of exports

Note: Period averages for 1980–1989, 1990–1999, and 2000–2002 calculated from annual data. Both net FDI (BoP) and gross fixed capital formation are in current US dollars. For 1980–1989 in ECA, GFCF was estimated using a three-year average share of GFCF in GDP over the 1990–1992 time period and back-calculating GFCF from GDP for the entire 1980–1989 period. GDP time series (for 1980–1989 ECA only) obtained from UN national accounts.

Sources: World Bank, WDI.

Sources: World Bank, WDI, and UN COMTRADE.

from developed countries embodied in imported intermediate inputs and backward linkages through exports. The magnitude of these links between increased trade in intermediates and productivity growth in developing countries has been studied in both cross-country analysis and country case studies.[13] While causation is difficult to establish, the evidence indicates that such links are important, and productivity growth associated with increased trade in intermediates is a potentially important source of growth.

Trade in new products

A large part of the expansion in exports in countries undergoing liberalization and successful trade expansion comes from products that were not traded—or minimally traded—prior to liberalization (see Kehoe and Ruhl 2002).[14] Growth in trade in new products

may have the important advantage of allowing countries to escape the deterioration in the terms of trade that would come from trying to increase market share in existing products.[15]

To assess this phenomenon, we reviewed the trade performance of the least traded decile of product categories. In East Asia and Pacific, those products that figured in the lowest 10 percent of all EAP manufactured exports to the world in 1981 grew to almost 40 percent by 2001 (figure 2.5). For the other five regions, the performance of products among their lowest initial 10 percent was also noteworthy. Countries are building dynamic new markets for their existing exports and developing new variations of old products to replenish the product cycle. This trend is also associated with increased trade in intermediates; detailed analysis indicates that many of the new export goods are intermediate inputs. Increased trade in new products is thus part of the virtuous circle linking trade and growth.

Investment, handmaiden of trade

Foreign investment has been a driver of integration, increased trade in manufactures, and vertical specialization. As tariff barriers have come down in manufactures, market-seeking, horizontal FDI that once led the way in the import-substitution process has faded in importance relative to efficiency-seeking, vertical FDI that looks to locate segments of production in the lowest-cost site. This form of investment is associated with the rise in production chains and trade in components and parts.

FDI has increased as a share of GDP in all regions. This trend abated somewhat since the East Asia crisis in 1997–98 and the global recession of 2001–02, but FDI growth is likely to resume with the recovery of the global economy in 2004. East Asia and Latin America—the largest markets—have had and have retained by far the largest shares of FDI throughout the period (figure 2.5).

In East Asia and Pacific, the increase in FDI supported the pattern of segmentation and relocation of production processes within the region. In the 1990s, a large part of the FDI into Latin America was due to the privatization process the region underwent during this period. There is broad correspondence between FDI trends by region and the share of parts and components intermediates in regional exports.

Technology transfer from developed to developing countries is linked to trade, especially through trade in manufactures and intermediates, and also through foreign direct investment.[16] The better economic performance of East Asia and Pacific can be seen as resulting from the emergence of a "virtuous circle" or synergy between increased specialization in production, increased trade in intermediates, increased foreign investment, increased factor productivity, and increased growth. This region started earlier and appears more successful than other regions in achieving and sustaining this virtuous circle.

Preferential Trade and Regional Outcomes

Many historical factors, not just preferential trading arrangements, contributed to these trends. In the next chapter we provide a more detailed analysis of the impact of RTAs on trade. Here we simply highlight that the nature of RTAs and the context in which they have been applied have varied enormously across regions and that regional agreements often follow, rather than determine, changes in regional trade patterns. This suggests that preferential trade agreements are just one of many factors affecting trade outcomes and that when implemented in a highly restrictive economic environment, they are usually inconsequential.

History shapes trading patterns

Differing regional performances in trade and growth have roots that go deeper than just boundaries on a map. Trade patterns—who trades with whom—have grown out of long political and economic histories that preceded the trends evident in the last two decades. The clusters of trading partners often bear little relationship to arbitrary definitions of regions (see Anderson and Blackhurst 1993, for an earlier analysis). Major trading blocs—that is, those countries that trade more with each other than with those outside their group—emerge from a cluster analysis. These blocs are not defined as traditional geographic political regions, but rather by statistical patterns in trade flows over decades.

The bipolar world of the 1960s

Coming out of the postwar period, the structure of world trade by the 1960s reflected a bipolar world, in which Europe and the United States had effectively formed blocs with some of their close neighbors, former colonies, and/or cold war partners; and with hub-and-spoke links to most of the developing countries. The two leading world trade blocs effectively accounted for 80 percent of global trade (figure 2.6). The European bloc was

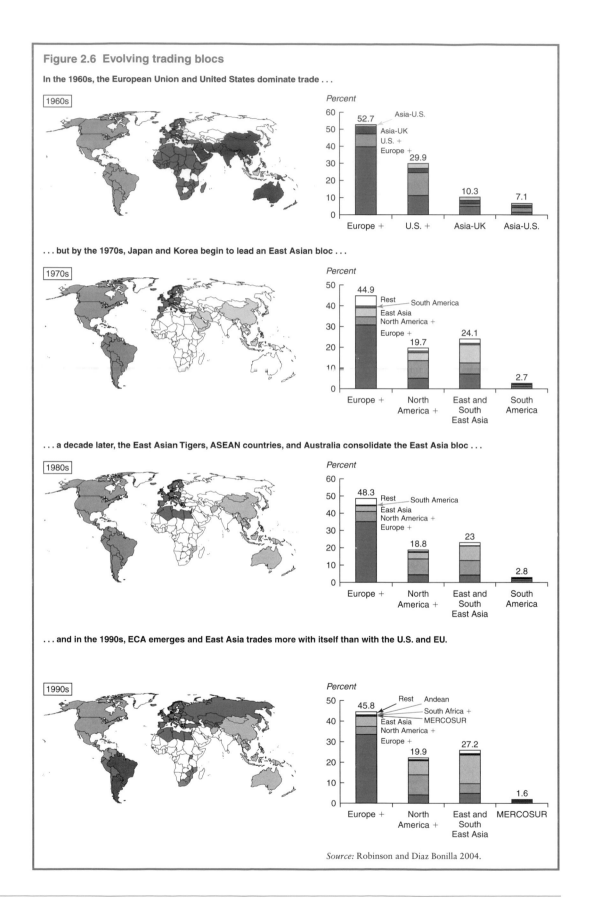

Figure 2.6 Evolving trading blocs

In the 1960s, the European Union and United States dominate trade . . .

. . . but by the 1970s, Japan and Korea begin to lead an East Asian bloc . . .

. . . a decade later, the East Asian Tigers, ASEAN countries, and Australia consolidate the East Asia bloc . . .

. . . and in the 1990s, ECA emerges and East Asia trades more with itself than with the U.S. and EU.

Source: Robinson and Diaz Bonilla 2004.

closely linked with countries in Africa and former colonies. The United States was closely linked to Latin America.[17] Britain still retained leadership in a small Asian cluster consisting of former colonies, China, and the rest of the Middle East, much as the United States led a cluster of countries closely linked to the post-WWII political order in the Pacific—Indonesia, Japan, Korea, and Taiwan. The dependent developing countries traded much more with Europe or the United States, and not as much among themselves.

The realignment and the emergence of East Asia in the 1970s and 1980s

In the 1970s and the 1980s, a realignment of world trade began. The European and U.S. blocs fragmented in the 1970s, and their dominance dissipated to 65 percent of global trade. The East and Southeast Asian countries left the European bloc and effectively formed a new bloc (East Asia).[18] This bloc consolidated in the 1980s, increasing the share of within-bloc trade and expanded membership to include Australia and New Zealand. Its export share shifted toward the United States (36.2 percent in the 1980s compared to 26.4 percent in the 1970s). It also represented a growing share of total world trade—23 percent in the 1980s compared to 16 percent in the 1970s.

Consolidation and diversification in the 1990s

By the 1990s, earlier trends blossomed into a tri-polar world. One new element was the breakup of the Soviet Union and Moscow's central management of trade in Eastern Europe. Trading patterns began gravitating toward the EU. A second new element was the emergence of a new grouping: Argentina, Brazil, Paraguay, and Uruguay (i.e., MERCOSUR).[19] Finally, detailed analysis indicates a nascent bloc forming around South Africa, including the SACU countries.

These global trading patterns are revealing: First, today's tri-polar world of global commerce does not signify that the world is evolving into three disparate, autarchic trading

blocs. To the contrary, trade among these blocs is intensifying, becoming more diversified, and linked with a web of business ties across oceans that bind the world market together. Second, in the 1990s, the emergence of new poles of commerce—MERCOSUR and South Africa—indicates that the process of segmentation and new bloc formation in world trade is still evolving. Third, it is clear that many of the emerging preferential arrangements have deep roots in historical trading patterns, but that some of the more recent bilateral FTAs are going beyond these historical patterns.

RTAs in different regions have different impacts

Patterns of regional integration tend to confirm the view that usually trade has preceded trade agreements. For *East Asia*, integration with the global economy was a strong impetus for regional integration. Exports to the world produced demand for imports from neighboring countries. As Korea matured and China opened, internal regional growth assumed its own dynamic. As a share of GDP, intra-regional trade in 2002 was 26.5 percent, twice as high as in the next highest region, yet regional trade preferences were very modest at best.

In fact, regional preferential trading arrangements followed rather than preceded this regional integration. The ASEAN Free Trade Area (AFTA), established in 1992, accelerated these tendencies and contributed to Southeast Asia's integration, but much of the tariff reduction has accompanied rather than preceded these patterns of regional integration. However, ASEAN leaders accepted in the Bali Declaration the need to pursue deeper integration and to create a single market to enhance the competitiveness of the region. The importance of preferential trade in the region was dramatically increased by the signing of a FTA between ASEAN countries and China.

Regional arrangements were critical for the successful integration of *Eastern Europe* into the world economy, but have not been as successful in the CIS countries. With the assistance of the EU in its Europe Agreements and with the aspiration of WTO membership, the Eastern European countries have moved swiftly toward integration. The CIS has been burdened with incomplete reforms, a poor investment climate, and a plethora of trading arrangements that have been implemented only partially. The combination has weighed down the subregion's performance.

In *Latin America,* the intra-regional share of exports in GDP in 2002 remains only one-fourth of East Asia's share. Since the 1960s, with the formation of the Latin America Free Trade Area (LAFTA), the region has struggled to expand trade. This proved futile as long as import substitution policies were in place and state enterprises were used as instruments of industrial policy. Early attempts in Central America and the Andean countries failed because of the inherent difficulty in managing potential trade diversion and location of industries within the regions behind high external protection barriers.[20]

This situation changed with the wave of unilateral reforms in the 1985–95 period. Mexico's reforms paved the way for the later creation of NAFTA in 1994, and reforms in Brazil and Argentina led to the creation of MERCOSUR in the same year. Similarly, the Central American countries, with a second go, managed to put in place a successful common market in the 1990s. As a result, intraregional regional trade has proceeded *pari pasu* with growth in the external markets.

In the *Middle East,* intra-regional trade has failed to gain dynamism. Because countries begin with broadly similar production and export structures, the scope for using regional trade to establish patterns of specialization and diversification in manufacturing production is limited. Intra-regional trade cannot be a substitute for extra-regional trade.

Several countries signed bilateral trade agreements with the EU as part of the Euro-Mediterranean agreements. Jordan and Morocco also signed agreements with the United States. All countries in the region entered into the Pan-Arab Free Trade Agreement and most participated in the sub-regional customs union, the Gulf Cooperation Council. Even so, these agreements have not been sufficient to overcome the effects of high border barriers and restrictions on services. The Euro-Med agreements with the EU have fallen short in their aspirations because of restrictions on trade in agriculture, services, and labor; lack of harmonization of standards; and stringent rules of origin.[21]

Regional agreements in *South Asia,* as with Latin America in the 1960s and 1970s, floundered on the shoals of high protection. The 1993 South Asia Preferential Trade Agreement (SAPTA) was stillborn, given continuing high levels of protection, a lack of meaningful concessions, domestic political problems, hostility between India and Pakistan, India's ban on imports of all consumer goods (from SAPTA countries until 1998 and from the rest of the world until 2001), and India's control over major primary goods (Baysan 2004).

Recently, however, unilateral trade reforms in India and Pakistan, political rapprochement, as well as concerns about rising preferential tariff arrangements in other parts of the world, led to the formation of the SAFTA Agreement in January 2004 (Newfarmer 2004).

In *Sub-Saharan Africa,* regional trade agreements are common and reflect an aspiration to overcome the limits that small sovereign states impose. These include SACU—one of the oldest customs unions in the world—CEMAC, COMESA, ECOWAS, and the East African Community. Although average applied MFN tariffs were cut by half between the 1990s and 2003, non-border barriers restrict internal trade. The recent regional trade agreements have had more impact on outward-looking MFN trade liberalization, and thus on external trade, than on intra-regional trade. The economic impact of these agreements appears to have been small, especially compared to pre-independence arrangements that essentially validated existing economic links (SACU, the West African

Economic and Monetary Union, and CEMAC). The EPAs under negotiation with the EU may reinforce this outward-looking pattern of trade integration, but the hope is that they will also aid Africa's own regional integration if they succeed in fostering economic reform and performance.[22]

The situation is different for agriculture and food products. Here margins of preference are more substantial in all regions except South Asia. The average margin of preference in the high-income region is similar to that in East Asia, Eastern Europe, and Latin America. Again, preferences are greatest in those regions showing the lowest degree of regional integration—the Middle East, and Sub-Saharan Africa.

Trade preferences have had very little impact on the high levels of intra-regional trade in manufactures in East Asia and Eastern Europe. Regions that offer substantial trade preferences behind high external barriers have not fared well in stimulating the growth of intra-regional trade.

Conclusion

Developing countries have increased their share of global trade as multilateral trade negotiations have led to sustained reductions in border protection for manufactured products. At the same time, and for a variety of reasons, the preferential trade agreements have proliferated. While the number of preferential agreements has increased rapidly, their trade coverage is substantially less than their official span of influence. Because many tariffs have come down close to zero, rules of origin restrict preferential access, and many products within agreements are excluded. Nonetheless, RTAs are leading to a more complex trading system and inefficiencies in customs administration; high tariffs in certain regions still risk significant trade diversion.

Notable differences are emerging between North-South bilateral agreements and South-South arrangements. North-South agreements are considerably more ambitious in content and coverage than South-South arrangements and reach deep behind the border to include services, protection of investment rules, and intellectual property rights.

In general, the wave of preferential trading arrangements followed—rather than preceded—an intensification of regional trade. Regions with the lowest external (MFN) border barriers ironically have developed the deepest intra-regional links and have been best positioned to diversify and exploit the emergence of global production chains in the manufacturing sector. East Asia is the starkest example, but Eastern Europe, in the wake of the dissolution of the Soviet Union, and Latin America, with the end of import-substitution industrialization, are not far behind.

What are the economic consequences of these arrangements? That is the subject of the next three chapters.

Notes

1. The recent accession of 10 new members to the European Union reduced the total number of RTAs in force from 285 to 229.

2. In fact there are only 12 countries that are not recorded as being party to a RTA, and many of these are small islands and principalities. The 12 are American Samoa, Bermuda, Channel Islands, Guam, Isle of Man, Monaco, Mongolia, N. Mariana Islands, Palau, Puerto Rico, Timor-Leste, and the Virgin Islands.

3. We are indebted to Gaspar Fontini of the European Commission's Directorate General for Trade for this formulation.

4. The U.S. Trade Representative is required to officially notify the U.S. Congress of its intent to negotiate FTAs.

5. See Weintraub (2004) and Schott (2004) for a more detailed discussion.

6. In the course of this discussion, the EU is treated as a single entity. For example, an EU-Mexico agreement is classified as bilateral.

7. The provision for regional cumulation in the rules of origin, particularly full cumulation, will tend to offset the hub-and-spoke system. See Brenton and Imagawa (2004). The EU, following substantial criticism of the hub-and-spoke system that emerged in Europe in the late 1990s, moved to create pan-European cumulation, although in terms of the more limited partial cumulation.

8. See Grether and Olarreaga (1999), who include GSP preferences but a smaller sample of countries.

9. In other words, 88 percent of intra-regional trade takes place among RTA partners.

10. This section benefited from the World Bank's regional chief economists at a workshop titled *Regionalism, Trade and Development,* May 5, 2004. Sadiq Ahmed, Harry Broadman, Alan Gelb, Homi Kharas, Mustafa Nabli, and Guillermo Perry made presentations that became the basis of this discussion.

11. The announced reforms were to reduce "supplementary duties" that were, in legal terms, additional to ad valorem tariffs; the economic effect is to reduce effective tariffs.

12. Hummels, Ishii, and Yi (2001) define an index of vertical specialization (VS). For direct effects for country k:

$$VS_k = \frac{\mathbf{u}\mathbf{A}^M\mathbf{X}}{X_k}$$

where u is a 1 x n vector of 1's, A^m is the n x n imported coefficient matrix, X is an n x 1 vector of exports, n is the number of sectors, and X_k is the sum of exports across the n sectors. When indirect effects are added,

$$VS_k = \frac{\mathbf{u}\mathbf{A}^M[\mathbf{I}-\mathbf{A}^D]^{-1}\mathbf{X}}{X_k}$$

the index becomes: , where I is the identity matrix and A^D is the n x n domestic coefficient matrix. Typically, given data limitations, measures of vertical specialization are imperfect. For example, a sector which produces both for exports and domestic markets, which is common given the aggregation available for sectoral data, is assumed to have the same production technology, particularly use of imported intermediates, for goods sold in either market. Even with these limitations, the measures provide a good picture of the changing role of trade in intermediates.

13. Winters (2004, 10–11) reviews the literature on links between trade in intermediates and productivity growth.

14. See Kehoe and Ruhl (2002). They present limited empirical evidence and then suggest a theoretical model that captures the phenomenon. Increased trade in new products is difficult to capture in standard models of world trade, so such models will tend to overstate terms-of-trade effects from changes in trade.

15. See Hummels and Klenow (2002).

16. Winters (2004) surveys work on the links between trade, productivity, and growth in developing countries. See also Nishimizu and Robinson (1984), and Esfahani (1991) who consider the links in semi-industrial countries. Schiff and Wang (2004) consider the link between TFP growth and regional trade links. Keller (2002) considers the mechanisms involved.

17. The definition of "closely linked" is countries that have such large trade shares with their bloc partners, particularly the United States and Europe, that adding them to the bloc increases the average within-bloc trade share.

18. Plus one region, "rest of Middle East and North Africa" (MENA), which is closely linked to Europe, but has significant trade with East and Southeast Asia.

19. The within-bloc trade share for MERCOSUR of 23 percent is lower than its trade share with Europe (27 percent), but given the increasing trend of its within-cluster trade share and the legal formation of MERCOSUR in 1995, it makes sense to designate it as a bloc. Latin American countries fall into three groups. One group is linked closely with North America, including RB de Venezuela, Colombia, and rest of Central America. The MERCOSUR countries define a second group, a trade bloc with diversified exports (a slightly higher share to the EU than to the United States). Finally, the third group is a heterogeneous collection of countries (Peru, Chile, and Other Andean Pact) with exports largely to the EU, partly to East and Southeast Asia, and with little trade among themselves.

20. IDB, Beyond Borders, 2002.

21. Chief Economist, MENA, 2004.

22. Chief Economist, Africa, 2004.

References

Acemoglu, D., S. Johnson, and J. A. Robinson. 2001. The Colonial Origins of Comparative Development: An Empirical Investigation. *American Economic Review* 91, no. 5: 1369–1401.

Anderson, Kym, and Richard Blackhurst, eds. 1993. *Regional integration and the global trading system.* New York: St. Martin's Press.

Baldwin, R. 2003. Openness and Growth: What's the Empirical Relationship? National Bureau of Economic Research, Working Paper no. w9578.

Baldwin, R., and A. Venables. 1995. Regional Economic Integration. In *Handbook of International Economics, vol. 3,* eds. Grossman and Rogoff, Amsterdam: North Holland Press.

Baysan, T. 2004. South Asia: Lessons and the Way Forward. Mimeo, World Bank, Washington, DC.

Bhagwati, J., and A. Panagariya, eds. 1996. *The Economics of Preferential Trade Agreements.* Washington, DC: American Enterprise Institute Press.

Brenton, Paul, and Hiroshi Imagawa. 2004. Rules of Origin, Trade, and Customs. In *Customs Modernization Handbook,* Conference edition, eds. Luc De Wulf and Jose Sokol. Washington, DC: World Bank.

Burfisher, Mary, Sherman Robinson, and Karen Thierfelder. 2004. Forthcoming. Regionalism: Old and New, Theory and Practice. In *Agricultural Policy Reform and the WTO: Where Are We Heading?* Eds. G. Anania, M. E. Bohman, C. A. Carter, and A. F. McCalla. Cheltenham, UK & Northampton MA, US: Edward Elgar.

Destler, I. M., and Peter J. Balint. 1999. *The New Politics of American Trade: Trade, Labor, and the Environment.* Washington, DC: Institute for International Economics.

Esfahani, H. S. 1991. Exports, Imports, and Economic Growth in Semi-Industrialized Countries. *Journal of Development Economics* 35.

Falkenberg, Karl F. 2004. EPAs and Doha Development Agenda—Parallelism or Crossroads Trade Negotiations Insights 3, (July) (4). www.ictsd.org.

Frankel, J. A., E. Stein, and S-J. Wei. 1996. Regional Trading Arrangements: Natural or Supernatural? *American Economic Review* 86, (2): 52–56.

Grether, Jean-Marie, and Marcelo Olarreaga. 1999. Preferential and Nonpreferential Trade Flows in World Trade. In *Trade rules in the making: Challenges in regional and multilateral negotiations,* 159–79. Washington, DC: Brookings Institution Press and Organization of American States.

Hinkle L., and M. Schiff. 2004. Economic Partnership Agreements between Subsaharan Africa and the EU: A Development Perspective on the Trade Components, *Africa Region Working Paper* (draft). February, World Bank, Washington, DC.

Hummels, David, Jun Ishi, and Kei-Mu Yi. 2001. The nature and growth of vertical specialization in world trade. *Journal of International Economics* (Netherlands) 54 (June) (1): 75–96.

Hummels, David, and Peter J. Klenow. 2002. The variety and quality of a nation's trade. National Bureau of Economic Research, Working Paper Series 8712, January.

IDB. (Inter-American Development Bank). 2002. Beyond Borders: The New Regionalism in Latin America. Economic and Social Progress in Latin America. Inter-American Development Bank, Washington, DC.

Kehoe, Timothy J., and Kim J. Ruhl. 2002. How Important is the New Goods Margin in International Trade? University of Minnesota.

Keller, Wolfgang. 2002. Trade and the Transmission of Technology. *Journal of Economic Growth* 7, (1): 5–24.

Kiener, Christophe. 2004. Economic Partnership Agreements: A New Approach to ACP-EU Economic and Trade Cooperation. Paper presented to the EU-World Bank Retreat on Preferential Trade Agreements, July.

Mansfield, Edward D., and Jon C. Pevehouse. 2000. Trade Blocs, Trade Flows, and International Conflict. *International Organization* 54 (Autumn) (4): 775–808.

Martin, W., and F. Ng. 2004. Sources of Tariff Reductions. Background paper.

Melo, J. de, and A. Panagariya, eds. 1993. *New Dimensions in Regional Integration.* Cambridge: Cambridge University Press.

Newfarmer, R. 2004. SAFTA: Promise and Pitfalls of Preferential Trade Arrangements. Background paper for Global Economic Prospects 2005, May, World Bank, Washington, DC.

Nishimizu, Mieko, and Sherman Robinson. 1984. Trade Policies and Productivity Change in Semi-Industrialized Countries. *Journal of Development Economics* 16, (1–2): 177–206.

OECD. 2003. Regionalism and the Multilateral System. OECD, Paris.

Robinson S., and C. Diaz-Bonilla. 2004. The evolution of global trading blocs in the past forty years: Who trades what with whom, and why. Background paper.

Robinson, S., and K. Thierfelder. 2002. Trade liberalization and regional integration: the search for large numbers. *Australian Journal of Agricultural and Resource Economics.* 46, (4) 585–604.

Sapir, Andre. 1998. The Political Economy of EC Regionalism. *European Economic Review.* 42, (3–5): 717–32.

Schiff, M., and L. A. Winters. 2003. *Regional Integration and Development.* Washington, DC: World Bank.

Schiff, M., and Y. Wang. 2004. North-South Technology Diffusion, Regional Integration, and the Dynamics of the 'Natural Trading Partners' Hypothesis. World Bank, June, Washington, DC.

Schott, Jeffrey J. 2004. Free Trade Agreements: Boon or Bane of the World Trading System. In *Free Trade Agreements: US Strategies and Priorities,* ed. J.J. Schott. Washington: Institute for International Economics; Song and Xu. 2000.

Ullrich, Heidi. 2004. Comparing EU Free Trade Agreements–Services. European Centre for Development Policy Management. July.

USTR. 2004. Free Trade with Chile, Trade Facts. www.USTR.gov.

Weintraub, Sidney. 2004. Lessons from the Chile and Singapore Free Trade Agreements. In *Free Trade Agreements: US Strategies and Priorities,* ed. J. J. Schott. Washington: Institute for International Economics.

Winters, L. Alan. 2004. Trade Liberalization and Economic Performance: An Overview. *The Economic Journal*, 114 (February): F4–F21.

Winters, L. Alan, Neil McCulloch, and Andrew McKay. 2004. Trade Liberalization and Poverty: The Evidence So Far. *Journal of Economic Literature*, XLII (March): 72–115.

Wonnacott, Paul. 1996. Beyond NAFTA—The Design of a Free Trade Agreement of the Americas. In *The economics of preferential trade agreements,* 79–107. College Park: University of Maryland, Center for International Economics; Washington, DC: AEI Press.

World Bank. 1999. Trade, Global Policy, and the Environment. World Bank Discussion Paper No. 402. Washington, DC: World Bank.

World Bank. 2003. *Trade, Investment, and Development in the Middle East and North Africa: Engaging the World*. Washington DC: World Bank.

_____. 2004. *East Asia Integrates: A Trade Policy Agenda for Shared Growth*. East Asia and Pacific World Bank Region, World Bank, Washington, DC.

WTO (World Trade Organization). 1999. Trade and Environment. Geneva: WTO.

3

Regional Trade Agreements: Effects on Trade

Regional trade agreements (RTAs) can have positive or negative effects on trade depending on their design and implementation. Analysis in this chapter confirms that gains from a preferential trade agreement cannot be taken for granted; moreover, even in agreements with positive impacts on average incomes, not all members are assured of increases. The interesting policy question then is not whether RTAs are categorically good or bad, but what determines their success?

The broader policy context in which an RTA is designed and implemented is crucial. Agreements that have been designed to complement a general program of economic reform have been most effective in raising trade. When RTAs have tended to be fruitless, it is often because of the lack of a coherent program of reform.

For an RTA itself, the most important ingredient for success is low trade barriers with *all* global partners. Most-favored-nation (MFN; i.e., nondiscriminatory) liberalization, which creates more trade, is the fastest and most efficient way to increase intraregional trade. In addition, agreements that minimize excluded products expand the scope for positive net benefits through competition and trade creation.

Recent research has added nonrestrictive rules of origin to the list of successful factors; local firms must be able to effectively source materials at the lowest cost. Such rules of origin are an essential element of agreements that expand both regional exports and exports to the rest of the world.[1]

RTAs can be a springboard to global markets, but here too, low MFN trade barriers are necessary for success. RTAs can help countries integrate with global markets, but no agreement provides guarantees, so design and implementation matter.

The Impact of RTAs on Merchandise Trade and Incomes

RTAs cover much more than trade barriers
RTAs have increasingly been designed to cover much more than formal trade policies (see chapter 2), and RTAs are signed for a variety of reasons. The impact of these agreements on trade determines the extent to which broader political and social objectives are achieved. It is difficult to identify an agreement that has fostered wider political objectives without achieving economic integration. It is clear that the political context and broad economic environment in which integration takes place are crucial for determining the trade impact. Success derives from a strong willingness to liberalize and to accept the subsequent economic adjustments, accompanied by intense mutual economic dialogue and communication and genuine efforts toward mutual understanding. Severe macroeconomic disturbances and a turbulent investment climate can easily disrupt trade and derail an agreement.

The simplest measure of integration is the trend in the share of imports from regional partners in the total imports of a region. Successful regional agreements might be expected to increase trade between partners relative to those countries' trade with the rest of the world. But three important caveats need to be understood.

First, successful regional integration is typically accompanied by reductions in tariffs for all partners. Hence, regional trade shares may not rise even though the volume of regional trade is increasing. Second, regional trade agreements that provide for the removal or reduction in trade costs other than those associated with formal trade policies (such as improved customs procedures), may stimulate trade from all sources. Third, many agreements cover nontrade issues such as investment, services, and labor, and these can have important consequences for growth and incomes. These are analyzed in subsequent chapters, but it is important to bear in mind here that an agreement may be successful even if the propensity for members to trade among themselves does not increase markedly.

Trade performance in several regional trade agreements shows that the increase in intra-regional trade shares of agreements signed in the 1990s has been substantial (figure 3.1). The share of intra-NAFTA (North America Free Trade Agreement) trade rose from less than 35 percent in the late 1980s to almost

50 percent in 1999. Over the same period, the importance of trade between MERCOSUR members doubled from 10 to 20 percent.

For many of the agreements signed in the 1990s, intra-regional trade shares were growing strongly before the agreements were signed (NAFTA, MERCOSUR, SAPTA, SADC). There may have been some anticipation effect in the year or two before signing, but this doesn't explain trend increases in shares commencing five or more years previous, as in the case of MERCOSUR. In many cases this increase in regional trade reflects the impact of unilateral, multilateral, as well as regional trade liberalization and the fact that agreements often follow growing trade relationships.

In Africa, the picture is mixed. The extent of regional integration among the Common Market for Eastern and Southern Africa (COMESA) members has been relatively static over the past two decades. In contrast the share of intra-area trade has increased substantially for Economic Community of West African States (ECOWAS) since the early 1980s and for SADC since the late 1980s. In East Asia, a region that has experienced substantial economic progress over the past 20 years, there has been little increase in intra-regional trade shares.

Given these disparate results, it is necessary to go beyond simple trade shares to identify the economic impact of regional trade

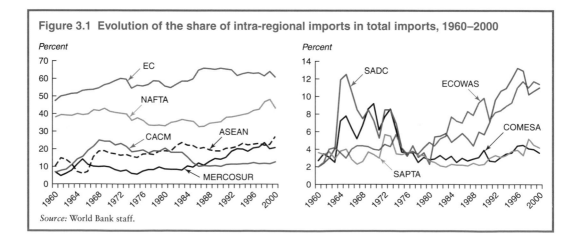

Figure 3.1 Evolution of the share of intra-regional imports in total imports, 1960–2000

Source: World Bank staff.

agreements. Because a decline in the share of extra-regional trade in total trade will be of less significance if the total value of trade is increasing, a logical (and commonly used) measure is the share of extra- and intra-regional trade in regional GDP (figure 3.2).

With the exception of MERCOSUR, all regions that have experienced an increasing share of intra-regional trade in total trade have also seen the ratio of extra-regional trade in GDP increase. The Association of Southeast Asian Nations (ASEAN) is an

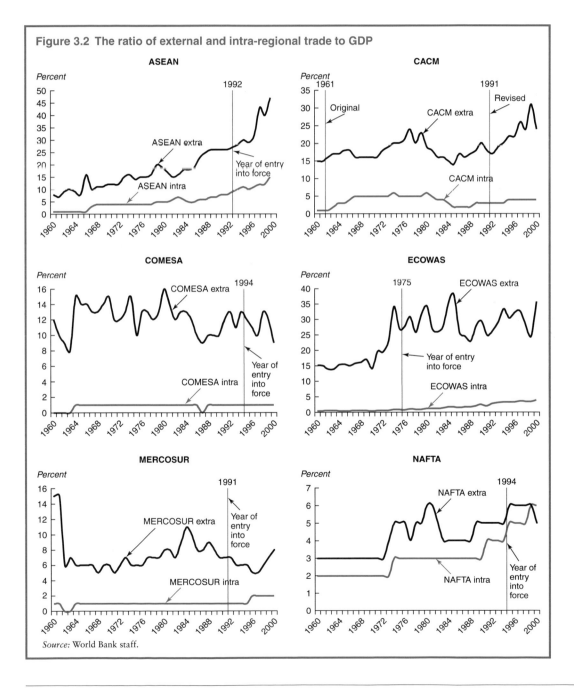

Figure 3.2 The ratio of external and intra-regional trade to GDP

Source: World Bank staff.

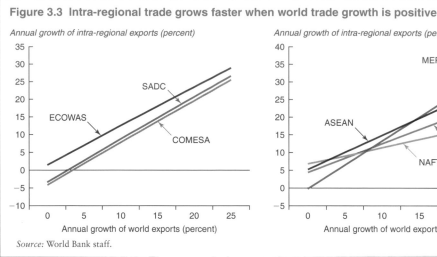

Figure 3.3 Intra-regional trade grows faster when world trade growth is positive

Annual growth of intra-regional exports (percent)

Annual growth of intra-regional exports (percent)

Annual growth of world exports (percent)

Annual growth of world exports (percent)

Source: World Bank staff.

interesting example. The share of intra-regional trade remained fairly flat during the 1990s. However, the ratios of intra-ASEAN trade to GDP and ASEAN imports from the rest of the world to GDP have both increased strongly. ASEAN appears to have been very successful.

In general, this suggests that external openness and the expansion of intra-regional trade go together. To take this analysis a little further, we plot the estimated relationship between annual changes in intra-regional trade and annual changes in the total volume of world trade, and we find a positive association in all cases (figure 3.3). Although crude, this analysis suggests that the successful expansion of trade among the members of a regional trade agreement tends to be associated with increasing extra-regional imports as a share of GDP and with the growth of world trade.[2]

Do regional trade agreements stimulate trade?

The analysis just discussed provides useful information, but it does not directly measure the impact of regional trade agreements. To isolate the role of policy—that is, RTAs—from other factors influencing trade patterns requires more sophisticated economic modeling. Different, yet complimentary,

approaches are available that we can crudely separate into *ex ante* general equilibrium simulation studies and *ex post* econometric analyses by using the gravity model (box 3.1).

The broad results[3] from general equilibrium exercises are that, first, excluded countries almost always lose. Second, for developing countries the bottom line determinant of positive income effects is the increase in market access. Third, in Free Trade Areas (FTAs) each country can always lower its tariff to ensure gains. This may be more difficult in a customs union. Finally, regional trade agreements are typically expected to create more trade than they divert, although this is not always the case.

These points are highlighted in figure 3.4, which summarizes model estimates of the impact of Chile signing FTAs with different regional groupings. Excluded countries lose in every case. Chile loses from an FTA with MERCOSUR. FTAs with larger markets bring bigger gains for Chile but also tend to entail larger losses for excluded countries. Large northern countries gain little from FTAs with substantially smaller southern partners.

A number of analysts have concluded that the numerous estimates from the gravity model generally support the contention that

Box 3.1   A primer on modeling of RTAs

A. Simulation studies: Looking forward to potential gains

The ex ante studies are based on a specific general equilibrium model structure that allows a rich analysis of the impact of RTAs at both the aggregate and sectoral levels. A key strength of this approach is its ability to highlight which sectors may expand and which may contract in the face of given resource constraints. The richness of the model structure, however, requires that many key parameters be selected, (often on the basis of an extensive literature search), with others being derived by a process of calibration to a single base-year observation; that is, the remaining parameters are derived such that the model replicates the situation in the base year. To a large extent the results of the impact of RTAs are determined by the choice of value for key relevant parameters (in this case the price elasticity of demand for exports). Also, given that parameters are chosen and not estimated, the statistical properties of the results are unknown.

The characterization of RTAs is often simple, with most studies focusing on the removal of tariffs but ignoring issues such as the rules of origin, product exclusions, and services. These simulation exercises answer the question, "What would be the impact of the preferential removal of tariffs against a limited set of trade partners, given the assumed model structure?" But they do not tell us whether particular agreements have *actually* created or diverted trade.

B. Econometric studies using the gravity model: Looking back at actual performance

The gravity model provides a useful framework for assessing the impact of policy variables on the behavior of bilateral flows between countries. Its name is derived from its passing similarity to Newtonian physics, in that flows between two countries increase in proportion to their economic mass (as measured by GDP) and are constrained by the friction between them (due to trade and other costs, which is proxied by distance). It is also common to use so-called dummy variables to capture geographical effects (such as whether the two countries share a border, or if a country has access to the sea), cultural and historical similarities (such as if two countries share a language or were linked by past colonial ties), and regional integration (such as belonging to a free trade agreement or sharing a common currency). A disadvantage of using dummy variables is that they may capture the impact of a range of other effects that occurred during the same time period as the RTA. For example, most applications do not distinguish the extent of multilateral trade liberalization. Ideally, specific trade policy variables would be included in the estimating equations, such the level of multilateral and preferential tariffs. However, the complexity of preferential trade arrangements precludes such an approach. A notable exception is the study done by Estevadeordal and Robertson (2004), who included a measure of preferential tariffs in their analysis of the impacts of RTAs on regional trade in Latin America.

Although widely used because of its empirical success, the gravity model had lacked rigorous theoretical underpinnings and was long criticized for being an ad hoc model. Recent theoretically grounded gravity equations are derived from models with strong constraints on preferences and technology, which undermines a straightforward interpretation of some of the estimated coefficients. Anderson and van Wincoop (2004) provide a good overview of this debate. Another weakness of many applications of the gravity model is the proxying of trade costs by distance, and the implicit assumption that cargoes traveling 1,000 miles in Africa face exactly the same trade costs as similar cargoes traveling 1000 miles in, say, Europe.

Sources: Inter-American Development Bank 2002 and Bank staff.

RTAs create trade.[4] This merits further analysis. Differing studies have produced sharply different results for the same agreement. For example, Bayoumi and Eichengreen (1997) find no evidence of trade diversion from enlargement of the European Union (to include Greece, Portugal, and Spain), whereas Wei and Frankel (1995) find "massive trade diversion." One way to digest this contradictory literature is to combine and assess these

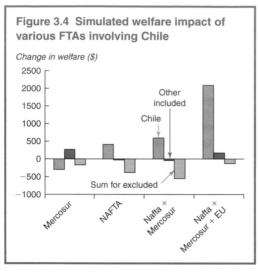

Figure 3.4 Simulated welfare impact of various FTAs involving Chile

Change in welfare ($)

Source: Harrison et al (2004).

results in a single statistical analysis, called meta-analysis (box 3.2). This meta-analysis of the literature on the impact of regional trade agreements on intra- and extra-regional trade indicates that although agreements typically have a positive impact on intra-regional trade, their overall impact is uncertain. Actual experience reinforces that there can be no presumption that a preferential trade agreement will be trade creating.

Do regional trade agreements benefit all members?

The attention in most of the econometric studies is on the impact of particular RTAs. Few studies have sought to estimate the impact of RTAs on individual members. This is despite the fact that studies of agreements that failed in the 1960s typically identify the lack of mechanisms for redistribution in the presence of asymmetric impacts as a crucial factor creating political tension and undermining commitment to the agreement (Greenaway and Milner 1990). We estimated gravity equations that identify impacts for individual members for each of 17 different regional trade agreements to determine whether the statistical evidence suggests that the agreement has created trade, diverted trade, or had no significant net effect on trade for each country.

For none of the agreements do we find unambiguous evidence of a net trade-creating effect extending to all members.[5] Thus even if an agreement as a whole creates trade, it is important that there are mechanisms to ensure that all members benefit.

Regional trade agreements and exports to the world

So far the analysis has concentrated on whether increases in intra-regional trade following the signing of a RTA are associated with falling imports from the rest of the world relative to a scenario in which the RTA was not signed. It is equally important to ask how regional agreements can be used as part of a broad approach to openness and especially whether they can provide a springboard to global markets for local exporters.

Applying the gravity model with an additional variable to capture overall exports of a member of a particular set of RTAs, we can assess whether these countries tend to export proportionately more than would "normally" be the case for a similar country that was not party to the agreements.[6]

These results, based on a sample period of 1948 to 2000, show that different agreements are associated with different propensities for higher-than-"normal" overall exports (figure 3.5). AFTA, EC, GCC, MERCOSUR, NAFTA, and SACU all appear to export significantly more than they would have done in the absence of the agreement. The countries that comprise these regional groups appear to have adopted policies that led them to be more export-oriented than they otherwise would have been. We cannot say, however, that it was the RTA alone that led to these policies. The variables that pick up changes in trade flows may be capturing the effects of unilateral and multilateral trade policies. Other agreements— CEMAC, CIS, COMESA, EAC, ECOWAS, and WAEMU—show a propensity to export significantly less than "normal." The Andean Community and SADC appear to export less when the whole sample period is considered, but not when the analysis is confined to the more recent sub-period, from 1980 to 2000. In

Box 3.2   Regional trade agreements in gravity models: A meta-analysis

Meta-analysis provides a means of assessing and combining empirical results from different studies. The approach takes as individual observations the point estimates of relevant parameters from different studies. This set of observations is then used to test the hypothesis that the relevant coefficient is statistically different from zero. Here we are concerned with two parameters. The first measures the impact of the agreement on total imports (which we label *overall impact*); a negative value for this parameter suggests that for the agreement concerned, the level of trade between a member and any other country is less than the normal level of trade that one could expect. Thus a negative value is evidence of trade diversion. The second parameter captures the impact of a regional trade agreement on the level of trade between partners (*internal impact*). In our analysis we have included 254 estimates of overall impact and 362 estimates of internal impact from

17 research studies. The table below reports the mean value of the overall and internal impacts, the standard deviation, the number of statistically significant estimates, and the total number of estimates of each impact.

Of the estimates of the overall impact, 76 percent are statistically significant, 42 percent are negative and significant, and 34 percent are positive and significant. For the internal impact, 66 percent of the estimates are statistically significant, 54 percent are positive and significant, and only 12 percent are negative and significant. The mean estimate of the overall impact is negative. The most robust estimates of the overall impact are negative. The mean value of the internal impact is positive. For both parameters there is a high degree of variance about the mean values. Within this analysis the estimates of 19 regional agreements were assessed; 10 exhibited on average net trade diversion.

Summary of the estimates by regional trade agreement

	Overall impact				Internal Impact			
	Mean Value	Standard error	Significant estimates	Total estimates	Mean value	Standard error	Significant estimates	Total estimates
Total	−0.31	1.12	194	254	0.79	1.30	238	362

Source: World Bank staff.

---

that period, the Andean Community also appears to have been more export-oriented than they otherwise would have been, perhaps reflecting substantial trade policy revisions.

Most of the agreements in which export propensities are lower also appear to generate fewer imports than would "normal" countries not participating in the agreements (CEMAC, CIS, COMESA, EAC, WAEMU). At the same time, those agreements that appear to be more export-oriented tend to be more open to imports (AFTA, EC, GCC, MERCOSUR since 1980, NAFTA, SACU). In many cases, there has been a strong impact on intra-regional trade. In general, members of regional agree-

ments that have been relatively open to imports have shown higher propensities to export to the global market than would otherwise be expected. Elsewhere, intraregional trade has been initiated, but imports have been diverted and exports suppressed.

The potential gains from larger markets and higher growth

Trade of RTA members will be affected through the changes in trade policies that take place, but will also change if there is an improvement in technology, higher investment, and a higher rate of growth. By crudely using dummy variables, gravity models provide a

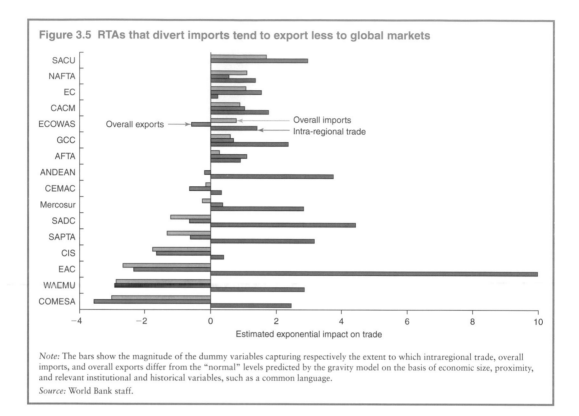

Figure 3.5 RTAs that divert imports tend to export less to global markets

Note: The bars show the magnitude of the dummy variables capturing respectively the extent to which intraregional trade, overall imports, and overall exports differ from the "normal" levels predicted by the gravity model on the basis of economic size, proximity, and relevant institutional and historical variables, such as a common language.

Source: World Bank staff.

measure of RTAs, which catches all of these factors through their impact on trade but cannot distinguish the precise mechanisms. Complementary approaches look at the impact of RTAs on these other factors.

Berthelon (2004), using cross-country regressions to estimate the effects of RTAs on growth during 1960–99, found that RTAs that enlarged the market substantially had substantial positive effects on growth. The results suggest, for example, that the FTA signed between Chile and the EU might be expected to increase the growth rate in Chile by 0.6 percentage points and in the EU by 0.005 percentage points. The larger market permits wider competition, larger scales, and greater specialization, all of which increase productivity and growth. South-South agreements face an uphill struggle in two respects: they generally entail much smaller markets, and they have less scope for realizing the gains from comparative advantage that different factor intensities would otherwise bring.

RTAs can also affect growth through technological transfer. Trade raises total factor productivity by providing access to a wider and more advanced range of technologies. The productivity of an importing country can increase through the importation of intermediate goods, which as a result of R&D in the exporting country, are either new and/or of better quality relative to existing products. In this way a country that is open to trade can benefit from R&D activities undertaken overseas. RTAs will have a positive effect if they stimulate imports from technological leaders. On the other hand, if the trade agreement leads to trade diversion away from more technologically advanced sources of inputs, then there could be a negative impact on productivity growth.

Schiff and Wang (2003) found that, for Mexico, trade with NAFTA partners had a large and positive impact on Mexico's total factor productivity (TFP), while trade with the rest of the

Box 3.3   Implementation matters

The European Union and agriculture
The founding treaty (the Treaty of Rome), and subsequent replacements, commit the European communities to "the harmonious development of world trade, the progressive abolition of restrictions on international trade, and the lowering of customs barriers." The European Union (EU) has failed to meet these objectives for agricultural products. There is little doubt that EU agricultural policy has been the source of considerable disharmony among trading partners.

Movement of Moldovan wine through Ukraine
Moldova is a major producer of wine. Although it has a free trade agreement with Russia, its main market, it costs more to ship a case of wine from Chisinau to Moscow than from Australia to Moscow (UNECE 2003). Why? Moldovan wine must pass through Ukraine, usually by rail. Although the two countries are party to the CIS free trade agreement, which provides for fair treatment in transit, the Ukrainian authorities, in addition to imposing delays and requiring unofficial payments, recently introduced an additional requirement that bulk wines must be transported in specially heated railway wagons, although a clear rationale for this is difficult to ascertain (World Bank 2004).

ASEAN and exclusions from preferences
ASEAN members initially were allowed to exclude certain products from tariff reduction, a right that they exercised liberally. In many cases the tariff reductions offered were of very limited value to other members. Thailand's offers, for example, included wood products that it did not import and that other members did not produce. Malaysia's list of products

for tariff cuts included a number of rubber products of which it was a major exporter. Indonesia, which lies on the equator, offered a 10 percent cut in the duty on snow plows (Balasubramanyam 1989). More recently, the trade elements of the agreement have been intensified with the launching of the AFTA (ASEAN Free Trade Area), the aim being to create a genuine free trade area. In 1995 the deadline for fully implementing AFTA was reduced from 15 to 10 years, although there has been some backsliding recently from agreed tariff-reduction schedules.

SADC and rules of origin
SADC initially agreed to simple, general, and consistent rules of origin similar to those of neighboring and overlapping COMESA. The initial rules required either a change of tariff heading, a minimum of 35 percent of value-added within the region, or a maximum import content of 60 percent of the value of total inputs. Subsequently, however, the rules were revised to include more restrictive sector- and product-specific rules. The requirement concerning change of tariff heading has been supplanted by detailed technical-process requirements, a much higher domestic value added requirement, and lower permitted import contents. The rules became much more similar to those of the EU and of NAFTA, reflecting in part the influence of the recently negotiated EU-South Africa agreement and the rules of origin governing EU preferences to ACP countries (Flatters and Kirk 2003). This example illustrates how sectoral interests and misperceptions of the role and impact of rules of origin can undermine RTAs.

Source: World Bank staff.

OECD did not. They suggest that this is because Mexico not only benefited from the content of trade with the NAFTA partners, the country also experienced closer contact and more information exchanges, especially among subcontracting firms, which are more integrated into the production networks of their Northern partners than was the rest of the OECD. They simulate the impact of NAFTA as a consequence and

find that it has led to a permanent increase in TFP in Mexican manufacturing of between 5.5 percent and 7.5 percent.

In a later study, Schiff and Wang (2004) look at the dynamic impact of North-South trade on technology diffusion to Korea, Mexico, and Poland from the EU, Japan, and North America. Using industry level data, they found that technology diffusion and productivity gains tend to be regional. A possible reason for this being that knowledge diffusion is also governed by close contacts and the hands-on relationships that are more likely with neighbors. Nevertheless, for all countries the biggest impact of trade on TFP can be guaranteed by removing trade barriers on knowledge-intensive goods from all countries.

Ingredients of Success
Open regions do better
RTAs are only effective for developing countries if implemented in conjunction with more comprehensive domestic reforms. At the same time, a successful RTA will contribute to the overall economic impact of that reform program. In Europe, the eight Central and Eastern European countries that recently joined the EU experienced strong growth in trade and investment inflows during the 1990s; yet two countries in the region, Bulgaria and Romania, having almost identical trade agreements with the EU but much less extensive domestic reform programs, saw a much weaker trade and investment response. Regional integration initiatives in Latin America in the 1990s have been much more effective than early efforts, reflecting broad and credible structural reforms in many countries (Devlin and French-Davis 1999). Given this context, there are a number of key features of RTAs that are likely to contribute to favorable trade outcomes.

The external trade regime is a crucial determinant of the success of RTAs for several reasons. First, trade diversion tends to fall with the level of the external tariffs maintained by member countries after they form a preferential trade agreement. The negative effects of trade diversion are offset or overcome if the preferential removal of trade barriers against some countries is accompanied by a degree of liberalization to all countries, whether undertaken unilaterally or through multilateral negotiations. If a country that enters into a free trade agreement increases its imports from all countries, not just its

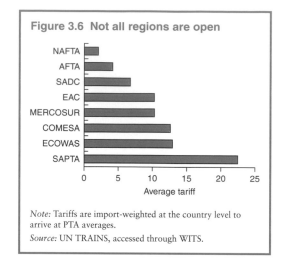

Figure 3.6 Not all regions are open

Note: Tariffs are import-weighted at the country level to arrive at PTA averages.
Source: UN TRAINS, accessed through WITS.

partners in the agreement, then it will experience an improvement in economic welfare. Therefore, countries forming preferential trade areas should simultaneously reduce the level of external protection facing nonmember trading partners. Risks of trade diversion are particularly high in the newly proposed South Asian Free Trade Area (SAFTA); (figure 3.6).

Second, where there are asymmetries in the level of external protection, it is important that the high-duty country reduce tariffs to avoid an adverse terms-of-trade shock. This is particularly relevant for developing countries seeking to sign agreements with the EU or the United States. In developed countries where tariffs on manufactured products are rather low (and high-duty agricultural products are typically excluded from regional preferences), trade diversion and trade creation are less likely to be significant. Thus with no trade being created in the developed market, the decline in domestic sales by firms in the high-tariff developing country may not be offset by a rise in exports to the developed country. Overall, the demand for goods produced in the high-tariff country may fall, and its terms of trade could worsen.

Third, low MFN tariffs (and nonrestrictive rules of origin) ensure that producers within the regional trade agreement will have access to competitively priced inputs. In today's globalized market, policies that significantly raise the input costs of producers will constrain their exports to both regional and global markets. Regional integration is more likely to be successful if it is achieved on the basis of strong competition and ease of access to low-cost inputs.

Trade liberalization is a crucial mechanism for increasing competition in domestic markets. Where it is not politically feasible to open up broadly to all external suppliers, a regional approach can provide a stepping stone toward the benefits of comprehensive liberalization. However, it is important to take the second step: Even in a large region such as the EU, competition from within the region has been found to be much weaker than that provided by external imports. Jacquemin and Sapir (1991), for example, found that profit margins in European countries were significantly dampened by external imports but not by intra-regional imports. And collusive agreements are more difficult to enforce for companies based in distant locations. Firms that face little competition in local and regional markets will have low incentives to achieve the efficiency necessary to compete in world markets.

Clearly RTAs may affect the setting of external tariffs. This is true by definition in the case of a customs union and indirectly true in the case of a free trade area. Recent research finds that World Trade Organization (WTO) members do not appear to have more liberal external trade policies than non-WTO members (Rose 2004), and that membership in a RTA has, on average, no clear effect on a country's trade policy (Nitsch and Sturm 2003). Foroutan (1998), on the other hand, concludes that countries in effective regional groupings, distinguished by the growth of intra-area trade, have undertaken more far-reaching trade liberalization. However, there are cases of liberalizing countries that did not belong to an RTA and of countries in an effective RTA that did not liberalize trade policy. The conclusion is that the acceptance of a liberal trade policy may be a requirement for the survival and deepening of a meaningful RTA, whereas belonging to a regional scheme constitutes neither a necessary nor a sufficient condition for an open and liberal trade regime.

In the 1960s and 1970s, preferential agreements among developing countries were typically accompanied by high external tariff barriers as part of an import substitution strategy. In contrast, agreements among more developed countries in the same period were more often associated with declining external barriers. For example, the simple average external tariff of the original six members of the European Union fell from 13 percent in 1958 to 6.6 percent after the Kennedy Round of General Agreement on Tariffs and Trade (GATT) negotiations. Agricultural products were excluded from these reductions, reflecting their exclusion from GATT negotiations until the Uruguay Round. The failure to reduce agricultural tariffs in Europe led to substantial trade diversion in agriculture with significant welfare losses for European consumers, especially the poorest, and a considerable hardship for poor farmers in developing countries.

Many developing countries have since reduced external tariff barriers both unilaterally and through multilateral negotiations. As a result, recent preferential agreements among many developing countries have been introduced or revamped with lower external barriers. This is particularly true in Asia and Latin America, where preferential and MFN tariffs declined in tandem after 1985, so that margins of preference remained stable or were slightly compressed (figure 3.7).

Paper agreements are not enough

Important aspects in the assessment of RTAs are whether their members have implemented their objectives under the agreement and the extent to which the objectives in the agreement have been met. Often the objectives in an agreement are defined by foreign ministers or even prime ministers, while the way that those objectives are to be carried out is determined later in negotiations between ministries. If tariff concessions are subsequently negotiated

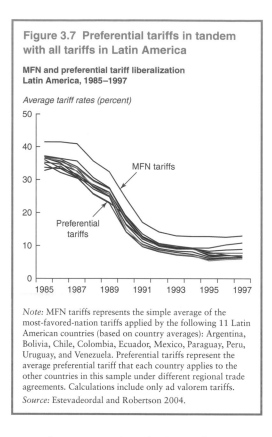

Figure 3.7 Preferential tariffs in tandem with all tariffs in Latin America

MFN and preferential tariff liberalization Latin America, 1985–1997

Average tariff rates (percent)

Note: MFN tariffs represents the simple average of the most-favored-nation tariffs applied by the following 11 Latin American countries (based on country averages): Argentina, Bolivia, Chile, Colombia, Ecuador, Mexico, Paraguay, Peru, Uruguay, and Venezuela. Preferential tariffs represent the average preferential tariff that each country applies to the other countries in this sample under different regional trade agreements. Calculations include only ad valorem tariffs.

Source: Estevadeordal and Robertson 2004.

sector by sector or item by item, the process becomes cumbersome and open to capture by domestic interests. The distinction is often made between agreements that reduce duties only on products specified in a positive list and other agreements, typically more liberal, implemented on the basis of a negative list of products excluded from tariff reduction.

Sectoral accords within RTAs can curb market forces and limit the benefits from competition. For example, Ozden and Parodi (2003) found that the auto agreement embedded in MERCOSUR between Argentina and Brazil compelled companies in both countries to balance trade, ensuring that production would not be reallocated to the lowest cost producer (Brazil); this move secured the support of the companies for the agreement. Because a new entrant would have to build plants in both countries (not just one), the agreement acted as a barrier to competition that favored insiders.

North-South agreements appear to have a better track record than South-South agreements. The comprehensive tariff objectives of most North-North agreements signed before the mid-1980s were implemented on or ahead of schedule (table 3.1). In contrast, South-South agreements reached during this period—most based on limited positive lists of products for tariff liberalization—had a very weak record of implementation. The delays in implementing initial regional tariff commitments "generally reflected a basic incompatibility between the inward-oriented development strategies of most members and regional liberalization"(De la Torre and Kelly 1992).

A larger number of South-South agreements signed or substantially revised in the late 1980s and early 1990s have sought a much broader degree of internal tariff liberalization, have been more effective in implementing agreed-on tariff reductions, and have tended to reduce external tariffs. For example, the GCC, launched in 1982, was originally intended to become a free trade area—a goal achieved by 1983. By the late 1980s, however, the objective evolved into formation of a customs union, which was established in 2003 (see World Bank 2003). However, table 3.1 also reports that substantial problems with implementation remain in many of the regional agreements involving developing countries.

Nonrestrictive rules of origin are integral to success

Preferential rules of origin are integral to preferential trade agreements. However, it has become increasingly clear that rules of origin can be designed in a way that restricts trade beyond what is necessary to prevent trade deflection or the transshipment of products from third countries through a member for the purpose of obtaining preferential duties. In addition, the proliferation of free trade agreements with accompanying rules of origin is increasing the burdens on customs services in many countries, and these burdens have consequent implications for trade.

Table 3.1 Implementation of tariff commitments by type of agreement, 1960–1999

Agreement	Objective on intra-bloc tariffs	Implementation record
North-North agreements reached from 1960–89		
ANZERTA (signed 1983)	Eliminate all tariffs by 1988	On schedule
European Economic Community (signed 1957)	Eliminate all tariffs by 1968	Ahead of schedule
U.S.-Canada FTA (1988)	Eliminate all tariffs by 1999	Ahead of schedule
EFTA (1960)	Eliminate all tariffs on manufactures by mid 1967	On schedule
South-South agreements, 1960–89		
Andean Pact (1969)	Eliminate tariffs on positive list	Postponed several times
Central American Common Market (1960)	Elimination of tariffs	Initially on schedule, most duties removed in the early 1970s, but restrictions reintroduced in the 1980s
EAC (1967–1977)	Establishment of a common market	The Community was dissolved
Latin American Integration Association	Liberalization of common lists of products by 1972	Common lists not liberalized on schedule
ECOWAS	Tariff liberalization by 1990	Progress negligible
ASEAN (1967)	FTA based on positive lists	Repeatedly postponed
GCC (1982)	FTA	Virtual elimination of all tariffs in 1983
South-South agreements, 1990–99		
AFTA (1992)	Gradual reduction of tariffs over 12–15 years according to member-specific schedules	Liberalization took place ahead of original schedule
CACM—Revised (1991)	Customs union	Implementation postponed; progress uneven among members
GCC	Customs union begins in 2003; completed by 2005	Customs union established on schedule
COMESA	Progressive tariff elimination to be completed by 2000	Implementation varies by country, 9 out of 20 members have moved to duty-free trade
MERCOSUR	Elimination of all tariffs by 1995	All lines, with the exception of sugar and automobiles, have been liberalized
SAPTA	Limited tariff concessions from a country-specific positive list	No formal schedules have been adopted
SADC	Tariff liberalization by 2008, with sensitive lists eliminated by 2012	Implementation delayed in some sectors due to lack of agreement on rules of origin
CEMAC (1999)	Economic Union	Tariffs liberalized according to schedule in nearly all lines
WAEMU (2000)	Economic and monetary union	Tariff liberalization mostly on schedule
North-South agreements, 1990–99		
Europe Agreements (Bulgaria, Romania)	Country-specific tariff removal schedules in preparation for the EU membership	Bulgaria mostly on schedule, Romania continues to have some unresolved issues
NAFTA	Tariff elimination in stages to be complete by 2008	On schedule
EU-Mexico	Progressive tariff elimination by 2010	On schedule
EU-South Africa	FTA establishment by 2012	Partial implementation pending official ratification
U.S.-Chile	Progressive tariff elimination by 2015	N/A

Source: World Bank staff.

In general, the rules of origin in North-South agreements are more restrictive than those adopted by South-South agreements (Figure 3.8). A feature of both EU and NAFTA agreements is the high degree of variation in rules of origin across product categories. Different rules are specified for different products: sometimes the rule may be a change of tariff heading, sometimes a change of tariff chapter; for other products there will be a value-added requirement; and in others the rules of origin may specify a particular technical process.

The amount of the required value added can vary across products. The change of tariff

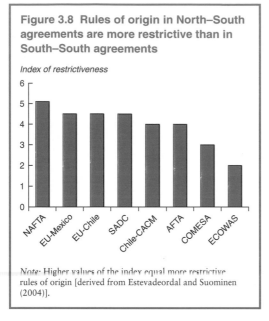

Figure 3.8 Rules of origin in North–South agreements are more restrictive than in South–South agreements

Index of restrictiveness

Note: Higher values of the index equal more restrictive rules of origin [derived from Estevadeordal and Suominen (2004)].

classification can be used to provide a positive test of origin by stating the tariff classification of imported inputs that can be used in the production of the exported good. Or it may be defined to provide a (more restrictive) negative test by stating cases where a change of tariff classification will not confer origin. For example, in the EU rules of origin, bread, biscuits, and pastry products (heading 1905 of the Harmonized System) can be made from imported products of any other tariff heading except those of chapter 11, which includes flour, the basic input to these products.

Specifying rules of origin on a product by product basis offers opportunities for sectoral interests to influence the specification of the rules in a protectionist way. The outcome of highly detailed product-specific rules of origin is typically a complex set of rules, which can be highly restrictive. Box 3.5 provides an example of the sort of complexity that can arise. Many agreements involving developing countries, on the other hand, tend to specify general rules that apply to all products. The AFTA, COMESA, and ECOWAS, for example, have a single value-added rule applicable to all products.

Anson and others (2004) and Carrere and de Melo (2004) estimate that the administrative costs of providing the documentary evidence to support the certificate of origin under NAFTA are in the region of 1.8 percent of the value of exports. The distorted impact of the rules, resulting from the need to use local and higher cost inputs to qualify, may be equivalent to an average duty of around 4.3 percent. Thus, restrictive rules of origin can very easily wipe out any margin of preference generated by a trade agreement. Other things being equal, compliance costs are lowest for rules involving a change of tariff heading, followed by value-added rules. Rules requiring a specific technical process have the highest compliance costs.

Estevadeordal and Suominen (2004) introduce a synthetic measure of the restrictiveness of rules of origin (the basis for figure 3.8) into a standard gravity model of bilateral trade flows. Their econometric analysis leads them to conclude that restrictive product-specific rules of origin undermine overall trade between preferential partners and that provisions such as cumulation[7] and *de minimis* rules,[8] which increase the flexibility of applying a given set of processing requirements, boost intraregional trade. Applied at the sectoral level, this approach yields support for the hypothesis that the restrictiveness of rules of origin for final goods stimulates trade in intermediate products between preferential partners and diverts trade away from nonmembers. Cadot and others (2002) find that for sectors where tariff cuts are larger than average, the rules of origin are more restrictive and the rate of use of preferences by Mexican exporters lower than average. They conclude that rules of origin are the "prime culprit" for the very modest impact of NAFTA on Mexican exports identified by other researchers.

Deeper agreements can lead to larger trade and income effects

In principle, agreements that address a wider range of barriers can have a greater impact on trade flows and incomes.

Box 3.4   Restrictive rules of origin under NAFTA—the case of clothing

Here is an example of what rules of origin look like; the following pertains to men's or boys' overcoats made of wool (HS620111).

> A change to subheading 620111 from any other chapter, except from heading 5106 through 5113, 5204 through 5212, 5307 through 5308 or 5310 through 5311, Chapter 54 or heading 5508 through 5516, 5801 through 5802 or 6001 through 6006, provided that: The good is both cut and sewn or otherwise assembled in the territory of one or more of the Parties.

The basic rule of origin stipulates change of chapter but then provides a list of headings and chapters from which inputs cannot be used. Thus in effect, the overcoat must be manufactured from the stage of wool fibers forward, because neither imported woolen yarn (HS5106-5110) nor imported woolen fabric (HS5111-5113) can be used. However, the rule also states that imported cotton thread (HS5204) or imported thread of man-made fibers (HS54) cannot be used to sew the coat together. This rule in itself is very restrictive; however, the rule is further complicated by requirements relating to the visible lining:

> Except for fabrics classified in 54082210, 54082311, 54082321, and 54082410, the fabrics identified in the following subheadings and headings, when used as visible lining material in certain men's and women's suits, suit-type jackets, skirts, overcoats, car coats, anoraks, windbreakers, and similar articles, must be formed from yarn and finished in the territory of a party: 5111 through 5112, 520831 through 520859, 520931 through 520959, 521031 through 521059, 521131 through 521159, 521213 through 521215, 521223 through 521225, 540742 through 540744, 540752 through 540754, 540761, 540772 through 540774, 540782 through 540784, 540792 through 540794, 540822 through 540824 (excluding tariff item 540822aa, 540823aa or 540824aa), 540832 through 540834, 551219, 551229, 551299, 551321 through 551349, 551421 through 551599, 551612 through 551614, 551622 through 551624, 551632 through 551634, 551642 through 551644, 551692 through 551694, 600110, 600192, 600531 through 600544 or 600610 through 600644.

This stipulates that the visible lining used must be produced from yarn and finished in either party's location. This rule may well have been introduced to constrain the impact of the tolerance rule, which would normally allow 7 percent of the weight of the article to be of nonoriginating materials. In overcoats and suits, the lining is probably less than 7 percent of the total weight. Finally, it is interesting to note that the rules of origin also provide very specific exemptions for materials that are in short supply or are not produced in the United States. In this regard, the rule reflects firm-specific lobbying to overcome the restrictions of these rules of origin when the original NAFTA rules were defined. The most extreme example is the following, where the apparel will be deemed eligible for tariff preferences if assembled from imported inputs of:

> Fabrics of subheading 511111 or 511119, if hand-woven, with a loom width of less than 76 cm, woven in the United Kingdom in accordance with the rules and regulations of the Harris Tweed Association, Ltd., and so certified by the Association.

Clearly, the job of the relevant official to check consistency and compliance with such rules is not a simple one.

_____

Source: World Bank staff.

Subsequent chapters elaborate on the potential economic impacts of dealing with many of the regional agreement issues introduced in chapter 2. Here we simply ask whether deeper agreements have a significantly greater impact on aggregate merchandise trade than more narrow trade agreements. Two studies[9] assume a productivity response to trade liberalization when other measures are included and ascribe the results to the deep integration measures. The calculations of these *ex ante* simulation studies illustrate the potential that deeper agreements may hold when they produce a productivity response, with changes in trade flows and incomes being a multiple of that under preferential tariff removal. However, because this result is inevitable from the way that deeper integration is modeled (i.e., inducing economy-wide increases in productivity), these results from one or another deep integration measure should be seen as indicative of potential rather than evidence of success.

Ex post exercises based on the gravity model will tend to capture all of the policy related impacts of a regional trade agreement on trade, not just the removal of trade policy variables. Several authors have tried to capture in an index the differences of depth between agreements; it is then used as the dummy variable in the gravity model to capture the impact of RTAs [Li (2000), Adams and others (2003)]. However, this approach presents the issue of how to weight different policy measures—for instance, should services liberalization get more weight than customs cooperation? Thus the value of the index would be dependent on the subjective weights that are assigned. The weights chosen by Adams and others lead to EFTA being ranked as much more restrictive than the Andean Pact or NAFTA. Further, many agreements appear extensive on paper but have accomplished little in practice.

Extensive monitoring of agreements is crucial to ensure effective implementation

In order to assess the impact of RTAs, information is needed on the extent to which the agreement's provisions are being implemented and how they are affecting decisions by producers and consumers. Given the need for monitoring, an implementation scorecard would be useful—such an approach has been adopted by the EU Commission which, as

part of its monitoring of the implementation of the single market, has introduced the "Single Market Scoreboard" (box 3.5). In addition to providing vital information, the scorecard is useful as a disciplinary measure—to shame governments with a record of poor implementation into action and to empower governments with good records of implementation to challenge those members who are not meeting their commitments.

More extensive monitoring could make an important contribution to the implementation of many trade agreements. Lack of effective implementation has been a major factor limiting the impact of many trade agreements in Africa, South America, South Asia, North Africa, and the CIS.

Conclusions: Preferential Trade Agreements and Economic Development

This review of the experience of preferential trading agreements over the past 40 years offers the following conclusions:

- There is no strong evidence to support the claim that a preferential trade agreement will be net trade creating or that all members will benefit. Positive outcomes depend on design and implementation.
- When embedded in a consistent and credible reform strategy, the key determinant of regional trade agreements' success is low levels of external trade barriers. While many developing countries have reduced tariffs, they remain high in many countries and regions, and the risk of trade diversion remains significant. Further reductions in applied MFN tariffs will be required to ensure that regional agreements are beneficial for those participating in them and to minimize the impact on the countries that are left out.
- Trade agreements that provide for comprehensive liberalization of trade across

all major sectors and nonrestrictive rules of origin are more likely to be successful. Agreements that devote considerable resources to negotiating limited positive lists or large negative lists and detailed product specific rules of origin limit the scope for gains.

- Effective implementation is crucial to positive outcomes, yet implementation is compromised by proliferation. If different

Box 3.5 Monitoring implementation of preferential trade agreements: "Single Market Scoreboard" in the European Union

The Single Market Scoreboard measures (1) the extent to which Single Market directives have been transposed into national law by each member state, (2) the average time it takes each member to transpose directives, and (3) the extent to which members are cooperating with enforcement and problem solving. This analysis by the European Commission is supported by regular surveys of businesses and individuals on perceptions of the Single Market and where it is not working. The Commission also monitors differences in prices of identical goods for indications that integration is leading to convergence.

The left figure below shows the implementation deficit for each member; that is, the proportion of directives that have not been notified as having been transposed into national law. The figure shows a substantial improvement in implementation since 1997; it also shows that the original six members of the EU and Greece are currently the worst offenders. Effective monitoring of implementation also requires that clear targets be established. In 2001, the EU Heads of State established an interim target of a 1.5 percent implementation deficit. As of July 2004, only five members had achieved this target.

A further measure of implementation is the extent to which agreed-on rules are being properly applied. In Europe, the Commission is charged with monitoring when Single Market rules are not being applied correctly; the Commission also takes infringement cases against member countries that are breaking EU laws. In terms of the number of infringement cases open in May 2004, Italy and France are the worst offenders (lower right figure).

Single Market Scoreboard

a. Implementation of single market directives by EU members

Percentage rate of nonimplementation

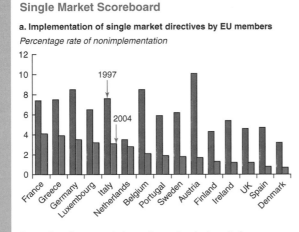

b. EU law breakers

Open infringement case (May 2004)

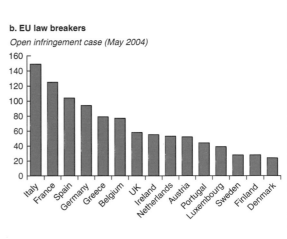

Source: http://europa.eu.int/comm/internalmarket/score/index en.htm#score.

agreements have different product coverage, different liberalization schedules, and different rules of origin, the ability of agencies such as customs to apply the agreements is severely undermined. The capacity to effectively implement is a crucial issue that countries should consider before signing an RTA.

- Monitoring can play an important role in providing for effective implementation, but often there is insufficient monitoring as well. Technical reviews are frequently not done, and when reports are made, senior officials fail to act on their recommendations.

Notes

1. Flatters and Kirk (2003).

2. The conclusion is unchanged if intra-EU and intra-NAFTA trade are excluded from the total of world exports.

3. Drawn from Burfisher and others (2004) and Harrison and others (2004).

4. For example, Ghosh and Yamarik (2004) suggest that "a consensus has emerged among researchers that RTAs are trade creating."

5. In this exercise, where the counterfactual is based on the historical pattern of trade flows, we assess how the regional trade agreement affected trade flows after its introduction. As a measure of robustness of the effects, we used three different estimation methods. Effects are considered statistically robust only if all three methods generate a significant impact of the same sign. The three methods are pooled OLS with robust standard errors. The second estimation method includes country-pair fixed effects using a specific OLS method. The third approach is a pooled Tobit estimation.

6. Here we follow Soloaga and Winters (2001), who include an additional dummy variable to assess the impact on the exports of members of regional trade agreements, although their focus is on the welfare effects of RTAs. However, here we apply a panel approach to a sample period of 1948 to 2000, covering bilateral trade between 178 countries with country-pair fixed-effects, which a number of authors, although not all, suggest is the preferred method. We apply the above equation. The regional dummies are time sensitive; that is, they are relevant only after the agreement has been signed. Using a different estimation technique, such as Tobit and OLS, and a different sample period can lead to different results for a particular agreement but the overall conclusion remains firm.

7. The basic rules of origin define the processing that has to be done in the individual beneficiary or partner to confer origin. Cumulation is an instrument allowing producers to import materials from a specific country or regional group of countries without undermining the origin of the final product. In effect the imported materials from the identified countries are treated as being of domestic origin of the country requesting preferential access. There are three types of cumulation, bilateral, diagonal (or partial), and full. The most basic form of cumulation is bilateral cumulation, which applies to materials provided by either of two partners of a preferential trade agreement. In this case originating inputs, that is materials, which have been produced in accordance with the relevant rules of origin, imported from the partner, qualify as originating materials when used in a country's exports to that Partner. Second, there can be diagonal cumulation on a regional basis so that qualifying materials from anywhere in the specified region can be used without undermining preferential access. Finally, there can be full cumulation whereby any processing activities carried out in any participating country in a regional group can be counted as qualifying content regardless of whether the processing is sufficient to confer originating status to the materials themselves. Under full cumulation all of the processing carried out in participating countries is assessed in deciding whether there has been substantial transformation. Hence, full cumulation provides for deeper integration among participating countries.

8. De Minimis or tolerance rules allow a certain percentage of nonoriginating materials to be used without affecting the origin of the final product. Thus, the tolerance rule can act to make it easier for products with nonoriginating inputs to qualify for preferences under the change of tariff heading and specific manufacturing process rules. This provision does not affect value added rules.

9. For example, Hoekman and Konan (1999) find that a free trade agreement between the European Union and Egypt limited to goods (but with substantial progress on removing regulatory barriers) could raise welfare by around 4 percent while an agreement that reduced barriers to services in Egypt could raise economic welfare by over 13 percent. Similarly, Brenton, Tourdyeva, and Whalley (2002) find that an EU-Russia FTA limited to tariff removal would increase welfare by around one-tenth of one percent while a comprehensive agreement removing technical barriers to trade and barriers to trade in services would raise welfare by more than 13 percent.

References

Adams, Richard, Philippa Dee, Jyothi Gali, and Greg McGuire. 2003. The Trade and Investment Effects of Preferential Training Arrangements—Old and New Evidence. Productivity Commission Staff Working Paper, Canberra, Australia.

Anson, Jose, Olivier Cadot, Antoni Estevadeordal, Jaime de Melo, Akiko Suwa-Eisenmann, and Bolorma Tumurchudur. 2004. Rules of Origin in North-South Preferential Trading Arrangements with an Application to NAFTA. Research Unit Working Paper 0406, Laboratoire d'Economie Appliquee, INRA, Paris.

Balasubramanyam, V. N. 1989. ASEAN and Regional Trading Co-operation in Southeast Asia. In *Economic Aspects of Regional Trading Arrangements*, eds. D. Greenaway, T. Hyclak, and R. J. Thornton. London: Harvester Wheatsheaf.

Berthelon, Matias. 2004. Growth Effects of Regional Integration Agreements. Processed.

Brenton, Paul, Natalia Tourdyeva, and John Whalley. 2002. Economic Impact of a FTA between Russia and the EU: Numerical Simulations Using a General Equilibrium Trade Model. Report prepared for the European Commission, Brussels.

Brenton, Paul, and H. Imagawa. 2004. Rules of Origin, Trade and Customs. In *The Customs Modernisation Handbook*, ed. L. De Wulf, and J. Sokol. Washington, DC: World Bank.

Burfisher, Mary, Sherman Robinson, and Karen Thierfelder. 2004. Regionalism: Old and New, Theory and Practice. Forthcoming in *Agricultural Policy Reform and the WTO: Where Are We Heading?* eds. G. Anania, M. E. Bohman, C. A. Carter, and A. F. McCalla. Cheltenham, UK: Edward Elgar.

Cadot, O., J. de Melo, A. Estevadeordal, A. Suwa-Eisenmann, and B. Tumurchudur. 2002. Assessing the Effect of NAFTA's Rules of Origin. Processed.

Carrere, Celine. 2004. "Revisiting Regional Trading with Proper Specification of the Gravity Model." *European Economic Review* (forthcoming).

Carrere, Celine, and Jaime De Melo. 2004. "Are Different Rules of Origin Equally Costly? Estimates from NAFTA." CEPR Discussion Paper No. 4437. London.

De la Torre, A., and M. Kelly. 1992. Regional Trade Agreements. Occasional Paper 93, Washington, DC: IMF.

Devlin, R., and A. Estevadeordal. Forthcoming. Trade and Cooperation: A Regional Public Goods Approach. In *Regional Public Goods: From Theory to Practice*, eds. A. Estevadeordal, Brian Frantz, and Tam R. Nnguyen. Washington, DC: Inter-American Development Bank.

Devlin, R. and R. French-Davis. 1999. Towards and Evaluation of Regional Integration in Latin America in the 1990s. *The World Economy* 22: 261–90.

Estevadeordal, A., and R. Robertson. 2004. Do Preferential Trade Agreements Matter for Trade? In *Integrating the Americas: FTAA and Beyond,* eds. A. Estevadeordal, D. Rodrik, A. M. Taylor, and A. Velasco. Cambridge, MA: Harvard University Press.

Estevadeordal, A., and K. Suominen. 2004. Rules of Origin: A World Map and Trade Effects. In *The Origin of Goods: Rules of Origin in Preferential Trade Agreements*, eds. A. Estevadeordal, O. Cadot, A. Suwa-Eisenmann, and T. Verdier., DC: Inter-American Development Bank.

Evenett, S. J., and W. Keller. 2002. On Theories Explaining the Success of the Gravity Equation. *Journal of Political Economy* 110 (2).

Foroutan, Faezeh. 1998. Does Membership in a Regional Preferential Arrangement Make a Country More or Less Protectionist? *The World Economy* 21(2):305–35.

Flatters, F., and R. Kirk. 2003. Rules of Origin as Tools of Development? Some Lessons from SADC. Paper presented at INRA conference on Rules of Origin, Paris, May 2003.

Ghosh, S., and S. Yamarik. 2004. Are Regional Trading Arrangements Trade Creating? An Application of Extreme Bounds Analysis. *Journal of International Economics* 63: 369–95.

Glick, Reuben, and Andrew Rose. 2002. "Does a Currency Union Affect Trade? Time Series Evidence." *European Economic Review* 46: 1125–51.

Greenaway, David, and Chris Milner. 1990. South–South Trade Theory, Evidence, and Policy. *The World Bank Research Observer* 5(1): 47–68.

Harrison, Glenn W., and David G. Tarr. 2003. Rules of Thumb for Evaluating Preferential Trading Arrangements: Evidence from Computable General Equilibrium Assessments. The Policy Research Working Paper 3142, World Bank, Washington, DC.

Hoekman, Bernard, and Denise Eby Konan. 1999. Deep Integration, Nondiscrimination, and Euro-Mediterranean Free Trade. Policy Research Working Paper 2130, World Bank, Washington, DC.

IADB (Inter-American Development Bank). 2002. *Beyond Borders: The New Regionalism in Latin America*. Washington, DC: IADB.

Li, Quan. Institutional Rules of Regional Trade Blocs and Their Impact on Trade. Processed.

Ozden, Caglar, and Francisco Parodi. 2003. Customs Union and Foreign Investment: Theory and

Evidence from Mercosur's Auto Industry. Working Paper, Emory University.

Palmeter D. 1997. Rules of Origin in Regional Trade Agreements. In *Regionalism and Multilateralism after the Uruguay Round: Convergence, Divergence, and Interaction*, eds. P. Demaret, J.F. Bellis, and G. Garcia Jimenez. Brussels: European Interuniversity Press.

Pelkmans, J., and Brenton, P. 1999. Bilateral Trade Agreements with the EU: Driving Forces and Effects. In *Multilateralism and Regionalism in the Post-Uruguay Round Era: What Role for the EU?* eds. O. Memdovic, A. Kuyvenhoven, and W. Molle. Boston: Kluwer.

Soloaga, Isidro, and Alan Winters. 2001. Regionalism in the Nineties: What Effect on Trade? *North American Journal of Economics and Finance* 12 (1).

Schiff, Maurice, and Yanling Wang. 2003. Regional Integration and Technology Diffusion The Case of the North America Free Trade Agreement. Policy Research Working Paper 3132, World Bank, Washington, DC.

Volker Nitsch, and Daniel Sturm. The Trade Liberalization Effects of Regional Trade Agreements.

UNECE (United Nations Economic Commission for Europe). 2003. Economic Survey of Europe. Processed.

Wonnacott, R. 1996. Trade and Investment in a Hub-and-Spoke System Versus a Free Trade Area. *World Economy* 19: 237–52.

World Bank. 2003. Trade, Investment, and Development in the Middle East and North Africa: Engaging with the World. Washington, DC: World Bank.

World Bank. 2004. DTIS Moldova, Case Study of the Wine Sector.

4

Beyond Trade Policy Barriers: Lowering Trade Costs Together

The removal of tariffs and quotas is a key feature of regional trade agreements (RTAs), but modern RTAs can, and are, being designed to achieve much more than that. Trade policies are only one element—and often a relatively minor one—of the overall costs of trade. Because logistical, institutional, and regulatory barriers are often more costly than tariffs and generate no offsetting revenue, cooperative governmental efforts to improve customs procedures, minimize the trade distorting impact of standards, and reduce transport costs may have a higher payoff than reciprocal reductions in overt trade policy barriers.

When RTA membership is part of a broad program of economic liberalization in which the objective is to attract international investment as much as to promote trade, a broad set of regulatory issues becomes paramount. Which are the most appropriate institutions to address these regulatory barriers? In certain cases, institutions at the regional level will provide for the most effective solutions, relative to both the multilateral and national levels.[1] RTAs can effectively promote dialogue and implement coordinated responses.

However, most RTAs have contributed little to reducing the associated trade costs, especially RTAs among developing countries. Many regional policy initiatives have foundered because of the lack of effective implementation, and crossing borders between most developing countries is still a major impediment to trade.

This chapter focuses on three key issues related to trade facilitation: *customs clearance, transport*, and *standards and their conformity assessment*. Coordinated action among developing countries is likely to be greatest with the first two issues, customs clearance and transport; examples of best practices in these areas are available and can be followed in regional trade agreements. Progress in reducing barriers is likely to facilitate trade to and from all trading partners with little or no scope to be discriminatory. And while cheaper, faster, and more predictable customs clearance and improved transport services have a direct impact on trade, they are also crucial elements of the investment climate.

Initiatives to deal with standards and conformity assessment on a regional basis are scarce; the most successful agreements have been between rich countries that are undertaking a deep integration process, as in the case of the European Union (EU). Nonetheless, systems of standards, quality assurance, accreditation, and measurement are crucial to competitiveness and sustained growth. Regional interventions can be useful if developed in a transparent way and with the participation of private groups (to ensure that procedures are not manipulated to serve a protectionist end). Initiatives targeted at a small number of key sectors and toward improving the quality of conformity assessment are likely to be the most useful.

Agreements that involve large markets and have differing levels of institutional capacity generally appear to have had the greatest success in dealing with these trade facilitation issues. This is because the more advanced partner tends to drive institutional improvements among the less advanced partners. (However, a real danger is that, in seeking greater access to industrial country markets through bilateral trade agreements, developing countries agree to apply a set of rules and regulations defined by the advanced country that are inappropriate for their level of development.) For many developing countries, agreements with industrial countries alone will not be sufficient, because the main source of higher trade costs are the borders and the weak transport systems they share with their developing country neighbors.

Progress often requires coordinated actions; for example, joint customs inspections must be allowed, common rules for transport must be established (including vehicle weight restrictions), and test results from partners' laboratories must be accepted. RTAs can provide a forum to enhance trust among trade partners that genuinely wish to move forward on these and other fronts.

The Costs of Trade

Despite globalization and the rapid increase in trade over the past 40 years, the costs of trading remain substantial—particularly for developing countries (box 4.1). Because of those costs, the actual volume of international trade is far less than economic theory would predict in the absence of significant barriers to trade [the case of the "missing trade" (Trefler 1995)]. And trade within countries is much more intense than between countries. If trade costs were insignificant, the propensities to trade nationally and internationally would be equal. In fact, crossing a national border appears to dampen trade flows even in regions such as the EU, where formal trade barriers and customs posts have been removed.[2] Finally, the retail prices of particular goods

tend to diverge with distance, and this difference is much higher when the two locations being compared lie on either side of a national border. If trade costs are low, then arbitrage should constrain such price variation (Engel and Rogers 1996).

The tax equivalent of trade costs can range from 30 to 105 percent, depending on the sector, according to estimates for imports by the United States (Anderson and van Wincoop 2004; Evans 2001). High trade costs discourage investment and constrain the ability of local firms to integrate into global production chains (Faini 2004). Given the magnitude of these barriers, ex ante simulation studies suggest that the benefits of lowering transaction costs, reducing insecurity, integrating services sectors, and increasing competition are multiples of reducing tariffs (Hoekman and Konan 1999). However, there is very little convincing ex post evidence of significant returns to regional initiatives that must deal with these issues, suggesting that substantial progress is difficult to achieve.

Ignoring institutional barriers during a tariff reform may undermine the objectives of reform—and indeed produce perverse results. For example, tariff liberalization in the face of border delays and customs corruption may have no impact on imports and may even reduce welfare if tariff revenues are replaced by longer waits to clear customs (Cudmore and Whalley 2003). In the absence of competition in the domestic transport sector, trade liberalization may simply lead to a transfer of revenue from the government to monopolistic transport owners. On the other hand, progress on many issues is not possible while high tariff barriers remain in place.

Cost raising barriers may be linked in circles of causation, with significant impacts due to scale economies in transport. For example, a reduction in tariffs or a decline in costs at the port may stimulate trade that can offer opportunities for transport companies to operate at more efficient levels of scale. And if there is effective competition in the transport sector, this could lead to lower transport prices and more

Box 4.1   Trading can be costly

Various policies and factors isolate national economies from world markets and thereby raise the cost of international trade:

- Tariffs, quantitative restrictions, and other border barriers—such as taxes on trade that raise the prices of imported goods relative to those produced domestically.
- Transport costs, both direct (freight and insurance) or indirect (inventory costs).

- Costs incurred when crossing a border due to documentation, delays, and bribes to corrupt officials.
- Compliance with national product standards and technical regulations.
- Insurance against risk, especially credit risk, and uncertainty associated with macroeconomic instability, lack of effective institutions, and unpredictable politics.

trade, and so on.[3] A reduction in corruption and delays at the border may stimulate trade, add to government revenues, and allow for a reduction in tariffs to achieve a given revenue target, which again stimulates trade.

Landlocked countries that face high barriers in moving their imports and exports through neighboring countries have no choice but to pursue bilateral or regional solutions.[4] These need not be embedded in a regional preferential trade agreement (PTA), but to be effective for small countries, agreements must provide for the settlement of disputes. Such provisions are likely to be more effective if they are part of a broad and comprehensive agreement.

Finally, removing institutional obstacles to crossing borders has a more certain benefit than reducing intra-regional barriers, because it saves real resources. Trucks that make more deliveries to the port are more productive. Interventions that lead to higher productivity have the greatest impact on trade and welfare—and on further increases in productivity. In contrast, removing revenue-generating tariff barriers on a preferential basis can lead to trade diversion and reductions in welfare.

Regional Agreements to Facilitate Trade and Transport

As countries develop their trade beyond the export of basic agricultural and extracted commodities, logistics requirements become

more important—and more costly. To compete in international markets and function within global production chains, firms need not only low transport costs and efficient ports, but also short transit times, reliable delivery schedules, appropriate storage facilities, and security (Carruthers and others 2003).

High transport costs, inefficient or corrupt customs, and long delays at borders reduce the trading opportunities available to many developing countries and can have significant economic and social costs (box 4.2). Conversely, better conditions tend to be related to higher levels of trade (Wilson and others 2003). Increasing the efficiency of customs, for example, can reduce costs and increase trade (figure 4.1). High transport and border crossing costs thwart, in particular, the poor landlocked developing countries.[5]

Regional integration can help promote more efficient and effective customs operations

Unlike many other factors that raise trade costs, there is broad agreement on what constitutes good customs procedures. Since its inception, the World Customs Organization (WCO) has developed best practices of customs policies and procedures. The Kyoto Convention commits its signatory members to implement these best practice principles and provides them with guidance in their efforts to improve national practices. While there is

Box 4.2   Border delays tax trade

Each day lost in transport delays is equivalent to a tax of about 0.5 percent (Hummels 2000). The situation in crossing borders between developing countries can be much worse.

- In Southern Africa, delays at the main border-crossing between South Africa and Zimbabwe (Beit Bridge) amounted to six days in February 2003, leading to an estimated loss of earnings per vehicle of $1,750, equivalent to the costs of a shipment from Durban to the United States.
- In Central Asia, on average, it takes more than 100 hours to cross the border between Uzbekistan and Turkmenistan. A truck traveling from Tashkent to Berlin, passing through Turkmenistan, Iran, and Turkey, will spend, on average, a third of total transport time waiting at border crossings (UNESCAP 2003).
- In the Andean Community, trucks spend more than half of the total journey time at border crossings (Pardo 2001).

- Crossing a border in Africa can be equivalent to the cost of more than 1,000 miles of inland transportation; in Western Europe the equivalent is 100 miles (Arvis 2004).

Border delays are associated with other trade costs as well, especially corruption in customs—and have been linked to the spread of HIV/AIDS. The World Bank has recently initiated a project in Western Africa to reduce, by the end of 2006, the average time for commercial vehicles to clear border formalities along the Lagos–Abidjan corridor by at least 20 percent, and average delays at the Nigeria–Benin border by at least 50 percent. These reductions are critical for this project and its mandate to reduce the incidence of sexually transmitted infection among commercial vehicle drivers.

Source: World Bank staff.

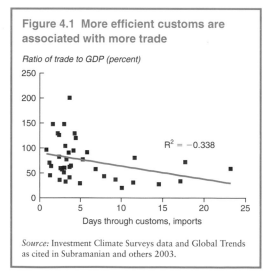

Figure 4.1 More efficient customs are associated with more trade

Ratio of trade to GDP (percent)

$R^2 = -0.338$

Days through customs, imports

Source: Investment Climate Surveys data and Global Trends as cited in Subramanian and others 2003.

other's problems and difficulties and can engender the sharing of best practices and positive experiences among members. This exchange is likely to be more relevant and better accepted inside the regional group of developing countries than examples from countries that are much more advanced and face very different implementation issues.

On the other hand, when regional units are made up of developed and developing countries, there is scope for financial support and technical assistance for less developed countries in their modernization efforts. The EU, for instance, provides assistance to the African, Caribbean, and Pacific (ACP) countries and incorporates customs technical assistance provisions in its Euro-Mediterranean Initiative. Such assistance will also be available under the Economic Partnership Agreements it intends to establish with regional groupings in Africa, such as ECOWAS. Similarly, Japan provides funding for capacity-building initiatives in APEC member countries.

much that countries can do individually to improve customs procedures, there is also scope for regional initiatives to modernize customs.

Contacts fostered by regional agreements can generate a mutual understanding of each

For a variety of reasons, tackling customs issues autonomously may be too daunting a task, and cooperation with trading partners may create the necessary momentum to overcome reluctance and opposition from domestic policymakers, customs officials, and traders. A review of a number of regional initiatives to modernize customs suggest the following areas in which RTAs can lead to improvements:

- *Align customs codes with international standards.* A good customs code supports efficient customs operations. It establishes the competence of the relevant authorities, promotes transparency and predictability of operational procedures and enforcement, encourages cooperation with the private sector, provides for effective appeals procedures, and enhances integrity. It would be advantageous for all countries to align their customs codes with international standards.
- *Simplify and harmonize procedures.* The recommendation here is to introduce a single customs document that limits the data requirement to a single set and adopts e-commerce techniques.
- *Bring all tariff structures in line with the international harmonized tariff classification* (HS). Many disputes can be avoided if all members of the grouping adhere strictly to an identical tariff classification.
- *Strive for transparency.* Increase the availability and accessibility of the legal text and regulations that traders and customs officials require and include other relevant information such as trade statistics.
- *Adopt and effectively implement the WTO Valuation Agreement.* Member countries can assist each other through effective mutual assistance agreements and shared databases.
- *Work together toward customs integrity.*
- *Establishment of joint border posts.* Joint border posts preclude multiple

examinations and lengthy border crossing procedures. A simple first stage would coordinate hours of operation and provide compatible computer systems on both sides of the border; these efforts would increase efficiency significantly.
- *Joint training centers.* Countries can join forces to operate regional training centers that can benefit from leveraged-up resources and can build cohesion between the customs officers of different customs services in the region.

Transport and trade facilitation initiatives raise productivity

In recent years there has been a development of a web of transport and trade facilitation (TTF) agreements aimed at easing the movement of goods and services across borders. Most of these agreements have been reached as part of, or in parallel with, an RTA.[6] Effectively implemented, TTFs can improve access to global markets for developing countries with poor transport systems—particularly landlocked countries.

TTFs often contain provisions to standardize customs procedures at borders and to harmonize customs documentation. TTFs can further facilitate trade by providing for the interoperability of transport resources and by fostering market access and competition in the transport sector.

Divergent national regulations for truck size and weight require vehicle checks on both sides of the border and often lead to overload charges and costly delays (box 4.3). In Southern Africa, for example, axle-load regulations are different in Namibia, Botswana, and Zambia (Röschlau 2003). Truckers who are in full compliance in one country can be prosecuted and fined across the border. Regulations concerning insurance, driver's licenses, and other documentation provide ample opportunities for cost savings. For example, the COMESA carrier's license system allows companies to operate regionally without having to pay for multiple licenses. And COMESA's vehicle insurance scheme enables

Box 4.3   Standardization and simplification can increase trade volumes: The case of the Trans-Kalahari Corridor

The Trans-Kalahari Corridor (TKC), the road route between Gauteng province (South Africa) and Walvis Bay (Namibia) via Botswana was opened in 1998, replacing the traditional longer route through western South Africa. Despite major road rehabilitation in 1999, traffic reached only 15 percent of the expected capacity. The major obstacles occurred at the border crossings. This led the TKC Corridor Management Group to seek a partnership with the customs administrations of Namibia, Botswana, and South Africa. This partnership resulted in agreements (October 2000) to extend the operating hours of customs at the Namibia/Botswana border from 22 to 24 hours to enable loading and unloading in Windhoek and crossing the border in the same day.

In August 2003, the TKC started a pilot phase to replace all existing transport documents with a single administrative document (SAD). To complement this effort, South African Customs developed a website with details on the SAD process. Border processing times were cut by more than half, from an average time of 45 minutes to 10–20 minutes. According to the United States Agency for International Development (USAID) estimations, reduced border delays created savings of $2.6 million per year along the corridor. As a result, the route had become economical, and traffic flows increased. Operators were moving about 620,000 tons annually along the TKC, about 65 percent of expected capacity, until the Botswanan government increased road user charges in February 2004. In some cases, road charges were multiplied by a factor of 10. The customs problem had been settled, but following this unilateral decision affecting the transport sector, traffic decreased significantly.

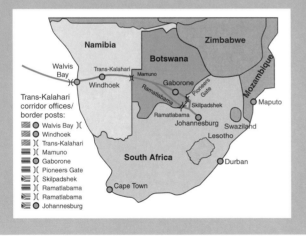

Trans-Kalahari corridor offices/border posts:

- Walvis Bay
- Windhoek
- Trans-Kalahari
- Mamuno
- Gaborone
- Pioneers Gate
- Skilpadshek
- Ramatlabama
- Ramatlabama
- Johannesburg

Source: World Bank staff.

transport operators to comply with insurance obligations throughout the region with a single policy. Similarly, ECOWAS's brown card system, introduced in 1982, has helped to reduce settlement time significantly. The success of such initiatives requires effective cooperation between different ministries (transport, interior) in the member states.

The impact of harmonizing customs procedures and transport rules may be limited unless there is competition in the domestic transport sector. In the extreme case of a domestic transport monopoly, the gains from lower operating costs and more efficient customs procedures may accrue to the transport company in the form of greater monopoly profits—with little impact on trade and poverty. Equally important is competition between routes and between different modes of transport. For example, Lao goods were almost exclusively exported through Vietnam until the Lao People's Democratic Republic developed alternative transit routes through Thailand. It now takes one day for an export container loaded with garments from Vientiane to reach a main international transport node at Bangkok, compared with three to four days to reach Danang (Banomyong 2000).

Although competition is often included in regional treaties (such as the 1982 ECOWAS convention regulating interstate road transportation or the 1993 COMESA Kampala Treaty),[7] effective implementation is rare. Because national authorities often fear a loss of sovereignty if they allow foreign operators in the market, a regional legal framework and effective enforcement mechanisms are necessary for successful implementation. In the case of the EU, full implementation was not achieved until 1985—28 years after the signing of the Treaty of Rome. Since then, the benefits have been substantial (box 4.4).

In several West African countries, transit regimes are governed by national, bilateral, or customs frameworks, rather than regional arrangements (UEMOA Commission 2000).[8] Many transport companies oppose the adoption of regional frameworks for fear of upsetting the "tour de role" system.[9] Bilateral transport treaties often predefine the transport share of both countries (normally 50-50); the exporter therefore has no choice in selecting a transport operator. The effect of this system is to protect less efficient operators. Even the more sophisticated North America Free Trade Agreement (NAFTA) has experienced difficulties in implementing cross-border trucking competition, following protectionist pressures from U.S. unions, concerns about truck safety, and Mexican driver qualifications and competence.

MERCOSUR countries implemented the "International Common Manifesto Cargo and Customs Transit Dispatch" (IMC/CTD) in 1991. This form harmonized and unified all

---

Box 4.4   Logistics costs in Europe have fallen in the last two decades

Since the late 1980s the proportion of company revenues spent on logistics in Europe has declined from 14.3 percent to 6.8 percent, a reduction that far exceeds the average level of EU external tariff on manufactured goods (Mentzoni 2003).

This development reflects the following important trends in the logistics industry:

- Centralization of inventory through a smaller number of warehouses;
- Increased outsourcing of logistics services to specialized companies; and
- Just-in-time supply policy (Ruijgrok 2001).

These changes have followed key policy initiatives. The removal of borders within the EU reduced uncertainty and the costs of international transport. At the same time, the EU acted to increase competition in the industry through the adoption of cabotage—a policy that enables carriers to operate

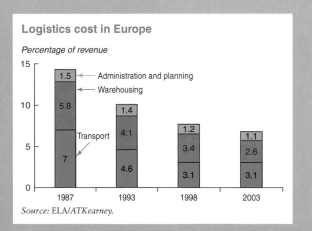

Logistics cost in Europe

Percentage of revenue

Source: ELA/ATKearney.

domestically in all member countries, regardless of their country of registry.

Source: World Bank staff.

information required by different border control institutions (customs, migratory; see Nofal 2004).

Regional cooperation reinforces transport and trade facilitation programs

Trade liberalization—whether unilateral, multilateral, or regional—may have a very muted economic impact in the presence of very high transport costs, weak logistical services, and long delays to clear customs. Conversely, in the presence of high trade barriers there may be little reason for traders to lobby for improvements in transport. And trade restrictions that limit quantities may undermine the incentive to invest in improved transport and trade facilitation services. Hence, actions to improve transport and reduce trade barriers are often complementary.

Trade facilitation can be effective even in the absence of a formal RTA. However, a formal agreement *may* help to entrench and enhance facilitation initiatives beyond what is possible through cooperation alone. In principle, unilateral and multilateral liberalization by itself should lead to larger trade volumes—and hence raise incentives to invest in trade facilitation. By inducing a more thorough dismantling of trade barriers among neighboring countries, regional cooperation can create a broader constituency for facilitating trade flows. Integrating fragmented markets can make infrastructure projects more viable, and thus promote a virtuous cycle of integration and growth.

Realizing the inherent potential of transport and trade facilitation requires both a sound institutional environment and a conducive economic one. RTAs can help address institutional gaps and reinforce the corridor approaches that are common in agreements between developing countries. At the same time, RTAs can provide a forum for the discussion and definition of norms and harmonized rules that are often necessary for effective implementation. Involvement of the private sector in these discussions is often a prerequisite for effective action (box 4.5). Finally, negotiating transport issues in a regional forum can act to depoliticize issues (Schiff and Winters 2002).

Despite the enormous potential for gains from regional initiatives to improve customs and transport services, progress in many cases has been slow. Trade costs remain very high for many developing countries. Many initiatives

---

Box 4.5   The case of the Northern Corridor Stakeholders Consultative Forum

Since 1999, officials dealing with transport, transit, and private operators along the Northern Corridor (including Ministry of Transport, Ministry of Trade, customs agencies, exporters, and importers associations, etc.) have been regularly meeting twice a year to discuss transit issues. This private-public sector alliance has produced the following positive developments:

- Elimination of charges on imports routed through the port of Mombasa (by Kenya Bureau of Standards and the Kenya Plant Health Inspectorate Service);

- Development of a one-stop processing center; and

- Reduction of the number of required stamps to go through Mombasa port (from 21 to 11).

As a result of this forum, national transit and trade facilitation committees are being established in the region. Private sector participation has been extended to include insurance clearing agents, bank associations, shippers' council, and the like. Public/private partnerships to tackle trade and transport facilitation are also being established in West Africa.

Source: World Bank staff.

to facilitate trade have suffered from a lack of effective implementation. In several agreements, disputes over implementation can only be raised at the political level, which often means that small landlocked countries have great difficulty in securing the necessary compliance from larger neighbors. In these cases implementation is very much a function of political will.

The possibility of taking legal action under regional treaties can help drive implementation of transport facilitation initiatives. The European Court of Justice has played an important role in the implementation of a common transport policy in Europe (Funck 1998). A regional court of justice has recently been established in the Eurasian Economic community of the CIS, another regional court exists in UMEOA in West Africa. While a regional court of justice does not guarantee implementation, it does create potential for more efficient enforcement than is available through less formal dispute settlement channels.

Standards, Conformity Assessments, and RTAs

The construction and implementation of systems of standards, quality assurance, accreditation, and metrology are crucial to competitiveness and sustained growth—and hence to development. Standards have become key elements for facilitating transactions and trade both within countries and in international exchange between countries. Standards support markets and provide for efficient transactions. Standards and technical regulations stipulate what can or cannot be exchanged, and they define the procedures that must be followed for exchange to take place.[10]

The ability of would-be exporters to comply with mandatory health and safety standards, as well as market-driven voluntary standards in overseas markets, is a major factor determining access to those markets. Divergent product standards and duplicative systems for assessing conformity with those standards can constitute substantial barriers to trade, but these may only become clear after other barriers have been addressed. Reducing tariffs and improving customs and transport can be likened to reducing the water level in a swamp only to find a range of previously covered "snags and stumps that need to be cleared away" (Baldwin 1970).

When producers must alter their product to meet divergent standards in foreign markets, they lose some of the benefits of larger scales of production. When the foreign government does not recognize standards-compliance tests performed in the exporter's home market, or the home country does not have the facilities to test the product, the exporter must foot the bill for additional tests in the foreign market. For example, in Moldova the certification of organic nut production exported to Germany has to be renewed every 6 months, and each visit from an international certifying company costs $5,000 plus $2,000 per production test—once before processing and once after processing. This can amount to $18,000 per year, which is a heavy burden for firms in an economy such as Moldova, an economy trying to compete in international markets. Upgrading testing facilities and measuring equipment is essential for reducing the costs of conformity assessments.[11]

To reduce the damping effect of divergent standards on international trade, WTO members have agreed to discipline the use of mandatory standards by governments. These are relatively modest provisions—they deal with transparency of standards regimes, equal treatment, and the need to justify standards that differ from internationally agreed-on norms. Efforts to reduce barriers to trade caused by standards and conformity assessment have been more extensive in a small number of RTAs, although empirical evidence identifying the benefits of these interventions is scant at best. The issue for developing countries is whether regional initiatives can provide for more efficient and effective standards and conformity assessment systems. These improved systems would allow governments to meet domestic objectives to raise health and safety levels, and at the same time, facilitate trade.

Different paths to better standards systems

Different approaches are available to raise standards and to address technical barriers to trade. Countries can unilaterally upgrade standards by adopting international standards. However, the technological content and the health, security, and environment objectives of the international standard may not be appropriate for developing countries, because the international standards are strongly influenced by the OECD countries. Further, some of the returns to adopting the international standard—in terms of greater market access—only materialize if the country's trading partners also accept products produced to that standard.

A second approach requires cooperation between countries to upgrade standards. Countries agree that products satisfying particular standards will be accepted in each other's markets. However, cooperation agreements do not discipline other market access barriers, so that returns from the upgrading of standards may be undermined if other barriers are raised to protect a particular sector once standards are harmonized. Typically, the dispute panels in cooperation agreements have a mediation role, not an arbitration role. For these reasons, and unless all parties are committed to the upgrading process, the process of standards upgrading could have important obstacles.

The upgrading of standards within a RTA is characterized by more formal institutions, a higher degree of enforcement, and greater trust originating from the frequent interactions between members and the comprehensive nature of the agreement. Members cannot use tariffs to prevent the entry of a product satisfying the regional standard; this increases the certainty that a country's upgrading efforts will be translated into greater market access. Within PTAs different approaches to standards have been followed, which reflect the

different levels of development and institutional capacities.

We start by discussing the EU experience, where integration has proceeded the furthest. The basis for the free movement of goods in the EU is the principle of mutual recognition of the regulations of partners or the recognition of equivalence. Although standards vary from one country to another, it is presumed that they are designed to meet the same regulatory objectives and to offer equivalent levels of protection to the public. Thus products produced in partner countries can be accepted with the assumption that those products will not undermine basic regulatory objectives concerning health, safety, and the environment.[12] Mutual recognition of regulations is the simplest approach to differences in standards: it is a powerful tool for removing barriers to trade in goods and services, and with this approach the difficulties of detailed harmonization measures, which intrude on national policy making, can be avoided.[13] However, mutual recognition of standards requires a high degree of trust between regulatory authorities (essentially the responsibility for protection of domestic consumers is, in part, transferred to the overseas partner). As such, mutual recognition can only work in regions comprising countries of similar levels of income that have comparable standards.

Effective institutions are also important. In the EU, governments can defer from nondiscrimination and the free circulation of goods for reasons of "public policy or public security" and protection of health as long as such restrictions are not a disguised restriction on trade. To ensure the latter, the EU has developed the following mechanisms for disciplining national regulations and interventions into product markets:[14]

- Infringement procedures, whereby the European Commission acts to enforce community law, although such procedures are very time consuming and costly, have an impact only after the event and are ad hoc.

- Notification procedures, whereby member states are required to notify all draft technical regulations for scrutiny by an EU Committee, whose objective is to prevent new regulatory barriers to trade. In practice, all new national regulations of EU member states have to pass an EU test regarding their impact on the free movement of goods.
- Notification of derogation procedures, which require member states to notify authorities of cases in which they wish to prevent the sale of goods lawfully produced or marketed in another member state, on the grounds of nonconformity and nonequivalence with domestic requirements. This ensures that any derogations from the principle of mutual recognition are transparent and subject to scrutiny.

While mutual recognition of regulations underpins the EU Single Market, it has been apparent for a long time that for certain products and for certain risks (when consumers are directly exposed to hazards), equivalence between levels of regulatory protection embodied in national regulations cannot be assumed. In these cases the EU seeks agreement among members on a common set of legally binding requirements. EU legislation harmonizing technical regulations has involved two distinct approaches, the "old" and the "new."

The old approach mainly applied to products (chemicals, motor vehicles, pharmaceuticals, and foodstuffs), involved extensive product-by-product or even component-by-component legislation, and was carried out by detailed directives. Achieving this type of harmonization was slow for two reasons. First, the process of harmonization became highly technical, with attention given to very detailed product categories. Consultations were often drawn out. Second, the adoption of directives required unanimity in the Council, which meant that they were slow to be adopted. The limitations of the old approach as a broad tool for tackling technical barriers to trade become apparent in the 1970s and early 1980s, when new national regulations were proliferating at a much faster rate than the production of European directives harmonizing regulations (Pelkmans 1987).

It became clear that the degree of intervention by the public authorities before a product was placed on the market needed to be reduced, and that changing the decision-making procedure to allow the adoption of harmonization directives by a qualified majority in the Council was needed. The "new approach" regulations indicate only "essential" health and safety requirements, allowing greater freedom to manufacturers to satisfy the essential requirements and to industries to flesh out product specifications in the form of voluntary standards. The new approach makes good use of established standardization bodies—European Committee for Standardization (CEN), European Committee for Electrotechnical Standardization (CENELEC), and the national standards bodies. Standardization work is achieved in a more efficient way, is easier to update, and involves greater participation from industry. Products that conform to the standards promulgated by the European standards agencies are presumed to comply with the essential requirements of the regulations. However, these standards are voluntary, and firms can produce to different standards if they can prove compliance with the requirements of the regulation.

MERCOSUR has followed the old approach of the EU and focused its limited resources on harmonizing national standards at the regional level (see Nofal 2004). MERCOSUR has formulated 366 common technical regulations and some 300 voluntary standards. The Andean Community has recently decided to focus regional harmonization on a targeted number of standards—those of the products most traded. Only 40 regional standards were created, although they cover 60 percent of trade.

When harmonized regulations are pursued, it is important to avoid overly bureaucratic mechanisms. Harmonization through the use of detailed regulations can lead to excessive intervention by public authorities before a product can be placed on the market and have a chance to prove its viability. Regulators should concentrate on defining essential health and safety requirements while allowing firms the flexibility to meet those requirements and not stifle technological change and competitiveness. The CIS, MERCOSUR, and Andean Community countries still apply an approach based on very detailed harmonized regulations. When a company wishes to introduce a new product, it is often necessary to change the existing regulations or wait for a new technical regulation to be promulgated, which can take considerable time and be very costly. A recent Peruvian technical regulation for gas containers specifies the minimum width of the walls, stating the exact thickness, which effectively prevents the use of new materials that might be lighter but thicker.

ASEAN is also following a policy of targeting key sectors, but it is harmonizing around international standards rather than promulgating its own standards. For 20 key product groups, members should adopt, as national regulations, the agreed-on international norms. Members that do not adopt any of the identified international standards as their national standards still need to accept products from partners that comply with these international standards—unless they can demonstrate an inability to adopt the international standard due to "climatic conditions or infrastructural reasons."

Here the contribution of the RTA has been to provide an enforcement mechanism through dispute settlement procedures, such that members who do not accept from partners products that satisfy an ASEAN standard are ultimately liable to fines for compensation or removal of concessions. Therefore, ASEAN countries can adopt the ASEAN standards with confidence that incurring the associated costs will not be undermined by subsequent denial of access to partners' markets.

In agreements where regional institutions are weak, especially free trade areas, barriers to trade can be removed when standards from different members are shown to be *compatible*. This is the approach of NAFTA and also tends to be applied in bilateral trade agreements that have a standards component, such as those between Chile and the EU and Chile and the United States.[15] The compatibility approach is the converse of the mutual recognition of regulations. Under the compatibility approach, the standards of a trading partner are assumed to be insufficient in their ability to satisfy the importer's regulatory objectives, unless proven otherwise.

Recognizing the results of conformity assessment in partners

Mutual recognition of conformity assessment [usually negotiated in the form of a mutual recognition agreement (MRA)] is necessary if nontariff barriers are to be fully removed. This ensures that the test results from laboratories in the exporter's home market are accepted by the importer so that the costs of duplicative testing can be avoided. This agreement does not require that both countries have the same standards nor that both countries be members of a PTA. For example, the EU and the United States, for certain sectors, accept the results of product tests (for compatibility with their own standards) that have been completed in the partner's laboratories.

If conformity assessment institutions are relatively weak, however, harmonization of standards may be a necessary step to facilitate mutual recognition of conformity assessment. This is the approach being followed in ASEAN. The Andean Community established a regulation for compulsory mutual recognition in 2003 for sectors covered by regional standards. MERCOSUR will proceed with mutual recognition of conformity assessment procedures in the near future. However, MERCOSUR is a perfect example of how the conformity assessment infrastructure is lacking: Policymakers prefer to harmonize standards before moving to mutual recognition of conformity assessment, but firms do not show much interest in standards because, in the absence of mutual recognition of conformity assessment, the returns to investment in standards are low. This suggests that improvements in the conformity assessment infrastructure are necessary.

Singapore has signed a bilateral trade agreement whereby the United States recognizes certifications provided by Singapore to some of its East Asian partners. This highlights that rules of origin can be an important element in an MRA. If Singapore has a comparative advantage in the region in testing and laboratory facilities and is well endowed with professional staff in this activity, then the U.S. agreement with liberal rules of origin (whereby the United States accepts tests from Singapore labs of products from other countries), may help to establish or enhance the position of Singapore as a regional hub for testing and conformity assessment. Rules of origin that restrict the testing and conformity activities to products produced only in Singapore would tend to constrain such a development. EU MRAs tend to have these restrictive rules of origin.[16]

Regional trade agreements can facilitate mutual recognition of standards

Effective solutions to problems arising from different standards require a high degree of dialogue and trust among trading partners. RTAs, while not the only path to trust, tend to promote dialogue and communication, which in turn build trust. This has been the case for member countries of MERCOSUR and the Andean Community, in which trust has grown as integration has deepened (Nofal 2004). Such trust needs to be nurtured through openness and transparency when new national regulations are being considered.

RTAs also can provide a favorable negotiating environment and so reduce politicization in standard disputes among members, making it easier to find common solutions for the removal of non-tariff barriers. The interactions that take place in an RTA often improve institutional relationships between the different standards bodies of member countries—and

sometimes even between the institutions of individual countries. These close relationships allow obstacles to be overcome in informal ways, circumventing cumbersome formal interventions. MERCOSUR has yet to adopt mutual recognition of standards, but many conflicts over standards have already been solved by telephone between relevant officials in member countries.

A degree of trust between public institutions and the private sector is also important if more flexible approaches, such as mutual recognition of conformity assessment and/or of regulations, are to succeed. Strong, centralized regulatory cultures tend to produce technical regulations that are too detailed and difficult to change. It is important to ensure the effective participation of the private sector and consumers so that the setting of standards and their enforcement reflect broad rather than narrow interests.

Successful cooperation in harmonizing standards depends on simple principles

To date, RTAs in the developing world have not realized their full potential for overcoming standards-related obstacles to regional or global trade, although some slow progress is evident, such as in MERCOSUR. That is likely to change as the WTO agreements on Technical Barriers to Trade (TBT) and Sanitary and Phytosanitary Measures (SPS) come into full practical application, and as the importance of reforming standards systems in developing countries gains prominence. In the meantime, several principles can contribute to successful cooperation in standards and conformity assessment procedures.

A first step for developing countries is to *identify priority sectors* for reform to keep costs low and gather momentum for further reform. The sectors to prioritize are those where trade costs resulting from differences in standards and conformity assessment procedures are higher and where trade between members is large.

Second, if international standards exist for these products and they are appropriate for all members given their level of development, then the simplest approach is to harmonize around these international standards. This will only be relevant if all members have the capacity to implement them. It is important to clearly define objectives before harmonizing standards so as to avoid overregulation. For example, requiring information on labels that the consumer is unlikely to understand will increase costs and contribute little to the objective of making information available to consumers.[17]

An open and transparent system, with standards published in an accessible official bulletin before being implemented, is essential if regional initiatives are to facilitate trade between members and preclude the difficulties facing exporters from outside of the region. Ensuring flexibility is also important; thus, regulations that set minimum standards rather than detailed requirements are less restrictive for firms. When countries face internal resistance to modernizing and adopting new standards, the compliance with standards can be offered on a voluntary basis. This allows those firms that are able and willing to satisfy the new standards to progress. Daskalov and Hadjikolonov (2002) show how such an approach made it possible for more advanced and competitive local producers in Bulgaria to quickly adopt European standards before they were formally introduced as mandatory Bulgarian standards.

In the short run, the greatest gain for many developing countries is likely to come from improvements in the testing, certification, and accreditation institutions to underpin greater enforcement capacity. Initiatives that improve these institutions are likely to have large payoffs by allowing governments to achieve more effectively their existing objectives concerning health and safety and facilitating greater exports on both a regional and a global basis. For example, most MENA countries require that testing be done at their national laboratories, which are usually less sophisticated than European testing centers and saddled with cumbersome procedures, pushing up

product costs (World Bank 2003). This hurts MENA exporters and prevents MENA countries from joining global production chains destined for EU markets.

Many developing countries are too small to efficiently offer a full range of these conformity assessment services. Often there are too many laboratories offering poor quality services.

RTAs can contribute to better conformity assessment first, and most simply, by facilitating dialogue and the sharing of technical knowledge. More ambitious initiatives can build regional accreditation bodies to increase efficiency and enhance the reputation of local certification bodies in the global market. An open regional market for laboratory services can lead to cheaper yet higher quality testing on the basis of specialization and economies of scale. However, it must be stressed that while the potential gains are large, there are very few successful initiatives that can provide useful guidelines. ASEAN provides an example where members are pushing forward with a number of initiatives, including cooperation on legal metrology, and efforts to enhance conformity assessment bodies to facilitate mutual recognition of test reports and certifications.

RTAs can also provide a framework for collaboration that increases the effective participation of developing countries in international standards organizations and at the WTO. This is important if international standards and conformity assessment measures are to reflect the interests of developing countries—and therefore make the TBT and SPS agreements relevant for the majority of WTO members. For this participation to be successful, the structure of international standards institutions needs to be modified to reduce the costs of representation of developing countries. The International Standards Organization (ISO) has moved one step in this direction by being the first standard institution to allow electronic voting. This could be extended to other institutions. Another possibility would be to allow RTAs to represent their members in standard-setting committees, which would reduce members' costs of representation.

Attempts to remove barriers caused by differences in standards and conformity assessment requirements will be more effective in a climate of trust and mutual understanding. Such a climate requires a genuine willingness to liberalize and is unlikely to result in agreements with many exceptions, frequent recourse to safeguard measures, and high barriers at the border that can be due to customs delays and inefficient port and transport services.

The lack of relevant examples of successful intervention at the regional level to deal with standards issues makes it difficult to derive clear proposals based on best practices. In this light the best recommendation is for developing countries to proceed with caution and concentrate on targeted coordinated action for which the institutional requirements are not extensive and the gains are clear.

Trade-Related Regional Cooperation Agreements

Countries can benefit from other forms of cooperation that are linked to trade directly through RTA arrangements or indirectly when they influence trade-related inputs or outputs.[18] Such trade-related cooperation can deal with shared resources, such as water, fishing areas, power, railroads, or the environment. Schiff and Winters (2002) make the case that in the presence of economies of scale or inter-country externalities, market solutions to problems are not necessarily the best, and regional cooperation can often pay large dividends.

When regional cooperation arrangements are embedded in RTAs, it may be easier to conclude and implement these arrangements. Increasing trade raises the level of salience of all aspects of regional cooperation and may foster greater high level attention to the regional arrangement and allow for more effective and informal dispute resolution. Moreover, agreements that cover more policy domains—for example, trade, transport,

power, and the like—allow countries to trade off gains in one area against losses in another, reducing or even eliminating the explicit compensatory schemes that would otherwise be needed (Schiff and Winters 2002).

Consider some examples. The Southern African Development Community (SADC) provided the coordination point for regional integration in a regional power cooperation agreement. The Southern African Power Pool (SAPP), launched in 1995, was designed to take advantage of power resources in the region and was the first formal international power pool outside of North America. The 12-country region has abundant hydropower resources, especially the Inga Reservoir, large reserves of cheap coal in South Africa, and the Karriba Dam on the Zambia/Zimbabwe border. The pool covers 6 million square miles and serves 200 million people. Utilities in the region had been trading electricity for decades through bilateral contracts, but these were cumbersome to administer. The objective for shifting to the pool was to create a more efficient regional market. The SAPP is modeled on the "loose" pools in Western Europe and the United States, which emphasize constant exchange of information to maximize the cost and reliability benefits from trading and system autonomy. Rather than relying on central dispatch, loose pools rely on long-term bilateral contracts drawn up with common designs and security standards plus some central services. Unlike in the developed world, SAPP membership is limited to national utilities. Each member must meet its Accredited Capacity Obligation, a requirement that each utility have capacity to cover its forecast monthly peak. Each member is also obliged to cover emergency energy up to six hours, to provide automatic generation control and other facilities in its control area, and to allow wheeling through its system. SAPP includes most Southern African Development Community (SADC) members and is predicated on the latter's institutions, including the SADC Treaty, the SADC Dispute Resolution Tribunal, the SADC energy ministers, and the

Technical and Administrative Unit. The energy ministers are responsible for resolving major policy issues.

Though still in its early stages, the pool's potential benefits include reducing or postponing new requirements for generating capacity and reserves, lower fuel costs, and more efficient use of hydroelectricity. A SADC electric power study conducted in 1990–92 estimated a savings of 20 percent ($785 million) in costs over 1995–2010.

Three factors were critical to the development of the regional agreement: The availability of complementary power sources, an active regional organization for economic cooperation, and the political will to support increased regional energy trade. SADC and its predecessor, the Southern African Development Coordination Conference, served as focal points for promoting regional integration and facilitating investments in the needed interconnection projects.

NAFTA offers another example. NAFTA has also fostered regional cooperation for the environment by tying essentially extraneous environmental issues to the trade and investment deal. This link helped to create the necessary political support for NAFTA in the United States, and it encouraged Mexico to accelerate their environment program in order to close the deal. The North American Agreement on Environmental Cooperation (NAAEC) was signed as one of the side agreements appended to NAFTA at the last moment. It created the Commission for Environmental Cooperation (CEC) in Montreal in early 1994 to carry out the provisions of the agreement. The CEC has a young but growing conservation portfolio, focused mainly on protecting habitats and species. A broad program of cooperation to protect North American birds is in place, aimed at identifying important bird areas across the three member countries and tying them into a protected network. A Biodiversity Information Network is under creation, and strategies are being developed for cooperation to protect marine and coastal ecosystems. The CEC has also coordinated measures to protect the monarch butterfly. Currently there is an active task force working to stop the smuggling of endangered species. Under this program, U.S. Fish and Wildlife officers are training Mexican officers.

While the trade agreements underpinning these regional cooperation initiatives were not essential to the actual activities, it is clear that they have provided useful political and institutional synergies.

Conclusions

One advantage of regional preferential trade arrangements is that they create opportunities to lower trade costs in areas other than tariffs and non-tariff barriers to trade. This review of trade facilitation, standards administration, and regional cooperation agreements points to several conclusions.

The potential to expand trade by lowering trade costs other than policy border barriers is great—and it may have a higher payoff to cooperative governmental efforts than reciprocal reductions in border barriers. This is because the costs of institutional obstacles, informal barriers, and sub-optimal regulatory scales are often higher than the costs associated with policy border barriers. Further, many of these barriers do not generate revenues but simply waste economic resources and directly constrain productivity. These issues are also important elements defining the investment climate.

RTAs can precipitate cooperation to lowering trading costs in these areas because RTAs raise the level of policy salience, spread information about members and about international markets, improve the institutional efficiency of countries (better coordination between the different institutions within a country and between countries), provide "institutional homes" for joint initiatives, and may facilitate dispute resolution across multiple areas.

Countries need not act in concert to reap the benefits of unilateral reforms; the chances of unilateral success are much improved, however, when policymakers are well informed about international standards and the trade-facilitation activities of other countries. In the absence of such information, and of the capacity to act on it, it is unlikely that a country, acting alone, will be able to match the benefits from participating in an RTA.

Finally, it seems clear that many RTAs are not realizing their potential as a forum for reducing trade costs. North-South agreements appear to have had somewhat greater success, perhaps because of the institutional interests and strength of the more advanced partner.

Notes

1. Lawrence (1997).

2. For example, McCallum (1995) reports results suggesting that Canadian provinces are more than 20 times more likely to trade among themselves than they are to trade with U.S. states after controlling for the main economic determinants of trade. Subsequently, Nitsch (2000) found evidence of substantial border effects in Europe, with internal trade being, on average, larger by a factor of 10 than trade with EU partners, although the magnitude of this effect did decline during the 1980s.

3. See, for example, Hummels and Skiba (2002).

4. GATT Article V mandates freedom of transit and national treatment of products in transit. However, this provision has never been invoked. The WTO framework provides little leverage for poor, landlocked countries to improve transit conditions.

5. Trade facilitation is of particular importance to landlocked countries, whose products must pass through numerous border crossings and checkpoints. Of the 50 least developed countries, 16 are landlocked: Afghanistan, Bhutan, Lao People's Democratic Republic, Nepal, Burkina Faso, Burundi, Central African Republic, Chad, Ethiopia, Lesotho, Malawi, Mali, Niger, Rwanda, Uganda, and Zambia. Even coastal developing countries may be effectively landlocked if they are not on major shipping routes and are served by inefficient and high cost coastal feeder services to main ports. Being landlocked has a significant and depressing effect on trade. For these countries, a regional approach may be the only way to improve access to global markets, since there seems to be little scope at present for solving transit issues within the WTO. Corridor solutions are efficient responses to the transport problems of landlocked economies with deficient infrastructure. By definition they require bilateral or regional intervention.

6. RTAs with TTF approaches include the European Union, MERCOSUR, Andean Community, SADC, COMESA, EAC, UMEOA, SAFTA, Eurasec,

and ASEAN. Two RTAs have no associated TTF: NAFTA and GCC. Three examples of TTFs existing independently of RTAs are ECO, ECOWAS, and the Northern Corridor Transit and Transport Agreement.

7. In treaties, competition is literally ensured through "equal treatment of carriers" or non-discrimination regarding carrier's nationality, known as respect of the third party rule.

8. According to UMEOA Commission (2000), 73 percent of the legal rules and customs governing transport and transit regimes were derived from bilateral treaties (34 percent), national legislation (24 percent), and customs (15 percent); 27 percent were derived from regional treaties.

9. Collusion between transport operators leads to agreement on price setting. National associations play a role in determining which goods a company will transport.

10. Standards can be mandatory as defined by governments (through technical regulations) so as to meet their objectives regarding health, safety, and environmental issues; as well as voluntary, reflecting the demands and tastes of consumers or the technological requirements of industrial purchasers. In addition to the writing of standards, an essential element of the system of standardization is conformity assessment, the technical procedures such as testing, verification, inspection, and certification, which confirm that products fulfill the requirements laid down in regulations and standards.

11. From The Republic of Moldova Trade Diagnostic Study, World Bank, 2004.

12. The principle of mutual recognition was developed on the basis of European Court of Justice case law, specifically, the Cassis de Dijon and Dassonville judgements. In the former case, cassis from France was prevented from being sold in Germany because it did not contain enough alcohol!

13. Mutual recognition of regulations has also been used within federal countries to remove barriers to inter-state trade. For example, Australia formally adopted mutual recognition in 1993 to remove regulatory barriers to the free flow of goods and labor between Australian states and territories. As in the EU, some harmonized regulations are promulgated at the federal level.

14. See Pelkmans and others 2000.

15. Bilateral trade agreements with the EU tend to contain support for developing capacity in the developing country, whereas those with the United States provide little such support.

16. Chen and Mattoo (2004) show evidence that MRAs promote trade, but that restrictive rules of origin lead to trade diversion, especially against developing countries.

17. Large companies in Brazil used their influence to their advantage in setting a voluntary labeling standard that requires water bottlers to include the results of numerous tests that are not understood by, or particularly relevant to, the consumer, but that constitute an effective barrier to entry to small companies that cannot afford the battery of tests required to provide the information. SEBRAI, a private institution that provides support services for small enterprises in Brazil, is working to improve access to certification and metrology for its client firms. Through "solidarity certification," for example, SEBRAI helps groups of small enterprises become certified at subsidized group rates. SEBRAI also provides bonds that subsidize small enterprises' expenditures for metrology services.

18. This section draws heavily from Schiff and Winters (2002).

References

Anderson, J., and E. van Wincoop. 2004. Trade Costs. NBER Working Paper 10480, National Bureau of Economic Research, Cambridge, MA.

Arvis, J. F. 2004. Transit and the Special Case of Land-locked Countries. In *Handbook of Customs Modernization*, eds. L. de Wulf and J. Sokol. Washington, DC: World Bank.

Banomyong, R. 2000. Multimodal Transport in South East Asia: A Case Study Approach. PhD thesis, University of Cardiff, www.bus.tu.ac.th/usr/ruth.

Baldwin, R. 1970. *Non-Tariff Distortions of International Trade*. Washington, DC: Brookings Institution.

CEC (Commission of the European Communities). 1998. *Technical Barriers to Trade, Volume 1.* Subseries III: Dismantling of Barriers of The Single Market Review. Luxembourg: CEC.

Cudmore, E., and J. Whalley. 2003. Border Delays and Trade Liberalization. NBER Working Paper 9485, National Bureau of Economic Research, Cambridge, MA.

Carruthers, R., J. Bajpai, and D. Hummels. 2003. Trade and Logistics: an East Asian Perspective. In *East Asia Integrates: A Trade Policy Agenda for Shared Growth*, eds. K. Krumm, and H. Kharas. Washington, DC: World Bank.

Chen, M., and A. Mattoo. 2004. Regionalism in Standards: Good or Bad for Trade? World Bank. Processed.

Daskalov, S., and D. Hadjinikolo. 2002. The Impact of Technical Barriers to Trade on Bulgaria's Exports to the EU and to the CEFTA Countries. In *Enlargement, Trade and Investment: the Impact of Barriers to Trade in Europe,* eds. P. Brenton, and S. Manzocchi. Cheltenham, UK: Edward Elgar.

Engel, C., and J. Rogers. 1996. How wide is the border? *American Economic Review* 86: 1112–1125.

Evans, C. 2001. Home Bias in Trade: Location or Foreign-ness? Staff Report 128, Federal Reserve Bank of New York.

Faini, R. 2004. Trade Liberalization in a Globalizing World. Paper presented at Annual World Bank Conference on Development Economics, Washington, DC, May 2004.

Funck, R. 1998. Integration of Transport Systems- the European Experience. Report for the EU-SADC Conference on Transport, Maputo, October.

Hoekman, B., and Konan, D. 1999. Deep Integration, Nondiscrimination, and Euro Mediterranean Free Trade. Discussion Paper 2095, CEPR, London.

Hummels, D., and A. Skiba. 2002. A Virtuous Circle? Regional Tariff Liberalisation and Scale Economies in Transport. In *Integrating the Americas: FTAA and Beyond,* eds. A. Estevadeordal, D. Rodrik, A. M. Taylor, and A. Velaso. MA: Harvard University Press.

Hummels, D. L. 2000. Time as a Trade Barrier. GTAP Working Paper 18, Center for Global Trade Analysis, Department of Agricultural Economics, Purdue University.

Lawrence, R. 1997. Preferential Trading Agreements: The Traditional and the New. In *Regional Partners in Global Markets: Limits and Possibilities of the Euro-Med Agreement,* eds. A. Galal, and B. Hoekman. London: CEPR.

McCallum, J. 1995. National borders matter: Canada-U.S. Regional Trade Patterns. *American Economic Review* 85: 615–23.

Mentzoni, J. T. 2003. Trade Logistics—A Study of Logistics Costs in Norwegian Wholesaler Industry. Processed. www.transportbrukerne.no.

Nofal, Beatriz. 2004. Constructing a deeper integration in MERCOSUR. Background paper for the *Global Economic Prospects 2005.* Washington, DC: World Bank.

Nitsch, V. 2000. National Borders and International Trade: Evidence from the European Union. *Canadian Journal of Economics* 33: 1091–105.

Pardo, M. 2001. Pasos Fronterizos en la Comunidad Andina. IADB. Processed.

Pelkmans, J. 1987. The New Approach to Technical Harmonisation and Standardisation. *Journal of Common Market Studies* 25.

Pelkmans, J., E. Vos, and L. Di Mauro. 2000. Reforming prodict regulation in the EU; a Painstaking Two-level Game. In *Regulatory Reform and Competitiveness in Europe, Volume I*, eds. G. Galli and J. Pelkmans. Cheltenham, UK: Edward Elgar.

Roschlau, F. 2003. Double Standards Cause Regional Transport Nightmares, e-corridor, Walvis Bay Corridor Group, number 3.

Ruijgrok, C. 2001. European Transport: Insights and Challenges. In *Handbook of Logistics and Supply-Chain Management*, eds. A. Brewer, K. Button, and D. Hensher, chapter 3. New York: Pergamon Press.

Schiff, M., and A. Winters. 2002. Regional Cooperation, and the Role of International Organizations and Regional Integration. Policy Research Working Paper 2872, World Bank, Washington, DC.

Trefler, D. 1995. The Case of the Missing Trade and Other Mysteries. *American Economic Review* 85: 1029–46.

UEMOA (West African Economic and Monetary Union) Commission. 2000. *Projet de Rapport de Synthèse Préparatoire à la Table Ronde des Bailleurs de Fonds sur les Infrastructures et le Transport Routier des Etats Membres de l'UMEOA*. Ouagadougou.

UNESCAP (United Nations Economic and Social Commission for Asia and the Pacific). 2003. *Transit Transport Issues in Landlocked and Transit Developing Countries*. New York, ST/ESCAP/2270.

Wilson, J., C. Mann, and T. Otsuki. 2003. Trade Facilitation and Economic Development; Measuring the Impact. Policy Research Paper 2988, World Bank, Washington, DC.

World Bank. 2003. *Trade, Investment, and Development in the Middle East and North Africa: Engaging with the World*. Washington, DC: World Bank.

World Bank. 2004. The Republic of Moldova Trade Diagnostic Study. World Bank, Washington, DC.

5

Beyond Merchandise Trade: Services, Investment, Intellectual Property, and Labor Mobility

As barriers to merchandise trade have come down and trade has expanded, policymakers and trade negotiators have turned their attention to services and trade-related regulatory issues. Of these, services, investment, intellectual property, and temporary movement of labor arguably have the greatest potential for affecting incomes and trade in developing countries. Agreements on these four issues are now becoming common in bilateral and some preferential regional trade agreements (RTAs).

North-South agreements, notably the bilateral free trade agreements of the United States and of the European Union (EU), have been the important drivers for services, investment, and intellectual property rights (IPRs). In broad terms, the United States, for example, offers access to its large market for goods in exchange for access to services markets in developing countries and their acceptance of rules governing investment and intellectual property rights. The EU market access agreements also cover many of these topics, if less specifically. Labor services—that is, the temporary movement of workers—are largely confined to professional and skilled workers, often intracorporate transfers. South-South agreements tend to feature services liberalization less prominently, and their rules governing investment, intellectual property, and even the temporary movement of workers, are commonly weak or absent altogether.

From a development perspective, the most potentially beneficial components of this set of issues are provisions that open services markets to additional potential suppliers through foreign subsidiaries (in GATS terminology, Mode 3) and the temporary movement of workers (Mode 4).[1] Services liberalization in preferential arrangements can enlarge the number of competitors and carries fewer risks of income losses than preferential merchandise trade because lifting most common restrictions does not cost the government revenue. Though multilateral liberalization is usually preferable even in services,[2] RTAs in services can be predicted, in general, to increase welfare. Similarly, preferential agreements that widen the scope for the temporary movement of workers have the potential to raise incomes.

In both services and labor mobility, however, agreements have yet to fulfill their development potential. Many of the North-South agreements are between countries with unusually open service sectors, so the additionality to the various parties is limited to a handful of relatively small sectors and to the credibility effects of locking in openness via treaties and "seals of approval" that investors might take as a sign of lower risk. Meanwhile, in many of the South-South agreements, where the potential scope for liberalizing measures is often far greater, RTA-driven additional liberalization has been sporadic. For labor services, both the

North-South and South-South agreements are confined to intra-firm movement of professionals, and neither agreement has substantially widened market access for the temporary movement of labor.

By contrast, North-South agreements regarding investment and IPRs have succeeded in promulgating comprehensive new rules that go beyond multilateral rules in the agreement on Trade Related Intellectual Property Rights (TRIPs). The United States and EU bilateral agreements have enhanced market access through negative-list and positive-list (respectively) pre-establishment rights, and the United States has implemented investor-state dispute settlement mechanisms that empower foreign investors to seek arbitration awards in cases of uncompensated expropriation or other violations of treaties.

Ironically, of the four areas, investment and IPRs are the two where the development potential is largely unproven. The investment provisions that enhance investor's rights have not been shown to increase the flow of investment to developing countries. Nor have stronger IPRs embedded in the TRIPS-Plus agreements been shown to accelerate technological flows to low-income countries—though it may do so for middle-income countries. On the other hand, because free trade areas that result in larger markets do attract additional investment flows, it may be that in combination with large, preferential trade areas, enhanced investor protections and IPRs do have a positive impact—but agnosticism seems warranted.

This chapter begins with a synoptic comparison of agreements and a focus on the regulation-intensive bilateral U.S. and EU free trade agreements (FTAs). Understanding the diversity and reach of these agreements permits us, in a subsequent section, to review the economic consequences of provisions that deal with services, investment, and intellectual property. A final section examines the treatment of movement of temporary labor.

Services, Investment, and IPRs in Regional Agreements

North-South agreements differ sharply in their coverage of services, investment, and intellectual property. At one end of the spectrum, U.S. FTAs usually involve the most explicit negotiations for market access in services and U.S.-style rules for investment and intellectual property. The EU market access agreements similarly contain market access provision in services, but tend to reinforce prevailing international rules for intellectual property; its Economic Partnership Agreements in Africa use development assistance in combination with trade preferences to promote rules beyond international agreements, including EU-style concerns for competition policy and geographical indications. At the other end of the spectrum, most South-South agreements are focused primarily on merchandise trade, and tend to treat services, investment, and IPRs unevenly, if at all. These distinctions should become clearer when we consider the U.S., EU, and South-South approaches in turn.

U.S. FTAs are rule intensive

Key features of the U.S. FTAs that cover services, investment, and intellectual property rights include:

- Opening services markets to competition from foreign suppliers or locking in prior autonomous liberalization, except in those sectors excluded (i.e., on a negative list). Because most of the countries with which the United States has concluded bilateral FTAs are already open in most sectors, the agreements generally lock in prevailing openness and affect changes in only a few still-restricted activities. Significant market openings took place in the Costa Rican telecommunications and insurance sectors and less dramatic market openings occurred in the banking sector in Bahrain. Provisions range from inclusion of insurance,

Table 5.1 Services, investment, and intellectual property: A comparison

Agreements	National and MFN/Treatment Market Access[a]	Rule of Origin (Nonrestrictive)[b]	Services — Pre-establishment & Limitations Market Access Exceptions	Services — Right to Provide Services w/o establishment[d]	Services — Ratchet Mechanism[e]	National Treatment/MF Post-establishment	Investment — Ownership Limitations[f]	Investment — Pre-establishment Limitations	Investment — Ban on Performance Requirements	Investment — Investor-State Dispute Settlement	Intellectual Property
U.S.											
U.S.-Jordan	Yes	Yes	Negative-list	No	No	Yes	Negative-list	Negative-list	TRIMS+	Yes	Yes[h]
U.S.-Chile	Yes	Yes	Negative-list	Yes	Yes	Yes	Negative-list	Negative-list	TRIMS+	Yes	TRIPS+
U.S.-Singapore	Yes	Yes	Negative-list	Yes	Yes	Yes	Negative-list	Negative-list	TRIMS+	Yes	TRIPS+
U.S.-Australia	Yes	Yes	Negative-list	Yes	Yes	Yes	Negative-list	Negative-list	TRIMS+	No	TRIPS+
U.S.-CAFTA	Yes	Yes	Negative-list	Yes	Yes	Yes	Negative-list	Negative-list	TRIMS+	Yes	TRIPS+
U.S.-Morocco	Yes	Yes	Negative-list	Yes	Yes	Yes	Negative-list	Negative-list	TRIMS+	Yes	TRIPS+
NAFTA	Yes	Yes	Negative-list	Yes	Yes	Yes	Negative-list	Negative-list	TRIMS+	Yes	TRIPS+
EU											
EU-South Africa	No	No	No	No	No	No	No	No	No	No[n]	Yes[i]
EU-Mexico	Yes	Yes	Standstill[c]	No	No	No	No	No	No	No[n]	Yes[i]
EU-Chile	Yes	Yes	Positive-list	No	No	Yes	No	Positive-list	No	No[n]	Yes[i]
South-South											
MERCOSUR	Yes	Yes	Positive-list	No	No	Yes	No	Negative-list	TRIMS+	Yes	No[j]
Andean Community	No	Yes	Positive-list	No	No	—	No	Positive-list	TRIMS+	No	No[k]
CARICOM	Not specified	Yes	Negative-list	No	No	No	Yes	Positive-list	No	Yes	No
ASEAN	Yes	Yes	Positive-list	No	No	No	No	Positive-list	No	No	No[l]
SADC	No	No				No	No	None	No	No	TRIPS
COMESA	Yes	No	Positive-list	No	No	No[g]	No	Positive-list	No	No	No[m]
Other											
Japan-Singapore	No	Yes	Positive-list	No	No					Yes	Yes
Canada-Chile	Yes	Yes	Negative-list	Yes	Yes					Yes	
Chile-Mexico	Yes	Yes	Negative-list	Yes	Yes					No	

a. Includes fair and equitable treatment.
b. Denial benefits only to juridical person that do not conduct "substantial business" in one of the member countries.
c. Provides for future negotiation of commitments à la GATS.
d. Right of non-establishment, that is no establishment required to supply a service.
e. Autonomous liberalization is automatically incorporated into the agreement.
f. Limits on equity shareholdings for companies in sectors other than those excluded from pre-establishment limitations.
g. COMESA does grant fair and equitable treatment to members, but not to non-members.
h. The IP provisions are considered TRIPs Plus. However the chapter coverage is less specific and comprehensive than other subsequent U.S. free trade agreements.
i. Requires only adherence to international conventions.
j. The MERCOSUR agreement does not include IP, but provides for interparliamentary committees to begin work on harmonization of IP laws.
k. Andean community regulates all patents.
l. ASEAN has a framework agreement.
m. Act 128(e) calls for adoption of new patent laws.
n. EU bilateral investment treaties provide for investor-state dispute resolution.

Sources: Legal treaties; Mattoo and Sauve 2004; re Velde and Fahnbulleh 2003; Mann and Cosbey 2004; Szepesi 2004a, 2004b; Abbott 2004a and 2004b; OECD 2003; information provided by governments.

financial advisory services, and selected telecommunications services to arguably relatively minor changes to the already open regimes, such as the commitment of Singapore to cease cross-subsidies in express mail delivery or the commitment of Chile to open selected insurance services (table 5.2).

- Ratchet provisions and negative-list exclusions. The ratchet clauses mean that new autonomous liberalization will automatically be subsumed under the terms of the agreements. Negative lists ensure that yet-to-be-invented new service areas are guaranteed to be covered by the treaty. Notable for their absence is the exclusion of labor services, except provisional visas for professionals associated with investing firms (discussed in the penultimate section of this chapter).
- Investment rights. Investment rights, with provisions for national treatment, nondiscrimination, pre-establishment provisions for companies based in each others markets, bans on trade-related investment measures (TRIM), and investor-state arbitration of dispute limited only by a negative list of exclusions.
- TRIPs-Plus provisions that provide stronger protections for IPRs than under the TRIPS agreement, with investor-state arbitration dispute settlement permitted in the event of disputes (subject to certain limitations).

Other noteworthy provisions (not the subject of this chapter) include labor protections and environment issues that figured prominently in the CAFTA, Chile, and Singapore agreements, among others. Signatory countries committed to enforcing their own labor laws in five areas: right of association, the right to organize and bargain collectively, prohibitions on forced labor, a minimum age for employment of children, and acceptable working conditions. Complaints can be filed, and if the agreed-on procedures to mediate the dispute fail, a panel of experts would review the case and, if warranted, impose a fine to be used for the enforcement of labor rights; that is to say, trade sanctions are not an agreed-on remedy (Weintraub 2004).

The FTAs involve innovations in trade law in two important areas: investment and IPRs:

Investment Access and Protections. The FTAs have incorporated the provisions of bilateral investment treaties (BITs), and in some cases, provided new measures covering investment (table 5.1). Agreements, especially post-NAFTA ones, include broad definitions of investment, comprising not only foreign direct investment (FDI), but also portfolio flows, private debt, and even sovereign debt issues as well as intellectual property (Mann and Cosbey 2004; Vivas-Eugui 2003). The inclusion of short-term debt, together with pre-establishment rights, led the U.S. Treasury to demand that Chile modify its controls on capital inflows that were

Table 5.2 Additional services liberalization in U.S. FTAs

	Chile	Australia	Bahrain	CAFTA	Morocco	Singapore
Banking			◆		◆	◆
Insurance	◆		◆	◆	◆	
Telecommunication	◆		◆	◆	◆	◆
Broadcasting & Audiovisual	◆	◆	◆			
Financial Advisory Services and Data			◆			
Retail/Wholesale Distribution				◆		
Restrictions on Foreign Directors & Managers				◆		◆
Express Mail Delivery						◆
Real Estate						◆
Legal Services						◆

Source: Legal treaties.

designed to curtail destabilizing hot money inflows.[3] Such broad definitions expose countries to dispute settlements across a range of assets that go far beyond multilateral commitments.

All agreements provide for treatment of foreign investors on the same basis as domestic investors (*national treatment*) and have provisos banning discrimination among investors from member countries (*MFN, or nondiscriminatory treatment*). For many of the initial FTA countries, these stipulations had been included in national legislations and/or had been incorporated into bilateral investment treaties, mainly on a post-establishment basis.

What is new is the extension of the *pre-establishment* right to invest in businesses and activities in all sectors, except where expressly prohibited via a negative list.[4] These pre-establishment rights lock in the right of Mexican and Canadian investors under NAFTA to invest in all activities in the United States. Exceptions for the United States include foreign investment with NAFTA guarantees in selected areas of communication, media, transportation, and social services. Pre-establishment rights mark a broad expansion of market access by foreclosing future government policies that would raise barriers to foreign investment. The rationale for accepting such disciplines is that it provides certainty on the rules of the game, which will in turn translate into increased investment inflows.

Another discipline more expansive than multilateral accords is in *trade-related investment measures (TRIMs)*. The WTO TRIMs agreement of 1995 attempted to clarify disciplines on government policies that require foreign companies to establish joint ventures, export in a certain portion of its sales or balance trade, use local inputs to achieve value-added objectives, or hire local staff. However, the agreement failed to provide adequate definitions of disciplines, and it presented poorly formulated implementation periods and inadequate notification and monitoring

procedures; the operation of the agreement was to be reviewed by January 1, 2000, but so far the review has not occurred (Bora 2003). All of the bilateral FTAs ban, in some form, trade-related investment requirements, such as by local content rules, value-added requirements, and restrictions on management. The U.S. bilateral agreements have, in effect, established a "TRIMs-Plus" set of obligations that includes outright bans on certain performance requirements, including exports, minimum domestic content, domestic sourcing, trade balancing, and technology transfer. In general, government procurement, environmental standards, some health measures, and requirements for local research and development (R&D) are all exempt (Te Velde and Fahnbulleh 2003).

Freedom to make transfers is a nontrivial investment right granted under the investment agreements. This assures investors that they will be able to transfer profits, make investments, or lend without government interference.

Finally, all U.S. agreements except the Australian FTA create an *investor-state dispute resolution* provision that permits investors to take foreign governments to dispute resolution for violation of the treaty's national treatment, nondiscrimination, or expropriation provisions, among others. NAFTA's Chapter 11 and Chile's Chapter 10 are the most widely known mechanisms, but these mechanisms are contained in the other bilateral agreements as well.

Intellectual Property Rights. The IPR provisions embedded in all recent U.S. FTAs go beyond the multilateral IPR standards established in the WTO's TRIPS Agreement. "TRIPS-Plus" elements found in many—but not all—of the IPR chapters include:[5]

- Extension of the patent term for delays caused by regulatory approval processes; extension of the term of copyright protection to life of author plus 70 years (compared to life of author plus 50 years in TRIPS).

- A requirement to provide patent protection for plants and animals.
- A limitation on the use of compulsory licenses for national emergencies and as antitrust remedies, and for public non-commercial use.

In the area of pharmaceuticals:

- An obligation to prohibit the marketing approval of generic drugs during the term of the drug patent.
- A five-year period of marketing exclusivity following the submission of safety and efficacy data to drug regulatory authorities (so-called data exclusivity). In addition, marketing exclusivity effectively applies across borders, so that marketing approval in one market—say, the United States—impedes registration of competing products in another market.
- An additional three-year period of marketing exclusivity based on the submission of new clinical data with respect to new uses of previously approved drugs. Exclusivity would also apply to drugs for which the patents have expired (although generic competition for previously approved uses would remain unaffected).
- Imposition of restraints on parallel importation, impeding the possibility that parties to the agreements open their markets to the import of products that have already been sold—possibly more cheaply—in foreign markets.

In the area of digital works:

- An obligation against circumventing so-called technological protection measures—devices and software developed to prevent unauthorized copying of digital content. Rules on the liability of Internet service providers (ISPs) when copyright infringing content is distributed through their servers and networks. These provisions are based on standards found in the U.S. Digital Millennium Copyright Act of 1998.

The inclusion of these services, investment, and IPR issues was a contributing factor to the breakdown in negotiations in the Free Trade Area of the Americas (Nogues 2004). We return to these issues below when considering the economic consequences of these arrangements.

EU FTAs take a different approach

In addition to market access in merchandise, the EU has focused heavily on services in its bilateral FTAs. The earliest (and least specific) is the South African agreement (1999) that contains only the promise of potential liberalization after discussions transpire in 2004 and 2005. In the EU-Mexico FTA, several general provisions were included (many ratifying GATS arrangements), as well as specific liberalization commitments in the financial sector. The EU-Chile agreement went further than the other two and included liberalization of telecommunications and maritime services (Ullrich 2004).

The EU agreements with Mexico and Chile differ from the U.S. agreements in important respects. First, the trade provisions are phrased on the basis of a positive list and implicitly exclude new products. Second, the treatment of intellectual property effectively reaffirms a multilateral approach to IPRs, because the agreements provide only the list of conventions that signatory countries have already ratified, those it intends to ratify, and those that it will consider ratifying in the future.[6] This approach differs from that taken toward the EU-accession countries, in which new entrants were required to apply the rigorous EU standards on data protection and marketing exclusivity; these have a major impact on generic producers.

The treatment of *investment* and capital flows in both agreements does not appear to be extensive. For example, the EU-Mexico agreement simply states that the existing restrictions on investment will be progressively eliminated and no new restrictions adopted; the agreement did not specify particular sectors or set a timeline for liberalization. The language in the EU-Chile agreement calls for the "free movement of capital relating to direct investments made in accordance with the laws of the host country." In both instances, the agreements allow for the use of safeguards in the event of monetary or exchange rate difficulties, and although the time limit is set at 6 months for Mexico and 12 months for Chile, it would allow for continuation of the safeguard after the time limit through its formal reintroduction. That said, many of the same investor protections found in U.S. FTAs are also found in EU bilateral investment treaties with developing countries.

The treatment of *dispute settlement* is similar in both agreements. In general, the EU has no special provisions pertaining to investment, but these are covered under the general dispute settlement provisions for all matters in the agreements (Szepesi 2004a and b). Dispute settlement is covered on a state-to-state level and is first attempted through consultations with a Joint Committee (Association Committee in the case of Chile) within 30 days of a party's request. If this step of "dispute avoidance" proves unsuccessful, the concerned party can forward its request to an arbitration panel comprised of representatives of both parties. The arbitration panel's decisions are binding, and the panel can also rule on the conformity of any measures undertaken as a result of its decision with the original ruling. Both agreements provide extensive detail on the process of appointing members to the arbitration panel, timelines for the panel's ruling, and compliance with the panel's decisions.

South-South agreements focus on expanding trade

Virtually all of the other major agreements contain references to *services liberalization*. Most agreements allow for national treatment, post-establishment nondiscriminatory provisions (table 5.1). At the other extreme, there are more limited agreements like Association of Southeast Asian Nations (ASEAN) and Southern Common Market Agreement

(MERCOSUR) that have delivered services liberalization additional to levels negotiated multilaterally or determined unilaterally. Regional agreements in services have competed to create complex structures of rules and commitments. But in many cases, the sound and fury of the negotiations has signified limited liberalization. Many agreements do not provide new market access beyond what countries have already scheduled with the GATS. In telecommunications and financial services, the GATS has in fact achieved a higher level of bound liberalization than that offered in most RTAs.

All South-South agreements have a relatively nonrestrictive definition of preferential access; by allowing firms from nonmember countries that have "substantial business" in member countries to invest through subsidiaries based in member countries, the number of potential competitions in the market is enlarged.

Agreements with negative lists have several advantages in terms of market access: they permit automatic liberalization of new service industries; they establish a stronger floor for liberalization by locking in the status quo; they are more transparent; and they may lead to a more productive internal dialogue with sectoral private interests (Mattoo and Sauve 2004). Ratchet mechanisms that allow new autonomous liberalization to be incorporated automatically into treaties are most likely to co-exist with negative list provisions. However, most of the South-South agreements have not liberalized many sectors, and some, like MERCOSUR, have not implemented accords in the way that was anticipated at signing (Nofal 2004).

Investment provisions have differed as well. South-South RTAs generally have been less ambitious with respect to investor protections. This is true for the right to provide services without establishing local affiliates. It is also true for investor-state dispute settlement. For the most part, only the United States and EU bilaterals have established sophisticated mechanisms to deal with disputes on investment. Some agreements provide for investor-state dispute resolution, though these protections are less strong than in the North-South Agreements.

Intellectual property rights, while mentioned in South-South agreements, rarely go beyond disciplines negotiated at the multilateral level, and they do not have the tightly formulated provisions that characterize the North-South agreements, notably those with the United States. MERCOSUR, for example, has agreed to establish a commission to examine areas of intellectual property harmonization, while ASEAN has a framework agreement. The Andean community has more detailed restrictions, but these are written less with the view of protecting intellectual property than of eliminating territorial restrictions on the use of patented technology; the restrictions were designed to end the restraints multinational companies put in their technology contracts with their foreign affiliates, which explicitly prevented them from using the patents in export production.

Economic Consequences of Services, Investment, and IPR Provisions in RTAs

New market access in services could promote growth

Services liberalization with proper regulation can be a powerful driver of economic growth and poverty reduction. At the sectoral level, removing barriers to competition can lower prices, improve quality, and add variety. Because of the linkage effects—the fact that producers require telephones, use finance, need adequate transportation services, and benefit from business services—improving service sector performance can generate huge economic gains. Mattoo, and others (2001) show that countries with fully liberalized financial and telecommunications sectors grew annually on average about 1.5 percentage points faster than other countries, controlling for other factors. These gains are not automatic—they require adequate regulation and a supportive

investment climate—but the potential gains are large (World Bank 2001).

Realizing these gains requires allowing foreign investors greater *market access,* and this is the most important provision in a preferential arrangement. Countries can open previously closed sectors to RTA partners as part of an agreement. Since today most countries accept, indeed clamor for, foreign investment in manufacturing and natural resources, RTA-driven reductions in entry barriers affect mainly services. Moreover, services now play a larger role in investment flows, and for some countries, such as Mexico, they have dwarfed investments in manufacturing. The great bulk of services investment are market-seeking, horizontal investments. These cover a vast range of large multinationals: Deutsche Bank, WalMart, Starbucks, Microsoft, and so on. These "mode 3" services require the commercial presence of affiliates, branches, or franchises to deliver the service. To be sure, some countries (such as India) have experienced substantial flows associated with call centers and data processing, and this new investment accompanies these cross-border supply ("mode 1") activities, though these activities remain small in comparison to trade through commercial presence.

Because preferential arrangements permit more suppliers to compete in the market, a country is almost certain to gain from preferential liberalization of the services trade, irrespective of the supplier. This is in sharp contrast to merchandise trade, where the income loss associated with trade diversion can occur with the loss in tariff revenue. In services, barriers to entry usually take nonmonetary forms such as regulatory restrictions on entry, foreign equity limitations, quotas on outputs and foreign service workers, and requirements on legal form of establishment. None of these generate revenue for the government, so removing these restrictions is less likely to produce income losses (with merchandise trade, income losses associated with trade diversion occur because the government loses the tariff revenue as trade is diverted to higher-cost sources of imports). Moreover, the scope for increased competition and exploitation of scale economies, as well as the possibility of inducing knowledge spillovers, strengthens the presumption that a country would gain from a preferential agreement in services.

Multilateral, nonpreferential liberalization is likely to produce *even larger* gains than preferential regional agreements. This is because multilateral liberalization opens the market to the largest number of competitors and permits consumers maximum choice; it allows imports from the most competitive source. It also leads to a less complex policy regime than a preferential arrangement, and therefore implies lower administration costs for government agencies and lower transaction costs for the private sector. Finally, it is possible that preferences could lead to a higher-cost firm gaining a competitive advantage relative to investors from outside the region. And first mover advantages and barriers to entry can make it difficult for lower-cost suppliers from third countries to enter the market. Inefficient suppliers from member countries might establish positions behind market barriers sufficiently high that new and even more efficient potential competitors would not choose to pay the cost of entry.

Rules of origin for services, as with merchandise trade, can play a significant role in determining the degree to which regional trading arrangements discriminate against nonmember countries, and hence the degree of competition in services associated with an RTA. For example, if one participant has a fully liberalized market, the adoption of a nonrestrictive rule of origin by the other participants can be likened to MFN liberalization. Service suppliers can enter the liberal jurisdiction and from there move to the other partner countries. Many governments take the liberal rules of origin one step further and extend regional preferences on an MFN basis under the GATS. This widens the number of competitors in the market and offers greater opportunities for securing access to the most efficient suppliers—particularly of infrastructural services likely to exert significant

effects on economy-wide performance. Because of the strong potential links to growth (World Bank 2002), the additional market access provided through RTAs could be important. Unfortunately, the actual additional liberalization has not yet matched this promise.

Nonetheless, restrictive rules of origin can limit the potential benefit to liberalization. Participants who seek to benefit from preferential access to a protected market and deny benefits to third country competitors are likely to argue for the adoption of restrictive rules of origin, based on criteria such as ownership or control considerations. This could be the attitude of regionally dominant but globally noncompetitive service providers toward third-country competition within a regionally integrating area.

Examples of restrictive rules of origin for services and investment can be found in MERCOSUR and the Andean Pact, both of which limit benefits to juridical persons that are owned and controlled by natural persons of a member country. The Hong Kong-China Free Trade Agreement, for example, features a detailed annex spelling out the set of criteria by which Hong Kong service suppliers may benefit from the terms of the agreement.

Do RTAs attract more investment?

RTAs can, in theory, promote more investment through new *trade rules* that create a larger market, new *investment rules that permit market access* by relaxing restrictions on market entry (such as discussed above for services), and *new investor protections*.

New trade rules that eliminate internal barriers create a larger internal market, which can raise the return to investment and create an incentive to invest for members and for third countries. Firms investing in the RTA countries can achieve economies of scale and scope in serving a larger market of potential buyers, may experience reductions in transactions costs, and if services are included, benefit from more efficient financial, telecommunications, and other services (Schiff and Winters 2003). Trade rules can induce greater efficiency in transactions with the global economy. Markusen (2004), for example, notes that inward investment to reach the local market may also include tapping into lower cost production sites within the new RTA to serve the wealthier parts. Japanese multinational companies might well locate in Mexico to reach the U.S. market, though the net effects might be diluted as U.S. firms also set up in Mexico. Frischtak (2004) found that MNCs in autos, textiles, and electronics reallocated their production to Mexico to serve the U.S. market.

The larger market can also increase productivity in other ways. Aside from economies of scale, a larger market can increase competition among a potentially larger set of suppliers, and take advantage of differing regional factor prices to drive productivity increases and hence more rapid growth; and the more rapid growth provides a dynamic attraction to intra-bloc and extra-bloc investment. If the RTA reduces border protection on investment goods and allows domestic producers to source cheaper and higher technology capital goods, members may benefit.

However, efficient results are not automatic. Even though investment may be destined for a larger market, border barriers may create incentives to invest in high-cost import-substituting activities that are not internationally competitive. Latin America's early experiments with admitting FDI behind high border barriers produced inefficient investment and a protectionist political economy that took decades to unwind (box 5.1). The formation of RTAs may increase both internal and external investment, but the resulting market size may not be sufficient to realize modern scales, and the high external tariffs drive up the costs of imported inputs. Indeed, the first Andean Pact in the early 1970s and the Central American Common Market in the 1960s failed to generate investment-related productivity gains.

RTAs may include new *investment rules to facilitate market access*. As with services, the decision to lift an administrative barrier impeding manufacturing investment or an investment in natural resources can create an opportunity for investors and hence prompt new investment. Most remaining restrictions today—equity ownerships limitation and bans on foreign investment in particular activities—are not restrictions on manufacturing, but rather on services (e.g., broadcasting, telephony, and airlines in the United States, among other countries) and natural resources (e.g., oil in Mexico). RTAs that reduce market

Box 5.1   Not all investment is good investment

Trade barriers in preferential arrangements can divert trade to higher-cost sources. No less important is the investment undertaken to produce the new trade. If trade policies provide high protection, they will limit competition, allow for shared monopoly pricing, and incur the inefficiencies of price distortions. This pattern of investment was common—and costly—in the period before high protection was brought down. Lall and Streeten (1977) who studied some 90 foreign investments using a cost-benefit methodology, found that more than 33 percent *reduced* national income; this was mainly from excessive tariff protection that allowed high cost firms to produce for the local market at very high

prices, even though they could have imported much more cheaply. (It turns out domestic firms performed even more poorly.) Encarnation and Wells (1986) found that between 25–45 percent of 50 projects studied (depending on analytical assumptions) reduced national income; again the main culprit was high protection. As average tariff levels have come down, these low-quality type of investments have faded in importance. Trade and tax policy often interact in ways that magnify their competition-restricting effects.

Sources: Lall and Streeten 1997; Encarnation and Wells 1986; Newfarmer 2001.

access barriers associated with restrictions on foreign entry are likely to have greater impact through this channel than through manufacturing.

Granting new *investment rights* may also attract additional investment, though here the case is more contentious. In general, the strongest investor protections entail nondiscrimination among all investors, provisions against expropriation, dispute settlement with eligibility for investor-state suits, and independent arbitration. The legal power granted to investors to sue governments under terms of the bilateral or regional agreements is arguably the strongest new protection in the trade agreements. These provisions differ in detail, but they closely mirror the bilateral investment treaties, even though they are anchored to the trade agreement.

Despite the proliferation of new protections to foreign businesses, the positive economic consequences have yet to be demonstrated. Theory would suggest that sound property rights are a foundation of any country's invest-

ment climate, and, other things being equal, stronger rights would lower risk and entice more investment at the margin. Since investors put money at risk against the promise of returns in subsequent periods, predictable regulation and protection of property rights are integral to the investment decision. However, the evidence for many of the same protections contained in the bilateral investment treaties is that these additional protections have no significant effects on inflows of FDI (box 5.2). To be sure, signing an FTA with new investor protections may enhance the credibility of a reform program, but evidence that these have observable consequences is scarce.

While the benefits of these protections in the form of new FDI inflow are open to question, the costs in the form of investor suits are nontrivial and growing. In NAFTA, for example, as of July 2004, there were 31 cases brought under Chapter 11 (including 14 against Mexico, 9 against Canada, and 8 against the United States). Six cases have been decided in favor of the investor, but the

Box 5.2   Do more investor protections mean more investment? Lessons from bilateral investment treaties

Does increasing investor protections produce the benefit of high investment? One test of this proposition was Hallward-Dreimeier's (2003) study of the enhanced investor protections through bilateral investment treaties for flows of FDI among signatory countries.[6] Analyzing bilateral flows of OECD members to 31 developing countries over two decades, she found that, controlling for a time trend and other factors, BITs had virtually no independent effect in increasing FDI to a signatory country from a home country. Said differently, countries signing a BIT were no more likely to receive additional FDI than countries without such a pact. Even comparing flows in the 3 years after a BIT was signed to the 3 years prior, there was no significant increase in FDI. This agrees with the findings of UNCTAD (1998) that the number of BITs signed by the host was uncorrelated with the amount of FDI it received.

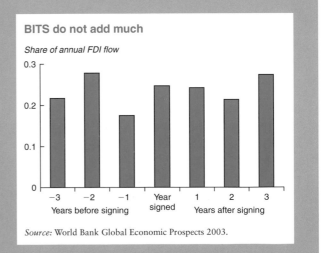

BITS do not add much

Share of annual FDI flow

Source: World Bank Global Economic Prospects 2003.

Sources: Hallward-Driemeier 2003; UNCTAD 1998.

amount awarded has been small compared to initial—and inflated—claims. Tribunal awards have totaled $35 million, compared to claims of $1015 billion. Under the similar BITs, 48 alleged BIT violations are under review arbitration at the International Center for Dispute Resolution. Cases have arisen out of the Argentine devaluation, the changes in tax policy perceived as adverse by investors, expropriations following conflict or coups, irregularities in bidding processes, and others (Peterson 2003a). In perhaps the most significant case to date, a tribunal in Stockholm ordered the government of the Czech Republic to pay one company, Central European Media (CME), $350 million for violation of a bilateral investment treaty that deprived CME from a stake in an English language TV station in Prague.

This amount was 10 times higher than previously known awards under arbitration cases and about equal to the entire public sector deficit of the Czech Republic (Peterson 2003b).

The legal and macroeconomic consequences of investment rights in treaties are largely unknown. They have not been thoroughly analyzed and tested in arbitration cases, and are without precedent. One could certainly speculate about adverse outcomes. For example, new rules for Chile could complicate management of short-term capital flows; in fact, the IMF expressed reservations to the U.S. government that the limitations that the U.S.-Chile bilateral FTA imposed on the Chilean government regarding short-term capital inflows reduced the government's ability to manage a macroeconomic crisis. Similarly, the breadth of definition of investment coverage opens the government to investor-state arbitration in event of default on debt or suspension of payments in emergencies—which may ultimately be unenforceable. For instance, Argentina's default has led investors to file nearly 30 arbitration cases; none of these appear to have been associated with nonpayment of debt. However, these debts are also subject to ongoing discussions between the government and creditors. By defining intellectual property as an "investment," a foreign investor who claims his intellectual property rights have been abrogated has recourse beyond the national court system to international arbitration proceedings under the investment provisions of the bilateral agreements.[7] These provisions have unquantifiable development benefits—and bring risk, which incurs uncertain costs.

The combination of changes in RTAs may have an effect on investment

Even if protections by themselves contribute little additional inflows, evidence is mounting that RTAs—that is, the *combination* of appropriate trade rules, liberalized market access, and investor protections—can have positive effects on inflows of foreign investment, provided that the investment climate is supportive and the size of the newly created market is attractive.

Indeed, Lederman, and others (2004) found that RTAs that formed large markets attracted FDI, (controlling for other factors that influence location), but that small markets had no effect. They also found positive effects for NAFTA, although the flow of FDI, even controlling for privatizations, appears to have surged in the first years but has not been sustained. Waldkirch's (2001) study, with less complete annual data, found that NAFTA increased FDI substantially, mostly from the United States and from Canada. Chudnovsky and Lopez (2001) found that FDI increased in the MERCOSUR, largely from outside sources, but that it often entered via acquisition, displaced domestic investment, and was tariff-hopping to produce for the local market—so it probably contributed to less to growth less than it otherwise would have. They also found that FDI inflows tended to locate in the larger countries, underscoring the need for stronger institutions and policies in the smaller countries.

Levy Yayati, Stein, and Daude (2004) used a gravity model to analyze the effects of RTAs on FDI inflows in 13 major agreements, and then applied their findings to a simulation for the FTAA. They found that RTAs have a strong positive impact on inflows, and that if these average magnitudes hold after the signing of an FTAA, the results would be substantial increases in flows to FTAA countries. However, the distribution is uneven, and countries with larger post-RTA market size, low inflation rates, strong domestic institutions, and open economics are likely to be the biggest beneficiaries.

To investigate further whether RTA formation can affect FDI flows in a consistent fashion, we examine the effects of RTA membership and other variables on FDI inflows for a panel of 152 countries over the 1980–2002 period. The sample takes into account 238 RTAs (both regional and bilateral), many of which overlap, that encompass the vast majority of sample countries.[8] In general, countries that are more open (measured as the sum of exports and imports over GDP), growing more rapidly, and are more stable (captured in less volatile inflation rates), attract greater quantities of FDI, controlling for growth rates of FDI to all countries and the world growth rate.[9] RTAs that result in larger markets do attract greater FDI. The interaction of an RTA signing and additional market size associated with the integrated markets is significant and positively related to FDI. On average, a 10 percent increase in market size associated with an RTA produces an increase of 5 percent.[10] This has important policy implementations: If a country seeks to use an RTA to attract investment, it should seek to amalgamate with the largest possible markets; RTAs among small market countries have little effect.

Two important caveats to this conclusion are worth underscoring: First, a preferential trading arrangement cannot compensate for an inadequate investment climate. Stein and Daude (2001) have shown that institutional variables that make up the whole of a country's investment climate—including political stability, government effectiveness, rule of law, and lower risks of expropriation—are all significantly associated with increases in investment flows, controlling for other determinants of FDI. These wash out the otherwise positive effects of RTAs. If the economy suffers from poor macroeconomic management, high levels of corruption, and poor infrastructure, an RTA by itself will not offset the disadvantages. To be sure, an RTA may help governments through their collective action to improve the investment climate and bring in more investment; but an RTA is no substitute for an adequate investment climate (World Bank 2004). Second, creation of an RTA will not have much effect on investment inflows from outside the region if restrictions on market access are severe and remain unchanged.

How do IPRs affect the price of technology?

Creation and enforcement of IPRs have an important role to play in development, but neither theory nor available studies provide much guidance on the likely outcomes of implementing in trade agreements the strongest of the IPRs or none at all. On the one hand, stronger IPR enforcement in general is likely to enhance the overall investment climate, especially for high technology firms. On the other, recognizing full patent protection for firms may require poor countries to pay higher prices, with little additional incentive either to innovate or to make investments in the local market.[11] Full enforcement of patents[12] could produce substantial financial flows, estimated roughly at $19 billion to the United States and $7 billion to Germany (World Bank 2001). Moreover, the administrative costs of upgrading IPR systems are not trivial (Finger and Schuler 2004).

It was the prospect that developing countries would have to pay higher prices for patented drugs that motivated the international community to agree to clarify flexibilities embedded in the TRIPS Agreement at the WTO Ministerial Meeting in 2001. The resulting Doha Declaration on TRIPS and Public Health reaffirmed the right of WTO members to use the flexibilities of TRIPS in the areas of compulsory licensing and parallel importation to "... *promote access to medicines for all.*"[13] In August 2003, WTO members created a special mechanism under the TRIPS Agreement that allows countries with insufficient manufacturing capacity to effectively use compulsory licenses by importing generic drugs.

At first blush, the TRIPS-Plus portions of the U.S. FTAs seem to circumscribe the policy space provided in the Doha Declaration. In particular, provisions on the link between patent status, marketing approval, and data exclusivity appear to put limits on the spirit of the Doha Declaration, because countries may be prevented from effectively employing compulsory licenses to introduce competition from generic drug producers.[14] To address these concerns, the U.S. bilateral agreements with Bahrain, CAFTA-DR, and Morocco contain side letters that share the understanding that the intellectual property chapters do not affect the ability of governments to "... *take necessary measures to protect public health by promoting medicines for all [...]*."[15] In other words, government can be justified as protecting public health, as permitted under the three FTAs. The United States Trade Representative office recently clarified: "... *if ... a drug is produced under a compulsory license, and it is necessary to approve that drug to protect public health ... the data protection provision in the FTA would not stand in the way.*"[16]

Notwithstanding the potential flexibilities provided by these side letters, they raise several questions. How widely will the parties to the three agreements define the "protection of public health"—or, what definitions would an arbitration panel use? Uncertainty in this respect may become itself a barrier to making use of the flexibilities and may open the door for restrictive interpretations by vested interests. Also, several of the other U.S. FTAs do not contain comparable side letters, raising questions about conflicts between intellectual property obligations and public health objectives in at least some of the affected countries.

The welfare effects of stronger and new copyright protection standards are ambiguous.

On the one hand, most countries have industries that rely on copyright protection and that may benefit from strengthened protection. And new technologies that greatly facilitate the copying of digital works pose challenges that policymakers need to address. On the other hand, copyright laws have historically sought to strike a balance between the interests of copyright producers and the interests of the general public. So-called fair use exemptions allow the copying of protected works for educational or research purposes. There are questions that new rules on the technological protection measures and the liability of Internet service providers could diminish the rights of consumers and the general public (CIPR 2002). Ensuring fair use of copyrighted material is particularly important for educational material. The opportunities and gains from the use of digital libraries, Internet-based distance learning programs, or online databases would be limited if access to such tools became unaffordable or otherwise restricted by copyright law.

Evidence is inconclusive about the responsiveness of FDI to intellectual property regimes. Although surveys of foreign investors typically indicate concerns for IPRs, this is often of secondary priority (Mansfield 1995). Maskus (2000) concludes that countries (especially low-income countries) should focus on their overall investment climate to attract more and high technology investment, rather than to fine-tune their IPRs. Nonetheless, some multinational companies (MNCs), when selecting an investment location among middle-income countries, clearly take into account the laws governing intellectual property. Other studies have found that weak laws and weak enforcement deter investment in middle-income countries,[17] but the results for low-income countries are inconclusive. Finger and Nogues (2002), in fact, argue that the introduction of patent protection for drugs in Chile made several multinational pharmaceutical companies stop production and investment and source this market from other locations. In summary, Fink and Maskus (2004) in their review of the evidence conclude: "... countries that strengthen their IPR regimes are unlikely to experience a sudden boost in inflows of foreign direct investment," but that IPRs can stimulate formal technology transfer through FDI and licensing.

All in all, the general conclusion is that countries have to develop an IPR strategy appropriate to their level of development, and then analyze carefully which if any IPR provisions ought to be contained in trade treaties or RTAs.

RTAs and Provisions for Movement of Labor

Using RTAs to promote movement of unskilled workers

Walmsley and Winters (2003) estimated that if a temporary visa system were introduced in those developed countries that permitted the movement of up to three percent of their labor force, world incomes would rise some $160 billion. Some 70 percent of the global welfare gains from increased migration would come from the movement of unskilled workers. To date, progress under the GATS Mode 4 negotiations in easing restrictions on the temporary entry of workers has been limited; the agreement has generally been used for skilled workers, not unskilled.

Regional agreements might offer a more promising venue for realizing the gains from

temporary movement of workers—that is, by going beyond the relatively limited scope of the GATS Mode 4 provisions. Regional agreements are often between countries with historical ties, and former migrants (or their children and grandchildren) tend to support increased opportunities for citizens of their home countries. Working on bilateral or regional levels may provide receiving countries with greater control over the numbers and nationalities of temporary workers. That is, receiving countries that wish to ensure maximum control in immigration decisions may prefer to design their policies without having to negotiate the terms with countries outside the region. Given both labor market and security concerns, this control may make it easier for countries to implement temporary programs for unskilled workers. Close neighbors tend to have a high proportion of immigrants in receiving countries. To what extent have RTAs facilitated labor movement?

Regional agreements treat labor movement in varying ways, ranging from full labor mobility to no provisions at all. As shown in table 5.3, RTAs treat labor in one of four different ways:[18]

- free labor mobility, with limited exceptions;
- temporary market access for certain (usually skilled) groups of workers;

Table 5.3 Summary of agreements by degree of labor mobility

Degree of labor mobility under agreement	Agreements
Full labor mobility	European Union, Agreement on the European Economic Area, European Free Trade Association, Australia-New Zealand Closer Economic Relations
Market access for certain groups	Caribbean Community, North American Free Trade Agreement, Europe Agreements, Group of Three, and Canada-Chile, U.S.-Singapore, U.S.-Chile, Japan-Singapore Free Trade Agreements
Based on GATS Mode 4, with additional provisions or limitations	ASEAN Free Trade Area, Euro-Med Association Agreements, New Zealand-Singapore Closer Economic Partnership, Southern Common Market Agreement, and EU-Mexico, EU-Chile, MERCOSUR, and US-Jordan Free Trade Agreements
No effective provisions for labor mobility	Asia Pacific Economic Co-Operation Forum, South Asian Association for Regional Cooperation, Central European Free Trade Agreement, and Common Market for Eastern and Southern Africa

Source: World Bank staff; Nofal 2004.

- temporary movement based on the GATS Mode 4 model, often with additional provisions or limitations;[19] and
- no provision in place for market access (beyond facilitating entry visas), or plans designated to be realized only in the future.

Most agreements do not override migration legislation, and parties retain broad discretion to grant, refuse, and administer residence permits and visas. It should be noted also that the right of labor mobility does not automatically entail the right to practice a certain profession; national regulations regarding licensing and recognition of qualifications are still applied.[20]

RTAs with full labor mobility

The EU, the European Economic Area and European Free Trade Association, and the Australia-New Zealand Closer Economic Relations Trade Agreement (ANZCERTA) allow for free labor mobility, with very limited exceptions.[21] The EU also allows the right to reside (with family), although residence permits are not required for stays of less than three months. The European agreements include exceptions for public services, public security, and/or public health works. ANZCERTA provides for both full market access and national treatment for all service suppliers, excluding a few sectors.

The migration provisions of these agreements facilitated regional integration by making it easier for firms from one country to transfer personnel to their operations in other countries in the region. The potential for workers to move to higher-paying jobs in other countries may have improved discipline in some labor markets. However, the EU agreements had almost no impact on stocks of permanent migration from other EU countries (figure 5.1), in part because several EU countries had already provided for free labor mobility. In addition, most of these countries are of similar income levels, so the incentive to disrupt family and personal relationships by moving for higher incomes was limited. The entry of less wealthy countries into the EU in the 1980s also did not result in greatly increased migration.

Several factors may explain this: among these, the free movement of workers from the

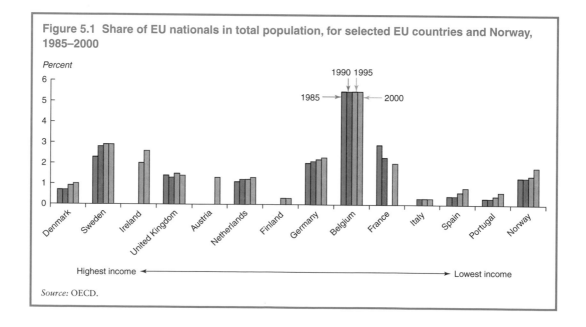

Figure 5.1 Share of EU nationals in total population, for selected EU countries and Norway, 1985–2000

Source: OECD.

new member states were subject to transitional periods; the EU's regional funds aimed at developing less prosperous regions combined with the prospect of a positive economic development in the new countries are likely to have thwarted a significant migration of labor. Greece, Portugal, and Spain underwent 6 years of transition, which limited the free movement of people after their entry to the EU. Even the richest EU countries (Denmark and Sweden) experienced only a slight rise in EU nationals as a share of population after the transition periods of the poorest EU countries (Spain and Portugal) expired.[22]

It remains to be seen whether the recent accession of Central and Eastern European countries to the EU will result in substantial migration. While this agreement will ultimately provide for full labor mobility, most of the original EU countries have taken advantage of provisions that delay this migration for a limited period (renewable up to 7 years). Most studies find that the accession agreements are unlikely to greatly boost migration to Western Europe. Forecasts of the additional migration due to expansion of the EU, which relies on both econometric models and opinion polls, generally find that migration will be limited to about 3–4 percent of residents of the 10 first-round East European nations within a decade of freedom of movement; this amounts to about 4 million people or 1 percent of the current EU population. Additionally, about half of these laborers are likely to return home within the 10-year period, meaning a net migration of 2 million persons (Martin 2003). However, some of the EU countries, particularly those bordering the Eastern European countries like Germany and Austria, could experience larger flows relative to population.

Box 5.3   Illegal migration: A growing global phenomenon

The number of migrant workers without proper work permits, so-called undocumented or illegal workers, is increasing. The International Organization of Migration estimates that each year, somewhere between 700,000 and 2 million people cross borders to take jobs without legal permission.*
Of this number, up to 500,000 seek entry into Western Europe and 500,000 into the United States, Canada, Australia, and New Zealand. In the United States, the stock of undocumented workers increased from an estimated 3.5 million in 1990 to 7 million in 2000, of which 69 percent were Mexicans (USCIS 2003). In Europe, illegal migrants numbered as many as 3 million by the end of the 1990s.* Countries in Asia have also experienced an increased number of irregular foreign workers in their labor force. In Singapore, undocumented workers accounted for 4.5 percent of the total labor force in 2000, and in Hong Kong (China), it was 2.3 percent. In Hong Kong (China), Korea, and Taiwan, there is one undocumented foreign worker for every three legal foreign workers. Thailand is one of the countries most affected by undocumented workers, with nearly 5.5 undocumented workers for each registered foreign worker (IOM 2003). In 2000–01, some 73,000 Chinese irregular migrants were assumed to be living in South Korea, and, in turn, China hosted some 50,000 irregular migrants.

Stricter enforcement of immigration rules may not have been successful in cutting off illegal migration, but it may have contributed to the very high costs involved, particularly between countries that do not have a common border. Today, irregular migrants from China wanting to enter the United States pay up to $35,000 to smugglers,† to Europe they pay in the range of $10,000–$15,000, and those seeking entry into Japan up to $10,000. The "fee" for moving from Lebanon to Germany varies between $5,000–$10,000; from India to the United States it is around $25,000, and from North Africa to Spain it is between $2,000–$3,500.

(Box continues on next page)

Box 5.3   *(continued)*

The vast majority of undocumented workers are unskilled for several reasons. Policies in most receiving countries offer greater opportunities for skilled workers to migrate legally than for unskilled. Many skilled workers, coming from middle- or upper-income households, may be less willing to experience the uncertainty inherent in breaking the immigration law (including the prospect of being jailed temporarily), than persons from lower-income households. Also, employers are more likely to offer unskilled jobs to undocumented workers, whose tenure is relatively uncertain, as skilled jobs may require a greater investment to apply technical backgrounds to the demands of specific jobs.

Efforts to control illegal entry have varied in effectiveness.[‡] Receiving countries have addressed undocumented workers by offering amnesties that generally involve the promise of regularization for undocumented workers who have been in the country for a period of time. For example, the U.S. Immigration and Regularization Control Act (IRCA) of 1986 regularized the status of undocumented workers who had been living in the country since before 1982, as well as undocumented agricultural workers. This program, which took effect mostly in 1989–91, granted a regular status to more than 2.5 million people, mostly from Mexico and Central America. However, this massive regularization program did not prevent Mexicans or other undocumented immigrants from continuing to cross the U.S. border. Similarly, in Europe, approximately 1.5 million undocumented migrants saw their status regularized under amnesty programs implemented by Belgium, France, Greece, Portugal, and Spain during the 1990s.[§]

Source: International Organization for Migration (IOM) 2003.

Regularization programs for undocumented are also present across developing countries. For example, in the 1990s, Argentina regularized undocumented workers from Bolivia, Paraguay, and Peru under bilateral agreements. Thailand had a similar program. Other countries have opted for more drastic measures to address undocumented workers. For example, Malaysia in 2002 deported hundreds of thousands of irregular migrants back to Indonesia and the Philippines, in reaction to rising levels of criminality; however, there was a slowdown in its economy given its dependency on foreign workers.

---

[*]IOM (2003). Unless otherwise noted, the data in this box are based on this document.

[**]The number may be even higher today. The United Kingdom may have up to one million irregular migrants (UK Immigration Service), France 500,000, Belgium 90,000 (Belgium Anti-racist Centre), and Ireland 10,000 (Irish Police). In terms of flows, some 100,000 irregulars are smuggled into Germany each year (German Police Trade Union), and some 95,000 irregulars from Albania, Romania, and Iraq alone enter Greece each year.

[†]Annually, some 25,000 to 50,000 Chinese irregular migrants enter the United States.

[‡]Hanson and Spilimbergo (1999) find that additional resources devoted to border enforcement in the United States have yielded only limited results, and Boeri and others (2002) find that tighter controls at a given entry point can be effective, but divert migrants to other points of entry. Worksite inspections can have a greater impact, but in the United States such efforts are very limited.

[§]Italy regularized 716,000 irregular migrants in three waves; Greece accepted 370,000 people (in 1997–98) mostly from the Balkans and Eastern Europe; Spain regularized 260,000 irregular immigrants mostly from Africa and Latin America; and Portugal regularized 61,000.

Some countries have recognized the need to manage both regular and irregular migration on a regional basis. Regional consultative processes, such as the Manila Process (1996), the Migration Dialogue for Southern Africa (MIDSA 2000), the Puebla Process (1996), and others have emerged—and all of them include consultations to deter human trafficking and the movement of undocumented workers. However, most of these groups are informal ones that mostly share information on migration-related issues and generally do not impose requirements on the immigration policies of the participating countries. It appears that neither unilateral policies nor consultative arrangements have had significant success in controlling the substantial pressures for migration to industrial countries.

Agreements that permit temporary access for certain groups

Several agreements provide for market access of certain groups of workers, usually the highly skilled. The most recent agreements have focused heavily on intra-corporate transferees, including managers and skilled technical staff.

The Central America and Caribbean Community (CARICOM) allows university graduates to move among member countries without passport requirements and allows university graduates, professionals, skilled persons, and workers from some selected occupations to work without a permit.

NAFTA, along with the Canada-Chile, U.S.-Chile, and the U.S.-Singapore Free Trade Agreements, do not provide for permanent migration, but allow for the temporary movement of business visitors, traders and investors, intra-corporate transferees, and professionals.[23] Visas are still required for all four categories, and work permits are required for all except business visitors.[24] Numeric restrictions on temporary entry are not allowed for the first three categories, but were imposed by the United States on professionals from Chile, Mexico, and Singapore, but not from Canada. U.S. professionals seeking to enter either market are not subject to numerical limits. In the Canada-Chile agreement there are no numerical limits to any of the four categories. Following the NAFTA agreement, the number of professionals entering the United States from Canada and Mexico increased substantially, and although the gap in favor of Canadians remained high, it narrowed considerably by 2002. Similarly, in the treaty traders and investors category, the ratio of Mexican over Canadian admittances into the United States increased from 0.4 in 1996 to 1.1 in 2002.[25]

The EU agreements with Central and Eastern European countries (prior to their 2004 accession to the EU) allowed for temporary entry of workers providing a service, managers and/or highly qualified employees, and company representatives negotiating for the sale or supply of services. Transition periods as well as restrictions for public service works and sectoral exclusions applied. They are still in force for the nonaccession countries, Bulgaria and Romania. The Japan-Singapore FTA provides for the temporary movement of natural persons for business purposes, including investors, subject to conditions for entry (such as pre-employment for at least one year for intracorporate transferees) and time limits of stay. The Group of Three (Colombia, Mexico, and Republica Bolivariana de Venezuela) facilitates temporary entry for business persons. As in other agreements, GATS Mode 4 restrictions regarding access to the employment market or permanent employment also apply. MERCOSUR also has provisions to facilitate the temporary entry of business persons and the exercise of temporary professional practices, and it is working on the issues relative to a "MERCOSUR National Residency" and a more flexible migratory regulation for MERCOSUR citizens (Nofal 2004). Other agreements among Latin American countries (such as the Mexico-Nicaragua, Mexico-Chile, Mexico-Bolivia, Mexico-Costa Rica, and the agreement between Central America and Dominican Republic) contain similar provisions.

Agreements based on GATS Mode 4

Several bilateral agreements, along with the ASEAN Free Trade Agreement (AFTA) and MERCOSUR, base labor mobility provisions on the principles of Mode 4 of the GATS. However, most of these agreements add provisions that allow for labor mobility in categories not covered by the GATS. For example, the U.S.-Jordan agreement facilitates visa arrangements for independent traders and persons linked to investment. The EU-Mexico agreement provides for a standstill and sets common regulations of work, labor conditions, and residency permits for temporary workers in each country. The AFTA since 1998 has covered all modes of supply, including services sectors not previously covered by the GATS. The Framework Agreement on the ASEAN Investment Area (1998) commits members to support freer flows of skilled labor, professionals, capital and technology among ASEAN members. By contrast, the Euro-Med agreements with Morocco and Tunisia do not provide for preferential access beyond GATS (the case for other Mediterranean agreements as well). The New Zealand-Singapore agreement generally follows the GATS model regarding labor mobility for service suppliers. MERCOSUR (and its agreements with Bolivia and Chile) is limited to the GATS provisions on the movement of

natural persons as services suppliers (Nofal 2004).

Agreements without effective provisions for market access

The Asia Pacific Economic Cooperation Forum (APEC), the South Asia Association for Regional Cooperation (SAARC), and Common Market for Eastern and Southern Africa (COMESA) do not provide for labor mobility. However, the first two have taken measures to facilitate business travel. Most of the members of APEC (except the United States and Canada) participate in the Business Travel

Box 5.4   U.S. temporary admission programs under NAFTA and unilateral policies

The U.S. has several visa categories for the admission of temporary workers. NAFTA provided for the temporary admission of professionals under TN visas and made it easier for Mexicans to take advantage of already existing visa categories for skilled workers and professionals. However, NAFTA made no provision for increasing admissions of unskilled workers to the United States. In contrast, the United States has unilateral programs that do allow for the temporary admission of unskilled workers, and these have grown from from about 14,000 in

1996 to about 66,000 in 2002. Moreover, the largest temporary business visitor program (B1 visa) is limited to six months (renewable, but total time cannot exceed one year), and generally is used for short-term trips to the United States. The other visas can be granted for one year or more, often with extensions. Thus more long-term unskilled Mexican workers have been admitted to the United States under unilateral programs than under programs initiated under, or supported by, NAFTA.

Temporary entry of Mexican workers to the United States (thousands of persons)	1996	2002
Program initiated under NAFTA		
Professional (TN visa)	0.2	1.8
Programs supported by NAFTA[a]		
Intracompany transferees (L1 visas)	4.8	15.3
Treaty traders and investors (E1, E2 visas)	1.0	4.0
Business visitors (B1 visas)	309.0	475.0
Unilateral programs		
Professionals with specialty occupations (H1B visas)	5.3	15.9
Agricultural temporary workers (H2A visas)	8.8	12.8
Non-agricultural temporary workers (H2B visas)	5.5	53.0

[a]These visa categories existed before NAFTA and apply to many countries. However, provisions of NAFTA make it easier for Mexicans to use them.
Source: USCIS 2002, INS 1997.

Card Scheme, under which holders of the card receive expedited entry at the airport, and are not required to submit separate applications for business visas. Members of the SAARC adopted a Visa Waiver Scheme in 1992, which exempts 21 categories of persons from visa requirements. Free labor movement is envisaged as a long-term objective of COMESA, to be accomplished by 2025. However, progress has been limited to date.[26]

To date: Limited labor integration

Most regional agreements have had little impact on increasing migration. First, the agreements with full labor mobility have been between countries of similar income levels, so there has been little incentive for migration. Most agreements, and particularly those agreements that include both industrial and developing country members, do not allow for permanent migration.

Second, while these agreements often provide for some temporary labor mobility, particularly for the service sectors, the provisions are generally restricted to higher-skilled workers. This is consistent with the trend in industrial countries of changing unilateral migration policies to attract higher-skilled workers—in principle on a temporary basis, but in practice allowing for the possibility to settle after some period of time. For example, the Temporary Immigration Program of Australia allows for unlimited visa renewal for skilled workers. In the United Kingdom, highly skilled temporary workers in certain occupations can settle after 4 years of continuous work. In Norway, temporary workers with special skills can be issued a permanent work permit after 3 years of stay. In Canada, the 2002 Immigration and Refugee Protection Act (IRPA) placed more emphasis on education, job experience, and language ability in allowing entry. This trend toward favoring higher-skilled workers limits the potential global gains from migration.

To the extent that developed countries have permitted entry for unskilled workers from RTA countries, it has occurred through parallel programs, many of which predated the RTA, such as programs in the United States with Mexico and in the EU with non-members of Southern Europe. Where industrial countries have allowed for some admittance of unskilled workers, the rules differ significantly from those governing admission of skilled workers. Unskilled workers legally entering host countries usually do so under seasonal work agreements, project (or guest) worker agreements, or specific provisions such as the working holiday maker programs (WHMP). Seasonal employment usually allows foreign workers to stay in the host country for periods between three months and one year, with work permits provided to foreign workers only in the event that no domestic labor can do the job and only in some specific sectors (such as agriculture, forestry, and tourism). Project worker agreements allow foreign workers entry for specific projects and usually include limits on the maximum stay and quotas (often determined on the basis of labor market conditions). WHMP allows young people (roughly 18–30 years old) to holiday and work for short periods, provided there is a prior bilateral working holiday agreement among the involved countries.

Developing countries' regional agreements also tend to discriminate in favor of skilled workers when providing for labor mobility. As mentioned above, CARICOM allows for the free movement of university graduates, other professionals, skilled persons, and workers from selected occupations. Several Latin American agreements (Group of Three, Central America-Dominican Republic, and agreements between Mexico on the one hand, and Chile, Nicaragua, Bolivia, and Costa Rica on the other) also provide for the movement of some skilled, not unskilled, workers.

Conclusions: Beyond Merchandise Trade

Agreements differ markedly in their treatment—to say nothing of their implementation—of non-merchandise provisions for services, investment, intellectual property, and temporary movement of workers. Differences between the United States and EU bilateral FTAs and other agreements are particularly vast.

In those areas where RTAs could seriously promote development—services liberalization and temporary movement of workers—results have ranged from mixed to missed opportunities. In general, the U.S. FTAs have prompted some additional services market openings in Bahrain, CAFTA, and Morocco, some changes in Singapore, but relatively few changes in Australia and Chile. To be sure, even those agreements that required no additional market opening could benefit developing countries, because investors may attach credibility to the lock-in effects of the treaty.

In the South, agreements that have substantially improved services access are relatively limited, and those with greater market access often have the most restrictive rules of origin for investor nationality. More common is the lack of progress on services liberalization.

More disappointing from a development perspective is the minimal attention given to creating opportunities for the temporary movement of workers, particularly unskilled workers. In neither North-South nor South-South agreements is there evidence of much activity. In the wake of the September 11, 2001, attacks on the United States, concerns for security have made cross-border movement of all persons subject to greater controls and scrutiny. This atmosphere does not bode well for expanding programs for temporary workers.

At the same time, in those regulatory areas where development benefits are largely unproven, the North-South bilateral FTAs are strengthening their rules. Strengthening the rules governing investment and intellectual property may contribute to better institutional environment, but the greatest gain is to be found in services. Enhancing protections offered to investors has not been shown to increase the flow of investment, and preventing the erosion of monopolistic returns to the owners of technology through enhanced IPRs is of doubtful development benefit for the average developing country.

Moreover, the downside risks of misjudgments in terms of adverse legal and economic ramifications are nontrivial, especially for unsophisticated governments. International treaty law in these areas is evolving fast and is being set through case laws of arbitration panels, whose judgments at times conflict (Ewing-Chow 2001). Governments may find themselves hauled before arbitration panels and compelled to pay large amounts of compensation for enacting regulations they had considered in their sovereign domain.

Broadly defining investment to include all capital flows and assets, including intellectual property, carries risks. For example, one potential risk, is the set of provisions associated with the U.S.-Chile arrangement. These provisions could limit a less sophisticated government's ability to deal with a financial crisis.

Realizing the promise of services, investment, IPRs, and labor mobility

Using RTAs as a lever to liberalize services has several advantages. The potential for improving economy-wide performance is often great. Moreover, most services liberalization is inherently multilateral. This is because member governments that open markets want to realize the immediate gain of full competition and so open markets to all comers, or because members adopt lenient rules regarding domicile of investors, thereby permitting external investors to invest in the region through subsidiaries located in member countries. Even if restrictions impede full MFN access, regional agreements can be cost-free stepping stones to open markets insofar as they do not carry the trade-diversion costs of lost revenues associated with tariff reductions for goods trade. More could be done in RTAs, particularly in South-South agreements, to realize these benefits.

Countries have to design strategies toward investment and intellectual property that are appropriate to their development priorities and then analyze carefully which elements, if any, ought to be contained in trade treaties. For some countries, improving other property rights—for example, land rights or small business assets—may have a higher priority than establishing market access rights for investors or rights for patent holders; for other countries, especially middle-income countries, these may indeed be a priority. Once a strategy is in place, it is possible to ascertain which of the new rules customarily associated with regional trade agreements make sense for development.

Evaluating the development benefit of any given RTA cannot rest solely on one component because often rules are accepted in one area to achieve market openings in partner countries in another. For example, the net development benefits of the investment and IPR components hinge critically on their appropriateness for development and the market access granted in product markets of partner countries.

A corollary lesson is that multilateral liberalization in goods markets is essential for reaping any gains from RTAs that contain new rules. Governments wishing to maximize gains from RTAs should ensure that new rules are consistent with extant border protection, and if not, they should consider lowering that protection. If a country has high tariff barriers and forms an RTA with a partner requiring investor protections and TRIPS-Plus, it may end up entrenching the businesses of that partner behind new barriers. It may confer first mover advantages in services and IPR restrictions in drug or other high technology manufacture, with reinforced barriers to parallel imports or new entry from third parties.

Finally, RTAs—and other regional cooperation agreements—do offer some important opportunities for countries to collaborate, especially in South-South agreements. To stimulate investment, particularly in services, they might adopt common standards that facilitate cross-border competition in services and investment. Adopting common technical standards for telecommunications, for example, has helped integrate markets and opens the way for competition. To adopt international norms regulating technology, new agreements could adopt their own IPR standards, with the advantage of foreclosing additional restrictions motivated by private interest groups in the North. At the same time, some regions may find opportunities to agree on common administration of patent and copyright law.

Notes

1. Agreements can also increase the number of competitors by allowing cross-border provision of services, Mode 1, such as supplying back office services. Restrictions on these tend to be less common than on supplying through commercial presence of a foreign subsidiary, Mode 3. One exception is supplying various types of insurance and reinsurance, which can be done cross-border, though a sales affiliate is normally required.

2. RTAs that restrict service providers to member countries by definition limit the number of potential competitors relative to multilateral liberalization. Even if later followed with multilateral opening, RTAs may confer on members first mover advantages, and, if some market barriers to entry remain, they will not be readily competed away; the result is higher prices to consumers.

3. According to the agreement, if Chile chooses to impose restrictive measures on capital flows it considers speculative, then special dispute settlement rules will apply.

4. For some FTA countries, pre-existing BITs had virtually the same rights; however, about half of the countries had no BIT prior to the FTA, and where BITS did exist, pre-establishments were often fewer and less extensive.

5. See Fink and Reichenmiller (2004) for a more detailed review.

6. These include, for example, TRIPS, the Paris Convention for the Protection of Industrial Property, the Berne Convention for the Protection of Literary and Artistic Works, the Rome Convention for the Protection of Performers, Producers of Phonograms and Broadcasting Organizations, and others also contains a list of new conventions that parties are expected to ratify within a specified timeline, such as the Budapest

Treaty on the International Recognition of the Deposit of Micro-organisms for Mexico and the World Intellectual Property Organization (WIPO) Copyright Treaty for Chile. Finally, the list includes several conventions that the member states are expected to ratify "as soon as possible" without mentioning a specific deadline, such as the WIPO Copyright Treaty for Mexico or the Madrid Agreement concerning the International Registration of Marks for Chile.

7. BITs customarily provide a definition of investment coverage, provide investor protections such as against expropriation, require national treatment for post-entry establishments, stipulate compensation for the expropriation of their investments, and provide for a dispute resolution mechanism. The latter usually permit the investor to sue the state for breach of treaty under binding arbitration. In some cases, treaties proscribe any government action that would reduce the value of the private investment, even if it were environmental, and establish grounds for compensation. Such compensation could either entail extensive liabilities for the host government or compel them to refrain from making certain policy choices.

8. The United States initiated the practice of defining investment to broadly include intellectual property in the late 1990s in negotiations of its bilateral investment treaties. See Vivas-Eugui (2003).

9. Some of the problems include the absence of data on implementation and the variable coverage of FDI provisions across agreements, which makes it difficult to distinguish the effects of investment rules from trade rules. Moreover, the absence on FDI data that would enable us to distinguish the effects of RTAs on differing type of investment—vertical or horizontal—limits the analysis. Nonetheless, the regressions are robust to variations in specifications.

10. The regression with fixed effects estimation of net FDI inflows is:

lfdi	Coef. Std. Err.	t	P>|t|
lgdp	.9404982 .2065772	4.55	0.000
lgnppc	−.1228465 .2008249	−0.61	0.541
open	.0051226 .0011387	4.50	0.000
growth	.0198651 .0040816	4.87	0.000
cpi	−.0196485 .0060906	−3.23	0.001
lfdiwld	.4472645 .0719058	6.22	0.000
growld	−.0611576 .0432152	−1.42	0.157
lftagdp	.0518633 .0163279	3.18	0.002

R-sq: within = 0.3973   corr(u_i, Xb) = -0.0410

between = 0.7469   F(28,2003) = 47.16
overall = 0.6690   Prob > F = 0.0000
F test that all u_i = 0: F(143, 2003) = 12.79
Prob > F = 0.0000

11. As mentioned earlier, this variable contains the sum of the host country's RTA partners GDP, excluding the host country itself. Thus if we consider Brazil as the host country and MERCOSUR as the relevant RTA, the variable lftagdp would be the log of the sum of GDP of Argentina, Paraguay, and Uruguay. This variable serves a twofold purpose in the estimation routine. First, since it is equal to zero prior to signing an RTA and carries a positive value afterwards, it measures whether signing an agreement has an effect on FDI inflows (i.e., including a dummy variable for RTA membership would be counterproductive in the presence of this variable, since it will capture the "threshold effect" of signing an RTA). Furthermore, this variable also captures the effects of participating in a larger market following the signing of an agreement. This is particularly important if a country is party to more than one agreement—the variable will then be a sum of all of its partners' GDP, reflecting the fact that the country has now created a larger market. The fact that this variable is positive and significant shows not only that signing an RTA will generally bring benefits in terms of greater FDI inflows, but also that larger market size of the country's partners tends to generate more incoming FDI.

12. See Finger and Schuler (2004) for a richer discussion of the the asymmetry in TRIPS; they argue that it protects the knowledge that businesses and individuals have in rich countries and that poor people buy, but not the knowledge that poor people generate and sell to the world.

13. In this sense, full enforcement is equivalent to a TRIPs standard (Maskus 2000, 183–85).

14. See paragraph 4 of the Doha Declaration on TRIPS and Public Health, available at http://www.wto.org.

15. Technically, the Doha Declaration does not address questions of marketing approval during the patent term and test data exclusivity. However, the provisions of the bilateral FTAs in these areas can still be seen as being at odds with the spirit of the Doha Declaration, to the extent that they preclude the effective use of compulsory licenses.

16. See the letter from USTR General Counsel John K. Veroncau to Congressman Levin dated July 19, 2004, available at *Inside US Trade*. Moreover, the side letters refer "*in particular* [to] *cases such as HIV/AIDS, tuberculosis, malaria, and other epidemics as well as circumstances of extreme urgency on national emergency.*" The language chosen mirrors wording in the Doha Declaration on TRIPS and Public Health, except that the latter employs the term "especially" instead of "in particular" and does not mention "circumstances of extreme urgency or national emergency." This difference in language may imply a narrower definition of public health and therefore flexibility to issue a compulsory license, but this is subject to

legal interpretation that must await actual cases of dispute settlement.

17. See the letter from USTR General Counsel John K. Veroneau to Congressman Levin dated July 19, 2004.

18. See the excellent studies in Fink and Maskus (2004) including particularly Fink (2004) for the U.S. and German MNCs; Smarzynska Javorcik (2004) for Eastern Europe; and Maskus, Dougherty, and Mertha (2004) for China.

19. The description on agreements that follows is strongly based on Nielson (2003) and a complement, in some cases, to the text of the agreements.

20. GATS (under "Mode 4") covers the movement of some temporary foreign workers among WTO members, specifically individual service suppliers. Although in theory GATS covers services suppliers at all skill levels, in practice WTO members' commitments have been limited to the higher skilled.

21. Some agreements include provisions facilitating mutual recognition (e.g., EFTA), and others have complementary arrangements (e.g., the ANZCERTA Services Protocol, the Trans-Tasman Travel Arrangement, and the Trans Tasman Mutual Recognition Arrangement together provide that persons registered to practice an occupation in one country can practice an equivalent profession in the other country).

22. ANZCERTA does not cover labor mobility other than for services suppliers, but under the Trans-Tasman Travel Arrangement (signed in 1973), nationals of each country have the right to visit, reside, and work in each other's country without time restrictions.

23. Between 1987–97, there was a total increase of 102,000 Greeks in the rest of the (11) European countries, which is an annual average of 10,000 only. In the case of Portugal, the annual average increase of Portuguese immigrants in the rest of the EU countries during 1986–97 was only 7,700.

24. In NAFTA, definitions for business persons and, in particular, a list of professionals are provided, as well as the minimum academic conditions that the latter must satisfy (in general, at least a baccalaureate degree, and sometimes complemented with some years of experience). The other agreements provide for a more flexible requirement, in that instead of listing the professions, they specify the academic and/or experience requirements that professionals must satisfy.

25. Business visitors need to demonstrate though that the proposed activity is international in scope and that they are not seeking to enter the local labor market. They need also to demonstrate that the primary source of remuneration, their principal place of business, and actual place of accrual of profits are from outside the territory they are seeking to enter.

26. Mexicans entering through this category into the United States increased to 4,000 business persons in 2002, from 980 in 1996.

27. Nonetheless, migration flows within COMESA have been substantial. The annual inflow of workers to South Africa from other African countries is estimated to have increased from roughly 500,000 in 1990 to more than 3.5 millions in 1995; most were temporary workers in mining and farming.

References

Abbott, Frederick M. 2004a. The Doha Declaration on the TRIPS Agreement and Public Health and the Contradictory Trend in Bilateral and Regional Free Trade Agreements. Quaker United Nations Office Occasional Paper 14.

————. 2004b. Towards a New Era of Objective Assessment in the Field of TRIPS and Variable Geometry for the Preservation of Multilateralism. Paper for The World Trade Forum 2004, Bern, Switzerland, June 4–5, 2004. (also forthcoming in *Journal of International Economic Law* No. 1 2005 Oxford.)

Bora, Bijit. 2003. The Agreement on Trade Related Investment Measures, 1995–2002. UNCTAD Discussion Paper Series No. 15, Geneva.

Boeri, Tito, Gordon Hanson, and Barry McCormick, eds. 2002. *Immigration policy and the welfare system.* New York: Oxford University Press.

Chudnovsky, Daniel, and Andres Lopez. 2001. La Inversión Extranjera Directa en el MERCOSUR: Un Análisis Comparativo. In *El Boom de Inversión Extranjera Directa en el MERCOSUR*, Siglo XXI, Buenos Aires 2001.

Commission on Intellectual Property Rights (CIPR). 2002. Integrating Intellectual Property Rights and Development Policy. Report of the Commission on Intellectual Property Rights established by the UK Secretary of State for International Development.

Encarnation, Dennis, and Louis T. Wells. 1986. Evaluating Foreign Investment. In *Investing in Development: New Roles for Private Capital?* ed. Theodore Moran. New Brunswick, NJ: Transaction Books.

Ewing-Chow, Michael. 2001. Investor Protection in Free Trade Agreements: Lessons from North America. *Singapore Journal of International and Comparative Law* 748.

Finger, Michael, and Julio Nogues. 2002. The Unbalanced Uruguay Round Outcome: The New Areas in Future WTO Negotiations. *The World Economy* 25.

Finger, Michael J., and Philip Schuler. 2004. Poor *People's Knowledge: Promoting Intellectual Property Rights in Developing Countries.* Washington, DC: World Bank.

Fink, Carsten. 2004. Intellectual Property Rights and U.S. and German International Transactions in Manufacturing Industries. In *Intellectual Property and Development: Lessons from Recent Research,* eds. Fink, Carsten and Keith Maskus. Washington, DC: World Bank, forthcoming.

Fink, Carsten, and Keith Maskus, eds. 2004. *Intellectual Property and Development: Lessons from Recent Research.* Washington, DC: World Bank, forthcoming.

Fink, Carsten, and Patrick Reichenmiller. 2004. Tightening TRIPS: the Intellectual Property Provisions of Recent US Free Trade Agreements. Report. World Bank.

Fink, Carsten, and Aaditya Mattoo. 2002. Regional Agreements and Trade in Services. Policy Research Working Paper 2852, World Bank, Washington, DC.

Frischtak, Claudio. 2004. Multinational Firms' Responses to Integration of Latin American Markets. *Business and Politics* 6:1.

Hallward-Driemeier, Mary. 2003. Do Bilateral Investment Treaties Attract Foreign Direct Investment? Only a Bit . . . and They Could Bite. Policy Research Working Paper 3121, World Bank, Washington, DC.

Hanson, Gordon H., and Antonio Spilimbergo. 1999. Illegal Immigration, Border Enforcement and Relative Wages: Evidence for Apprehensions at the U.S.-Mexican Border. *American Economic Review* 89 (5): 1337–57.

Immigration and Naturalization Service (INS). 1997. *Statistical Yearbook of the Immigration and Naturalization Service.* Table 40. http://uscis.gov/graphics/shared/aboutus/statistics/Nim97list.htm.

International Organization for Migration (IOM). 2003. World Migration 2003: Managing Migration Challenges and Responses for People on the Move. Geneva.

Lall, Sanjaya, and Paul Streeten. 1977. Foreign Investment, Transnationals, and Developing Countries. Boulder, Colorado: Westview Press.

Lederman, Daniel, William Maloney, and Luis Serven. 2004. Lessons from NAFTA for Latin American and Caribbean Countries: A Summary of Research Findings. World Bank, Washington, DC.

Levy Yeyati, Eduardo, Ernesto Stein, and Christian Daude. 2004. The FTAA and the Location of FDI. Paper for Central Bank of Chile and World Bank Conference on The Future of Trade Liberalization in the Americas, Santiago, Chile, March 22–23.

Mann, Howard, and Aaron Cosbey. 2004. International Investment Agreements: Trends and Impacts for Developing Countries Background paper for *Global Economic Prospects 2005,* World Bank, Washington, DC.

Mansfield, Edwin. 1995. Intellectual Property Protection, Direct Investment and Technology Transfer. IFC Discussion Paper No. 27, World Bank, Washington, DC.

Markusen, James. 2004. Regional Integration and Third-Country Inward Investment. *Business and Politics* 6 (1).

Martin, Philip. 2003. Economic Integration and Migration: The Mexico-US Case. Wider Discussion Paper No. 2003/35. United Nations University World Institute for Development Economics Research. Helsinki.

Maskus, Keith. 2000. *Intellectual Property Rights in the Global Economy.* Washington, DC: Institute for International Economics.

Maskus Keith, Sean Dougherty, and Andrew Mertha. 2004. Intellectual Property Rights and Economic Development in China. In *Intellectual Property and Development: Lessons from Recent Research,* eds. Fink, Carsten, and Keith Maskus. Washington, DC: World Bank, forthcoming.

Mattoo, Aadittya, R. Rathindran, and A. Subramanian. 2001. Measuring Services Trade Liberalization and its Impact on Economic Growth: An Illustration. Policy Research Working Paper 2655, World Bank, Washington, DC.

Mattoo, Aadittya, and Pierre Sauve. 2004. Regionalism and Trade in Services in the Western Hemisphere: A Policy Agenda. In *Integrating the Americas,* eds. A. Estevadeodal, Dani Rodrik, Alan Taylor, and Andres Velasco. Cambridge, MA: Harvard University Press.

Newfarmer, Richard. 2001. Foreign Direct Investment: Policies and Institutions for Growth. In *New Horizons for Foreign Direct Investment.* Paris: OECD.

Nielson, Julia. 2003. Labor Mobility in Regional Trade Agreement. In *Moving People to Deliver Services,* eds. Mattoo, Aaditya, and Antonia Carzaniga. Washington, DC: World Bank.

Nofal, Beatriz. 2004. Construyendo una intergracion mas profunda en Mercosur. Background paper for the *Global Economic Prospects 2005,* World Bank, Washington, DC.

Nogues, Julio. 2004. The Roles of Multilateralism and Regionalism for Latin America. Paper prepared for the Economic Commission for Latin America (ECLA). Santiago, Chile.

OECD. Trends in International Migration, various years.

OECD. 2003. Regionalism and the Multilateral Trading System. Paris: OECD.

Ozden, Caglar, and Francisco J. Parodi. 2004. Custom Unions and Foreign Investment: Theory and Evidence from Mercosur's Auto Industry. Paper for Central Bank of Chile and World Bank Conference on The Future of Trade Liberalization in the Americas, Santiago, Chile, March 22–23.

Peterson, Luke. 2003a. Emerging Bilateral Investment Treaty Arbitration and Sustainable Development Research Note, *Invest-SD News Bulletin*, International Institute for Sustainable Development (IISD). April. http://www.iisd.org/pdf/2003/trade_bits_disputes.pdf.

_____. 2003b. Czech Republic Hit With Massive Compensation Bill in Investment Treaty Dispute. *Invest-SD News Bulletin,* International Institute for Sustainable Development (IISD). March 21.

Schiff, Maurice, and Alan Winters. 2003. *Regional Integration and Development.* Washington, DC: World Bank.

Smarzynska Javorcik, Beata. 2004. The Composition of Foreign Direct Investment and Protection of Intellectual Property Rights: Evidence from Transition Economies. In *Intellectual Property and Development: Lessons from Recent Research*, eds. Fink, Carsten, and Keith Maskus. Washington, DC: World Bank, forthcoming.

Stein, Ernesto, and Christian Daude. 2001. Institutions, Integration, and the Location of Foreign Direct Investment. In *New Horizons for Foreign Direct Investment*. Paris: OECD.

Szepesi, Stefan. 2004a. Coercion or Engagement? Economics and Institutions in ACP-EU Trade Negotiations. European Center for Development Policy Management (ECDPM) Discussion Paper 56. Maastricht, Netherlands.

Szepesi, Stefan. 2004b. How Did David Prepare to Talk to Goliath? South Africa's experience of trade negotiations with the EU. European Center for Development Policy Management (ECDPM) Discussion Paper 53. Maastricht, Netherlands.

te Velde, Dirk Willem, and Miatta Fahnbulleh. 2003. Investment Related Provisions in Regional Trade Agreements. Paper prepared for the project on Regional Integration and Poverty. UK Department for International Development (DFID). London, October.

Ullrich, Heidi. 2004. Comparing EU Free Trade Agreements: Services. *ECDPM In Brief.*

UNCTAD (United Nations Conference for Trade and Development). 1998. *Bilateral Investment Treaties in the Mid-1990s.* New York: United Nations.

US Citizens and Immigration Services (USCIS, formerly the INS). 2002. *Yearbook of Immigration Statistics* (formerly Statistical Yearbook of the Immigration and Naturalization Service, INS). Table 27. http://uscis.gov/graphics/shared/aboutus/statistics/TEMP02yrbk/Temp2002list.htm.

US Citizens and Immigration Services (USCIS, formerly the INS). 2003. *Estimates of the Unauthorized Immigrant Population Residing in the United States: 1990 to 2000.* Office of Policy and Planning. Table B. http://uscis.gov/graphics/shared/aboutus/statistics/Illegals.htm.

USTR (United States Trade Representative). 2004. *USA—Chile Free Trade Agreement.*

Vivas-Eugui, David 2003. Regional and bilateral agreements and a TRIPS-plus world: the Free Trade Area of the Americas (FTAA). TRIPS Issue Papers 1. Geneva: Quaker United Nations Office.

Waldkirch, A. 2001. The 'New Regionalism' and Foreign Direct Investment: The Case of Mexico. Oregon State University Working Paper.

Walmsley, Terri Louise, and L. Alan Winters. 2003. Relaxing the Restrictions on the Temporary Movement of Natural Persons: A Simulation Analysis. Centre for Economic Policy Research Discussion Paper Series No. 3719. January.

Weintraub, Sidney. 2004. Lessons from the Chile and Singapore Free Trade Agreements. In *Free Trade Agreements: US Strategies and Priorities,* ed. J. J. Schott. Washington, DC: Institute for International Economics.

World Bank. 2001. *Global Economic Prospects and the Developing Countries 2002: Making Trade Work for the World's Poor.* Washington, DC: World Bank.

_____. 2002. *Global Economic Prospects and the Developing Countries 2003: Investing to Unlock Global Opportunities.* Washington, DC: World Bank.

_____. 2004. *World Development Report 2005: A Better Investment Climate for Everyone.* Washington, DC: World Bank.

6

Making Regionalism Complementary to Multilateralism

The emergence of a more proactive stance in multilateral negotiations by developing countries in parallel with an explosion of preferential regional trade agreements (RTAs) around the world raises an important question: Are these trends complementary, representing different paths to the same desired outcome of faster growth, development, and poverty reduction, or are they competing and incompatible? In principle, the best outcome for all countries would be a nondiscriminatory trading system; developing countries, in particular, would benefit from a nondiscriminatory trading system because most poor people and many poor countries might find themselves excluded from preferential deals. If the explosion in RTAs implies a higher probability that the majority of developing countries would face greater discrimination than under an MFN (or nondiscriminatory) regime, the world as a whole will be worse off, and individual developing countries may lose substantially.[1]

RTAs can be a complement to multilateral reform, but they are not a substitute. Consider a scenario, modeled in the first section of this chapter, in which each developing country signed an agreement with the United States, the European Union (EU), Canada, and Japan—the Quad. Each developing country could raise its real incomes by *individually* signing bilateral agreements with the Quad countries; and in some cases they would raise their real incomes more than they would through multilateral accords. But these gains

disappear if *all* developing countries were to sign such agreements. In fact, all developing countries would lose relative to a multilateral agreement and even relative to the baseline. This scenario underscores the fact that, while stalled collective action through multilateral channels creates a strong incentive for each developing country to sign a regional agreement, if every country does so, they all lose.

RTAs do alter the incentives for countries to participate in multilateral liberalization. RTAs can be a stumbling block to multilateral arrangements by creating incentives to resist the preference erosion that can occur through new multilateral liberalization. However, because the gains are often substantially larger in multilateral agreements, concerns over preference erosion may be limited to a few small countries that could conceivably block a multilateral agreement. Those recalcitrant countries resisting reforms are likely the beneficiaries of preferences associated with distorted agreements encompassing agriculture or the clothing and textile trade, not RTAs. Large developed countries may gain more from signing individual bilateral agreements than they would from a multilateral accord, because they can use the carrot of preferential access to extract concessions in nontrade areas from developing country partners that would be resisted in the WTO negotiating framework. But we see little evidence that the high-income countries have reduced their effort to bring the current multilateral negotiations to fruition.

From a development perspective, the WTO remains the best-available forum to discipline the use of trade-distorting policies. RTAs can complement the WTO efforts by cooperating on behind-the-border policies, especially on regulation-intensive issues such as services, trade facilitation, and the investment climate. Governments pursuing this agenda through RTAs must adopt rules that are appropriate to their own level of development. To be effective, the rules must target a priority concern, must be enforceable, and must avoid becoming a tax on scarce resources that would be better used elsewhere. Getting the rules "right" so that they promote development has implications for negotiations and enforcement of the resulting disciplines. The potential for inappropriate outcomes is higher in North–South RTAs because the asymmetry in negotiating power can overtake real development priorities.

Reinforcing the complementarity between regionalism and multilateralism and minimizing the latent tensions must begin with the completion of the Doha Development Agenda. If the Doha Development Agenda is completed in a way that actually promotes development, it would bring down tariffs, enhance the gains from open regionalism, and discipline any exclusionary effects of regional accords.

All countries could take steps to promote open regionalism—the developing countries, high-income countries, and the international community working together through the WTO. Developing countries are likely to have the greatest success in harnessing trade for growth and poverty reduction if they adopt a three-pronged strategy that involves autonomous liberalization, active multilateralism, and open regionalism.

High-income countries could promote open regionalism by including agriculture in RTAs. They could adopt more common and nonrestrictive rules of origin across agreements; and, to the extent that these rules set patterns common to most agreements, the burden on customs administration would be reduced. They could work with prospective partners to ensure that new regulations regarding investment and intellectual property are appropriate to the level of development, which would reduce risks of undue enforcement costs. Finally, they could provide trade-related technical assistance not only in the implementation phase but also in the negotiating phase, which could promote greater liberalization and supply response to new market opportunities in regional or global markets.

The international community, working through the WTO, can reduce discrimination in the system. The procedures associated with RTA disciplines as currently configured are ill-suited to limit either their proliferation or to control their discriminatory provisions. WTO members should establish stronger multilateral surveillance mechanisms to document, analyze, and monitor the effects of RTAs on nonmembers. Expanding the information on the impact of RTAs to stakeholders—firms, consumers, taxpayers—would also help ensure that the potential benefits of liberalization are both realized and distributed more equitably. Medium-term efforts should focus on implementing WTO disciplines on regional agreements.

Preferential Agreements within the Global Context

To place preferential trade arrangements in a multilateral context, we evaluate how different collections of trade agreements compare with multilateral alternatives. For this evaluation, we utilize the World Bank's global trade model known as LINKAGE, which has been used in previous *Global Economic Prospects*. The model is built around the GTAP database that is widely used to assess the global, regional, and country implications of alternative trade liberalization scenarios. However, the results described in this year's report reflect an update of the model's database, which has two notable differences. First, it has a new base year, 2001 (the old base year was 1997). Second, it has a new protection database that takes better account of preferential trade access. Box 6.1 provides a brief

Box 6.1   Impacts of the new GTAP database

The simulation results from the World Bank's LINKAGE model were presented in the past three issues of *Global Economic Prospects* (2002, 2003, and 2004) and were based on the use of various versions of Release 5 of the GTAP dataset.* An updated version of the data has become available; prerelease 6.04 was released in September 2004. The main innovations of the new dataset include a more recent base year (2001 instead of 1997), revised national input-output tables, and a new database for estimating the levels of trade protection. This last innovation is likely to have a large impact on trade scenarios. First, a brief digression on a technical issue regarding the new base year: The global database, to a large extent, is the outcome of merging national data. The national input-output tables have different base years and are virtually always in national currencies. Thus they must be updated to the given base year—2001 in the case of the new release—and converted to the database's common currency (i.e., the U.S. dollar). This has a practical implication because of movements in the value of the dollar. In 1997, the U.S. dollar was relatively strong (for example, $1.13 per euro), and it was much weaker in 2001 ($0.90 per euro). This means that the relative weight of countries will change between the two base years (holding growth constant). In fact, the global U.S. economy as a share of global output was around 32 percent in 1997 and only 27 percent in 2001. Thus the change in the value of the dollar will have some impact on the reported gains from trade reform, both globally and by region.

The more important change in the database relates to the change in protection. The new protection data relies on the MAcMaps dataset—a collaborative effort of CEPII (Paris) and the International Trade Centre (ITC, Geneva). Among the prominent features of the MAcMaps dataset is the incorporation of preferential tariff regimes and the conversion of specific tariffs to ad valorem equivalents; it thus represents a more realistic picture of the bilateral levels of protection. In summary, the new database will capture the

considerable reform between 1997 and 2001 (e.g., continued implementation of the Uruguay Round and China's progress towards WTO accession), and an improved treatment of preferential trade agreements.

The overall impact of these changes is that the World Bank's estimate of the global gains from global merchandise trade reform is now around $260 billion** (in 2015, relative to the baseline scenario), compared with around $380 billion using the 1997-based results from previous GEPs.*** The lower number reflects, to a large extent, the impacts of trade reforms achieved between 1997 and 2001 and the incorporation of preferences.**** The allocation of the gains across regions and sectors is broadly consistent with the previous results. Thus 41 percent (instead of 45 percent) of the gains from global reform accrue to developing countries, and agricultural reform generates some 47 percent (instead of 58 percent) of the global gains.

---

*The GTAP dataset is a product of the Global Trade Analysis Project (GTAP), based at Purdue University, with funding from an international consortium of international and national agencies (including the World Bank), universities, and research centers. Since its initial development in the early 1990s, the GTAP dataset has become the premiere dataset for undertaking global trade analysis. The current version includes a full social accounting matrix for 87 regions (of which 69 are individual countries), 57 economic sectors, and fully consistent bilateral trade flows.

**These results should still be viewed as preliminary as the GTAP consortium is preparing for the final release sometime before the end of 2004. The final release may result in some changes at the micro level, but will probably only have a relatively minor impact at the aggregate level.

***These gains refer to the so-called "static" effects, i.e., not taking into account dynamic effects such as improvements in productivity.

****There are other technical differences, including among others, the relative change of the value of the U.S. dollar as mentioned above. The LINKAGE model, apart from the change in the database, is identical to that used in the last *Global Economic Prospects*.

summary of these changes and the impacts of using the new database relative to the results outlined in previous *Global Economic Prospects*.

To assess the relative impacts of various RTAs, it is useful to develop a benchmark simulation (apart from the baseline). The benchmark simulation is a global reform

Table 6.1 Comparison of bilateral agreements to global trade reform
(change in real income in 2015 compared to baseline)

	Global (1)	Bilateral with Quad (2)	Bilateral minus large countries (3)	Global (4)	Bilateral with Quad (5)	Bilateral minus large countries (6)
		$ billion			Percent	
High-income countries	154.4	133.6	46.9	0.6	0.5	0.2
Low-income countries	16.6	−19.0	−1.9	0.9	−1.0	−0.1
Middle-income countries	92.2	−2.6	−4.7	1.2	0.0	−0.1
All developing countries	108.8	−21.5	−6.6	1.2	−0.2	−0.1
World Total	263.2	112.0	40.3	0.8	0.3	0.1

Source: World Bank simulations.

scenario in which all merchandise trade distortions are eliminated (services reform is left out for lack of sufficient data), domestic distortions in agriculture are removed (input and output subsidies, direct payments, and export subsidies), and import quotas in the textile and clothing sectors are removed. This scenario would be the ultimate long-run outcome of successful multilateralism. Under this reform scenario, the global gains in 2015 amount to $263 billion, or an increase of 0.8 percent in baseline income (table 6.1).[2]

How much do regional trade agreements benefit developing countries?

To examine how bilateral agreements affect developing countries, we look at three simulations: One in which *all* developing countries sign a bilateral agreement with Quad-plus countries (United States, EU, Japan, Canada, plus Australia and New Zealand);[3] a second simulation—similar to the first simulation—in which the large countries, such as Brazil, China, and India are excluded, which is perhaps a more plausible scenario; and a third in which *each* developing country/region signs an individual bilateral agreement with the Quad-plus countries, assuming other developing countries do not sign agreements.[4] Note that these scenarios *overstate* bilateral and multilateral effects because they assume that no sectors are exempt, and rules of origin are not restrictive. In reality, the United States and EU bilateral agreements usually exclude important sectors, such as sensitive agricultural products, or attach extended phase-in periods

beyond even our 2015 time horizon, and rules of origin tests often limit preferential market access.

The first simulation, in which all developing countries sign a bilateral agreement with the Quad-plus countries (columns 2 and 5 in table 6.1), shows that, as a group, developing countries are substantially worse off than with a multilateral agreement. Instead of gaining $109 billion from global reform, they lose $22 billion relative to a baseline scenario, with no change in protection. If one looks at individual countries (table 6.2), the effect is nearly universal; only a handful of developing countries—for example, Brazil and China—would gain from a full hub-and-spoke system of bilateral agreements, and all developing countries would lose compared to full multilateral trade.

It is interesting that some of the Quad countries would benefit from this strategy. Although the high-income countries would generally lose from this set of bilateral agreements compared to global reform, the impact is not uniform.[5] Both the United States and the EU (the most aggressive advocates of bilateral deals) would appear to benefit more from pursuing bilateral agreements with all developing countries than from global reform (table 6.2); the United States would gain an additional $7 billion (0.1 percent of GDP), while the EU would gain $27 billion (0.4 percent of GDP). Although they would have to open up their agricultural markets to some extent (assuming exemptions are disallowed), they would not have to dismantle domestic

Table 6.2 Comparison of bilateral agreements with global trade reform (change in real income in 2015 compared to baseline)

	Global merchandise trade reform (1)	Bilateral agreements between Quad and all developing countries (2)	Bilateral agreements between Quad and developing countries excluding large countries (3)	Bilateral agreements between Quad and each developing country (4)	Global merchandise trade reform (5)	Bilateral agreements between Quad and all developing countries (6)	Bilateral agreements between Quad and developing countries excluding large countries (7)	Bilateral agreements between Quad and each developing country (8)
	\$ billion				Percent			
Australia, Canada, and New Zealand	8.4	6.0	0.5		0.5	0.5	0.0	
United States	24.9	32.3	10.7		0.5	0.3	0.1	
European Union with EFTA	55.0	82.4	33.6		0.7	1.1	0.4	
Japan	29.7	25.0	4.8		0.5	0.8	0.1	
Republic of Korea and Taiwan (China)	26.4	−9.8	−2.3		2.5	−1.0	−0.2	
Hong Kong (China) and Singapore	9.8	−2.4	−0.3		2.3	−0.7	−0.1	
Brazil	8.0	1.5	−1.7	7.3	1.4	0.3	−0.3	1.3
China	14.1	9.7	−7.2	21.8	0.5	0.4	−0.3	1.0
India	4.3	−10.0	−3.1	2.1	0.5	−1.2	−0.4	0.2
Indonesia	3.6	−2.3	3.0	5.1	1.4	−0.9	1.2	2.1
Mexico	0.3	−1.5	−1.3	2.6	0.2	−0.2	−0.2	0.3
Russia	2.9	−1.7	−1.3	0.8	0.8	−0.5	−0.3	0.2
SACU	2.5	−0.3	0.8	3.7	1.8	−0.2	0.5	2.6
Vietnam	2.4	−0.2	0.6	0.9	5.0	−0.5	1.3	1.9
Rest of East Asia	19.6	−5.0	−2.8	7.4	4.7	−1.2	−0.7	1.8
Rest of South Asia	0.4	−3.2	−1.1	1.2	0.2	−1.3	−0.4	0.5
EU accession countries	0.8	−2.0	−0.5	0.9	0.2	−0.4	−0.1	0.2
Rest of ECA	2.3	−3.3	−1.3	0.4	0.5	−0.7	−0.3	0.1
Middle East	6.1	−2.7	−0.1	1.3	0.9	−0.4	0.0	0.2
North Africa	19.1	1.9	4.3	5.7	6.7	0.6	1.5	2.0
Rest of Sub-Saharan Africa	2.9	−3.0	−2.5	−0.2	1.1	−1.2	−1.0	−0.1
Rest of LAC	16.3	0.9	6.4	9.6	1.6	0.1	0.6	0.9
Rest of the World	3.0	−0.3	1.2	4.0	1.3	−0.1	0.6	1.8
High-income countries	154.4	133.6	46.9		0.6	0.5	0.2	
Low-income countries	16.6	−19.0	−1.9		0.9	−1.0	−0.1	
Middle-income countries	92.2	−2.6	−4.7		1.2	0.0	−0.1	
All developing countries	108.8	−21.5	−6.6		1.2	−0.2	−0.1	
World Total	263.2	112.0	40.3		0.8	0.3	0.1	

Source: World Bank simulations.

129

support programs. Hence the EU and the United States improve market access in highly protected markets in developing countries, but they do not face the full force of competition between themselves, particularly in agriculture, nor the full brunt of competition in developing countries. For example, when India opens up to Quad country imports, Quad country exporters do not simultaneously face increased competition from developing country exporters as they would in a multilateral agreement. In agriculture, Quad producers will face greater competition from relatively efficient developing country exporters, but some of the fiercest competition will be among themselves. And the terms of trade losses that they would suffer from removing agricultural protection between Quad countries is muted when signing the bilateral agreements. Note that this is not the case with Japan, whose agriculture is relatively more threatened by developing country market access; it would gain more from a multilateral agreement, although it nonetheless gains significantly from bilateralism. It is the Quad-plus agricultural exporters—Australia, Canada, and New Zealand—that would prefer multilateralism, because the gains from access to European, Japanese, and the American markets, and the dismantling of distortionary agricultural support programs would be highly beneficial for their farmers.

Were the large developing countries[6] to be excluded from the hub-and-spoke bilateral arrangements (perhaps a more plausible scenario), the broad conclusions still hold, but are muted (columns 3 and 6). First, many developing regions still lose in absolute terms compared with the baseline scenario. Second, all lose relative to the gains from a global reform scenario, though for some, the hub-and-spoke gains approach those in the global reform scenario (e.g., Indonesia, and to a lesser extent, the rest of LAC and rest of the world regions). The gains for the high-income countries, on the other hand, are significantly lower when the large developing countries are

excluded—not surprising given their weight in global trade with the Quad countries. Finally, the impacts on the excluded countries are mixed: Brazil and China, which would gain in a full hub-and-spoke system, lose when excluded. The other excluded regions—India, Mexico, Russia, rest of East Asia, and rest of South Asia—would see a dampening of their losses.

This adverse outcome from bilateral agreements with the Quad raises the question of why developing countries are so anxious to pursue them. There are a number of possible reasons, not necessarily mutually exclusive. First, countries may hope to maximize their benefits through first-mover advantages. Second, countries aim to guarantee market access on a permanent basis. Third, there might be a desire to pre-empt other countries. Fourth, a bilateral agreement may be used as leverage to facilitate domestic reforms. And fifth, other components of an agreement (for example, services, trade facilitation, and so on) may have significant benefits in addition to simply improving market access for merchandise goods. Focusing on the first of these possible reasons, we use the model to simulate the impact of *each* developing country signing an agreement with the Quad countries, but with no other country doing so. The results (table 6.2 columns 4 and 8) provide some justification for developing countries' pursuit of RTAs with the Quad if they believe they can do so exclusively, or at least capture a "first mover" advantage by getting there first. About one-half of the developing regions would be better off with a bilateral agreement than with a global agreement; the winners (relative to global liberalization) include China, Indonesia, Mexico, Southern African Customs Union (SACU), rest of South Asia, and EU accession countries. Losers include Brazil (slightly), India, Russia, Vietnam, rest of East Asia, rest of ECA, Middle East, North Africa, rest of Sub-Saharan Africa, and rest of LAC.

A few cases deserve special mention. The rest of the Sub-Saharan Africa region could suffer losses from a bilateral agreement with the Quad. Because this region already has relatively free access to the Quad markets, opening up to permit greater imports from the Quad worsens their terms of trade and negates any gains from the bilateral agreement. Russia and the Middle East are dependent on energy exports and these face low tariffs in industrial countries (even if energy is heavily taxed), so these regions have little to gain from additional market access. These cases highlight one of the key findings from recent *Global Economic Prospects*, that developing countries have much to gain from greater market access to other developing countries. First, because protection is, on average, higher in developing countries, and second, because of the high growth potential of developing countries over the next decade compared with the industrial countries.

The idea that a single developing country or region would be able to sign bilateral agreements with the Quad countries without other developing countries doing the same over the next decade is unrealistic. Indeed, the increase in the number of agreements over the last decade means that a portion of any first-mover advantage has been eroded already. But as a conceptual exercise, it does help illustrate what may have motivated some developing countries to aggressively pursue deals with one or more Quad members.

To summarize, developing countries could gain an (unweighted) average of 1.7 percent in real income from a global agreement (figure 6.1). But if all developing countries sign bilateral agreements with the Quad, creating a complex hub-and-spoke system, developing countries actually suffer losses averaging 0.4 percent (1.0 percent for the low-income countries alone). While some individual developing countries might have gained from entering exclusive agreements with Quad countries, RTA proliferation has already eliminated that first-mover advantage. Moreover, RTA-induced structural changes could produce disincentives for achieving broad-based multilateral

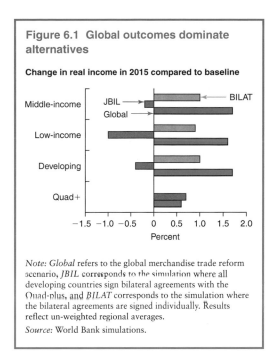

Figure 6.1 Global outcomes dominate alternatives

Change in real income in 2015 compared to baseline

Note: Global refers to the global merchandise trade reform scenario, JBIL corresponds to the simulation where all developing countries sign bilateral agreements with the Quad-plus, and BILAT corresponds to the simulation where the bilateral agreements are signed individually. Results reflect un-weighted regional averages.
Source: World Bank simulations.

reforms (box 6.2). The implications are clear: The most development friendly outcome is associated with global reform, and a full set of bilateral agreements would leave virtually all developing countries worse off than at present.

Countries are also pursuing other RTAs, both North-South and South-South. These agreements are linked to the ongoing talks on the Free Trade Areas of the Americas (FTAA), the ASEAN+3 negotiations, and the EU's various agreements/negotiations with the EU-accession countries toward the east, partners around the Mediterranean, and in Sub-Saharan Africa toward the south. Chapter 2 of this report documents the large number of existing or prospective agreements among developing countries. Figures 6.2 and 6.3 summarize the overall impacts from simulating selected North-South and South-South agreements.[7] Some of these proffer relatively significant gains (for example, a broad free trade region in East Asia), but are nonetheless clearly inferior to the gains from global merchandise

Box 6.2   Regional trade agreements, structural change, and congruence

While impact assessment of RTAs and global agreements often focus narrowly on the real income impacts, from a political economy point of view, the main drivers of these agreements typically will be at the micro or institutional level, where it is easier to identify the potential winners and losers. Moreover, the macro analysis typically ignores the transitional costs. A final issue deals with the compatibility of partial reforms (as represented by preferential trade agreements) with multilateral reforms, which is arguably where the world economy is heading. In other words, how compatible are the structural changes induced by a partial reform with the structural changes one would anticipate from a multilateral reform? For example, what if a country such as Vietnam has a regional comparative advantage in agriculture, but a global comparative advantage in apparel? Would a regional agreement then make it more difficult to achieve a multilateral accord?

The figure above provides a summary indicator of the congruence or compatibility of the bilateral agreements—both the individual (BIL) and joint (JBIL). The indicator measures the average structural change of moving from the baseline to the partial agreement, and then moving from the partial agreement to global free trade, relative to the structural change induced by the global agreement. If the partial agreement is compatible (or congruent) with the global agreement, this measure is 1; that is, the two-step structural change is identical to the one-step structural change from implementing directly a global free trade agreement. For example, a global agreement of a 50 percent tariff cut is largely congruent with a 100 percent tariff cut and would most

Joint bilateral vs. bilaterals

Index (1 → fully congruent)

Source: World Bank simulations.

likely lead to a 50 percent change in our structural adjustment measure.

For most of the developing regions, the joint bilateral agreements are broadly consistent with the global agreement, with the structural index varying from around 1 (or near perfect congruence) to a high of around 2—for example, for Middle East and North Africa. On the other hand, the individual bilateral agreements are clearly not congruent with a global agreement. The pattern of structural change induced by the individual bilateral agreements is markedly different from what one would anticipate with a global agreement. Developing countries therefore face a tradeoff. They can get short-term benefits from signing a bilateral agreement with the Quad—assuming other countries do not—but the longer-term gains from a global agreement may be more difficult to attain because the patterns of capital and labor allocation would be misaligned by the partial agreement.

trade reform. Two additional comments regarding the results of these regional simulations are suggested by the figures.[8] First, when North-South agreements are implemented simultaneously, the gains are dampened relative to when they are implemented in isolation—a reflection of the impacts of trade diversion. In the case of the South-South agreements, the weak gains reflect, in part, the preferences already granted in many of these regions as well as a lack of distinct comparative advantage.[9] This again emphasizes that broad South-South and North-South trade reform is needed to reap significant gains.

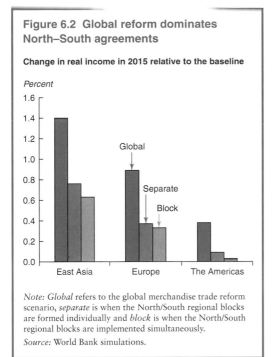

Figure 6.2 Global reform dominates North–South agreements

Change in real income in 2015 relative to the baseline

Note: *Global* refers to the global merchandise trade reform scenario, *separate* is when the North/South regional blocks are formed individually and *block* is when the North/South regional blocks are implemented simultaneously.

Source: World Bank simulations.

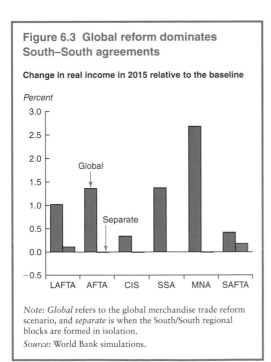

Figure 6.3 Global reform dominates South–South agreements

Change in real income in 2015 relative to the baseline

Note: *Global* refers to the global merchandise trade reform scenario, and *separate* is when the South/South regional blocks are formed in isolation.

Source: World Bank simulations.

Building Blocks versus Stumbling Blocks

Whether regional agreements are *building blocks* or *stumbling blocks* to open global markets—the terms Jagdish Bhagwati (1991) used—remains a central question.[10] Proponents of the *stumbling block* theory emphasize that: (1) RTAs may promote costly trade diversion rather than efficient trade creation, especially when sizable MFN tariffs remain—these tariffs create vested interests to maintain preferential margins in "their" markets; (2) proliferating regional agreements absorb scarce negotiating resources (especially in poorer WTO members) and crowd out policymakers attention; (3) competing RTAs (especially different North-South combinations) may lock in incompatible regulatory structures and standards, and may result in inappropriate norms for developing country partners; and (4) by creating alternative legal frameworks and dispute settlement mechanisms, RTAs may weaken the discipline and efficiency associated with a broadly recognized multilateral framework of rules.

Building block proponents stress that moving forward in smaller steps is often easier to accomplish, and it creates a certain reform momentum: (1) regional/bilateral agreements can help sensitize domestic constituencies to liberalization and keep the stakes lower to allow for incremental progress on trade; (2) expanding the number and coverage of RTAs can erode vested opposition to multilateral liberalization because each successive RTA reduces the value of the margin of preference, thereby reducing the discriminatory impact; (3) RTAs are often more about building strategic and/or political alliances or locking in domestic reforms than about actual trade liberalization, and so are not necessarily competitive with multilateral efforts; (4) regional arrangements can provide an incubator for developing country firms/producers to learn to trade with RTA partners without facing full global competition; and (5) for some issues, such as regulatory cooperation, RTAs may be a viable and more manageable alternative to the WTO, where "lowest common denominator" outcomes tend to prevail.

One strand of analysis in the literature explores theoretical bargaining models to shed light on these divergent perspectives. For example, Saggi (2004) considers how RTA formation affects incentives to participate in multilateral trade liberalization. Using a stylized three-country oligopoly model of intra-industry trade, he reasons that while formation of RTAs can reduce tariffs in the short run, in the long run it hinders multilateral trade liberalization because it lowers the incentives for nonmembers to pursue multilateral cooperation. In a three-country model, where country size and costs differ, Saggi and Yildiz (2004) look at tariff outcomes under two different sets of rules: One where countries can form RTAs, and another where they cannot. They find that free trade is less likely to occur as an outcome when countries can join RTAs as well. Moreover, the outcome depends on size and cost features: When countries are relatively similar, the RTA option tends to lower world welfare; whereas with larger differences among countries, welfare increases. In the latter case, gains are somewhat larger for the small country getting access to the larger country (because it gains more in new export earnings and loses less in domestic surplus) than for the country with lower costs (because gains from expanded market access increase when their own costs are lower and partner costs are higher). Aghion and others (2004) construct a dynamic bargaining model to assess the relative effects of simultaneous multilateral liberalization or sequential bilateral liberalization, and they identify situations in which the latter can lead to worldwide free trade. Their model concludes that, as long as large coalition payoffs are higher than if all countries were combined in alternative coalition structures, the outcome is likely to end up in global free trade, regardless of sequencing.

The Saggi findings support the empirical evidence that North-South RTAs with small developing countries yield the biggest benefits for developing country participants. This intuition comes from the fact that most empirical models derive their impact from the effect of RTAs on prices and quantities of traded goods. But when one partner is much smaller than the other, its participation in an RTA has virtually no impact on prices, and any incremental exports it sells are a tiny share of the large country trade flows—so the resulting gains or losses for the larger partner are also small. Support for this conclusion comes from the computable general equilibrium model (CGE) simulations on the impact of RTAs; in most cases, the net impact on the Northern partner has been exceedingly small, whether measured in terms of trade flows, terms of trade, or welfare changes

This result in turn has implications for how RTA proliferation affects incentives to pursue multilateral liberalization. If the impact of additional North-South RTAs on the industrial partner is indeed quite marginal, then it seems likely that the *economic* consequences of these agreements would not dampen their willingness to pursue multilateral deals. As we see below, neither the EU nor the United States seem to be less disposed toward multilateral negotiations because of their RTAs or the RTAs of each other.

Other studies show less sanguine results. Limão (2003) notes that North-South RTAs can involve more than just the mutual lowering of tariffs; industrial countries often lower their tariffs and expand market access in exchange for cooperation in a variety of nontrade areas, such as labor standards, intellectual property, migration, security, and so forth. Limão models the interaction between such RTAs and multilateral liberalization, and concludes that pursuit of RTAs creates a strategic incentive for industrial countries to maintain their multilateral tariffs at a higher level than they otherwise would—to hold back tariff concessions in the multilateral arena in order to have bargaining room for negotiating RTAs. In the case of the United States, multilateral trade liberalization commitments are less deep for products that are produced by regional firms.[11]

A more compelling argument is that developing countries with preferential access may have a vested interest in perpetuating the tariff walls that screen out competing countries from preferred markets. In fact, Barbados, Jamaica, and Mauritius have all been outspoken opponents of the agricultural liberalization that would erode their preferences in EU sugar markets, and Bangladesh has advocated measures that would delay the phaseout of the textile and apparel quotas required under the WTO Agreement on Textiles and Clothing. Nonetheless, this seems confined to a handful of relatively small countries heavily dependent on a narrow range of preference-benefiting products.

An illuminating example of how preferences can be a stumbling block to multilateral liberalization is provided by rum. Low valued bottled and bulk rum is one of the largest exports from several Caribbean countries to the United States. It enters the United States duty-free under the Caribbean Basin Initiative. In 1994 there was a single tariff line for rum in the U.S. schedule (HS 22084000) with a tariff of 37 cents/liter. As result of WTO discussions, the United States and EU in 1996 agreed to phase out all tariffs on rum and other "white spirits" by 2000. Caribbean governments were concerned that this would be costly to Caribbean exporters because they would have to compete with the rest of the world in the U.S. market. In response to this concern, the United States agreed to substantially liberalize the duties on expensive rum but to maintain duties on low-valued rum. As of 2003, the U.S. schedule now has four tariff lines for rum, two for high-valued rum with no MFN tariff charged, and two for low-valued rum with an MFN tariff of 23.7 cents/liter.[12] Since then, the imports of rum from the affected Caribbean countries have fallen sharply, apparently replaced by imports from Mexico—another bilateral RTA partner. So efforts to prevent erosion of preferential access may have only limited the impact temporarily.

An increase in RTA activity may be associated with multilateral trade negotiations.

Mansfield and Reinhardt (2003) argue that multilateral trade negotiations motivate countries to conclude RTAs; the motivation is for increased negotiating power and the desire to obtain or maintain preferential access to markets. They also note that as WTO membership expands, larger membership reduces individual countries' ability to influence the content and pace of MFN liberalization and makes it more difficult to formulate coordinated positions. Finally, they find that countries use RTAs to increase leverage against third parties with which they are embroiled in a WTO dispute. In their empirical analysis they conclude that countries are more likely to form RTAs when: (1) GATT/WTO membership rises; (2) a multilateral round is taking place; and (3) parties have recently been involved in a GATT/WTO dispute in which they lost.

Others have argued that RTAs are a mechanism to enhance the pressure to move on the multilateral front, and they act as laboratories for international cooperation on behind-the-border policy issues. This line of reasoning has a long history. Winham (1986) and Lawrence (1991) have both argued that the creation and subsequent expansion of the European Economic Community (EEC) motivated earlier General Agreement on Tariffs and Trade (GATT) rounds—the objective being to reduce European external protection. More recently, Schott (2004) noted that the United States has pursued bilateral trade agreements over the last two decades in part to complement and cajole progress at the multilateral level. He argues that tensions from the GATT meetings in 1982 were the impetus to pursue bilateral deals with Canada and Israel; he also claims that the start of the NAFTA negotiations in 1991 reflected some frustration over failure to conclude the Uruguay Round negotiations on time in late 1990. In the early 1990s, the United States also began to pursue broader umbrella regional initiatives, including Asia Pacific Economic Cooperation (APEC)— whose members have never formally committed to a binding RTA—and the FTAA.

In short, there is only limited evidence from the theoretical literature and a handful of empirical studies that the proliferation of RTAs affects multilateral liberalization either way. On balance, the evidence does point to tactical behavior in trade negotiations, which seems to provide mild additional incentives for greater liberalization. The exception is for small countries that suffer from preference erosion—a nontrivial obstacle to future liberalization.

The Competitive Liberalization Game: The Case of Doha

The rapid proliferation of RTAs may have affected the *negotiating* dynamics of the Doha Round, and it is unclear whether the increase in bilateral deals is in response to slow progress in the Doha talks. Concerns over RTA proliferation played a role in the launch of the Round and came back full force after the failure of the Cancun ministerial. Consider the actions of the major players in the global and regional game.

The U.S. pursuit of like-minded partners
With the change in U.S. administration in 2001 and the subsequent congressional approval of the Trade Promotion Authority in 2002, the pace of bilateral, regional, and multilateral efforts increased. Then, in the absence of progress on the Doha agenda in Cancun in September 2003, the U.S. Trade Representative (USTR) indicated that the United States would pursue deals with "like-minded" partners, and the result has been an unprecedented spurt of U.S. negotiating activity. The United States had negotiated RTAs with six countries/groups by 2004 (Australia, Bahrain, Central America and Dominican Republic, Chile, Morocco, Singapore), and another dozen are under negotiation, including SACU (Botswana, Lesotho, Namibia, South Africa, and Swaziland), Colombia, Ecuador, Panama, Peru, and Thailand. As discussed in chapters 2 and 5, the United States is pursuing new rules in key areas (investment, intellectual property,

and services liberalization)—areas where multilateral efforts have gone slowly or halted altogether—while developing countries seek market access.

Eligibility is not guided by a single criterion or ranking system (box 6.3). Political criteria include national security-cum-foreign policy concerns (a major factor in the recent agreements and ongoing discussions with Arab countries), while others reflect a mixture of classic market access goals and a desire to export U.S. regulatory standards (for instance, in the area of investment and IPRs—see chapter 5). The U.S. decision to pursue bilateral arrangements in Latin America also has the effect of putting pressure on Brazil and other countries, which are seen to be impeding progress on the now-stalled negotiations on the FTAA. Reaching these agreements does not appear to have reduced the United States' participation in the WTO negotiations, nor to have had much effect on the content of its negotiating position.

Recent EU regional initiatives
Having been a leading (and early) player in the RTA game, the EU had established many RTAs prior to the launch of the Doha Round (see chapter 2). Since then, it has pursued market access agreements with a few individual partners (notably Chile and Mexico, with South Africa predating 2001) as well as MERCOSUR. The EU has preferred to negotiate with blocs of countries and has encouraged the Mediterranean countries to sign agreements with one another; the EU made the RTA with Gulf Cooperation Council (GCC) countries conditional on the adoption of a common external tariff by the GCC and supported the development of a web of bilateral RTAs between Southeastern European economies. The recent Economic Partnership Agreements (EPAs)[13] were launched to replace the Cotonou agreement with the African, Caribbean, and Pacific (ACP) group in a WTO-compatible set of agreements, and the EPAs are seen by the EU as a development-promoting vehicle rather than as a way to gain additional market access.

Box 6.3 Choosing partners: Selection criteria for U.S. RTAs

The U.S. choices of developing country RTA partners reflect a range of different objectives, which makes categorization difficult. In a report prepared for the U.S. Congress, U.S. General Accounting Office (GAO) (2004) reports that early RTA proposals were (according to the USTR) based on evaluation of 13 different factors (without any formal weighting scheme) that covered five themes: Congressional guidance, business interests, political will of partners, security and foreign policy concerns, and regional parity. Following consultations with relevant agencies, there is now a shortened list of six factors to guide the choice of future U.S. FTA partners: country readiness (political, trade, and legal), economic/commercial benefit; benefits to broader trade liberalization strategy (including success in meeting WTO obligations and support of key U.S. positions in FTAA and WTO negotiations); compatibility with U.S. interests (including foreign policy positions);

congressional/private sector support; and U.S. government resource constraints. The report emphasizes that the selections are not mechanical and argues that trade strategy and foreign policy factors dominate the selection criteria.

Schott (2004) identifies the same broad criteria, but also notes the role of partner choice in selection of U.S. FTA partners. Current U.S. law requires that potential partners must request negotiations with the United States, rather than the other way around. He notes that most of these requests reflect concerns over discriminatory treatment (from other agreements, especially NAFTA) and serve to demonstrate commitment to domestic audiences who may need to be convinced of the benefits of reform trade and domestic policies.

Source: Schott 2004.

These agreements do not appear to have altered the EU's approach to the Doha Round. After the conclusion of the Mexican and Chilean bilateral deals, the EU had declared it would negotiate no new trade agreements, save for the EPAs that were necessary to replace the Cotonou agreement set to expire in 2008. However, this stance may be short-lived. In September 2004, the incoming EU Trade Commissioner announced that he would review this policy and consider launching new negotiations.

Japan is a latecomer but moving quickly
Until recently, Japan remained disengaged from the RTA trend and instead pursued a voluntary approach that centered on APEC. A distinguishing feature of APEC is that it focuses primarily on exchanging information and identifying good practices in the trade policy (and other) areas. While it also sets specific targets for trade policy (e.g., free intra-APEC trade by 2020), implementation of the

good practices and targets are left to individual members. The primary enforcement devices are mutual surveillance and peer review. More recently, it appears that competitive pressures that emerged from the more intensive activity by the United States—also an APEC member—and the concern that even in the Asia region there was a risk of being left out of the new generation of RTAs, have prompted new Japanese activity. Japan completed the negotiation of its first RTA with Singapore in 2002. Negotiations with Mexico are advanced. The competitive disadvantage in Mexican markets relative to the United States and the EU is a strong inducement, with Japanese products facing an average customs duty of 16 percent (Tojo 2004). Negotiations are beginning with Republic of Korea, which are considered important because Japan-Korea could form the basis of a future East Asian economic zone. Talks have also begun with three individual members of ASEAN (Thailand, Malaysia, and the Philippines), and consultations have been initiated over how to move forward with a proposed Comprehensive Economic Partnership between Japan and the full ASEAN group. Finally, there are preliminary discussions and analysis of a possible ASEAN+3 RTA (including China, Republic of Korea, and Japan) in the context of efforts to strengthen economic relations among this group.

Developing country objectives and negotiating strategies

Developing countries have three general approaches to RTAs. Some have adopted an aggressive approach and pursued a serial RTA strategy; that is, they negotiate a string of agreements and use the sequence to demonstrate their commitment to trade reforms by locking these in and increasing the incentive for excluded countries to negotiate. Harrison, Rutherford, and Tarr (2002) have labeled this negotiating dynamic "additive regionalism." Its most prolific proponents include Chile, Mexico, and Singapore, which have pursued RTAs with most of their geographic neighbors, as well as with many of the other major players (Schott 2004). The idea is that negotiating additional RTAs will progressively lower the effective average tariff (reducing potential trade diversion costs) and assure stability of market access for partner countries. A second, much larger group of countries has pursued a strategy more explicitly regional in focus, which seeks to deepen ties with neighboring countries; examples include ASEAN, the GCC, MERCOSUR, and SADC. A third group has focused on negotiating North-South RTAs, often in parallel with their regional integration efforts with neighbors; examples are the southern Mediterranean countries with the EU and the US-CAFTA agreement. The ACP-EU Economic Partnership Agreements are another example.

Additive regionalism could create adverse global effects by reducing the incentives for countries to participate in multilateral liberalization efforts. That has not been the case with Chile, Mexico, or Singapore. The fact remains

that these countries still have incentives to see lower barriers in the many countries with which they do not have RTAs and to harness the multilateral process to achieve movement in areas outside of the RTAs, such as agriculture and anti-dumping. The WTO provides a forum to achieve these objectives at a lower cost than negotiating a plethora of bilateral RTAs. Countries pursuing such strategies are very much a minority—most developing countries are not in this game (box 6.4). Chile, Mexico, and Singapore are all economies that moved substantially toward free trade and thus have already captured most of the potential gains from unilateral trade reforms. From a global point of view, therefore, these are not countries that have a vested interest in maintaining high MFN barriers. These countries are examples of open regionalism.

The determinants of the multilateral negotiating stance of the broader group of developing countries are more varied. For a handful of countries, existing preferences under unilateral accords as well as multilateral and regional agreements are openly driving their opposition to multilateral liberalization. For some other developing countries, it is possible that RTAs are undermining their interest in multilateral negotiation, either because they mistakenly see RTAs as an alternative, because they feel subsumed in large coalitions with other countries, or because they do not have the resources to negotiate with both the WTO and with potential regional partners.

This discussion suggests a few impressionistic conclusions. It is hard to argue that competitive liberalization through RTAs has much influence on the behavior of the major players in the WTO, either in their fundamental negotiating positions or their willingness to compromise to achieve a result. As evident in the July WTO Framework Agreement, major players are still working with commitment toward an agreement in Doha. To be sure, for smaller countries with scarce negotiating capacity, RTAs do absorb resources that could be devoted to multilateral negotiations; but these countries tend to participate in the WTO

Box 6.4 Sequencing of RTAs: Is there a good practice?

Debates over trade liberalization have often included extensive discussions of whether there is a preferred (or even optimal) sequence for reforms. Theoretical guidance for policymakers in the design of RTAs speaks to two dimensions of the question—the choice (and sequence) of partners over time and the substantive coverage of an RTA (and the sequencing of inclusion of different elements)—that have implications for the debate. On the former, the sequencing of partners may affect incentives of members to pursue MFN liberalization. Thus as discussed elsewhere in this report, the formation of large blocs creates incentives to join for smaller countries that trade heavily with members—what has been termed "domino regionalism" (Baldwin 1993). The EU is the best example of this phenomenon: EFTA countries that were not in favor of the EU integration model ultimately concluded that the costs of staying out were too high. Whether this process makes RTAs more or less receptive to MFN reforms depends in part on the preferences and interests of those who join the bloc over time—which in turn will affect the willingness of incumbent countries to accept new members.

On the product/policy coverage issue, the conventional wisdom appears to be that agreements should first focus on trade liberalization and then move on to behind-the-border areas—that is, go from shallow to deeper integration. There is no theoretical justification for this, however, and there is a well-documented history that, in the case of the EEC, many policymakers were of the view that the two needed to be pursued in tandem. The rhetoric of policymakers and their advisors often suggests that deeper integration is necessary to attain free trade. During the period leading to the creation of the EEC,

Jelle Zijlstra, the Dutch Minister of Economic Affairs argued that credible tariff removal required common policies on taxes, wages, prices, and employment policy. Similarly, the Belgian government felt that policy harmonization was required to equalize costs, and that without it, a customs union would not be feasible because countries would impose new forms of protectionist policies. French officials persistently demanded harmonization in social policies—equal pay for both sexes, a uniform work week—as a precondition for trade liberalization—French standards in this area were higher than in other countries (Milward 1992).

Recent research on the effects of, and interplay between, efforts to liberalize trade and investment in services (and FDI more generally) suggests that countries may be better of pursuing both shallow and deeper forms of liberalization in tandem. Hoekman and Konan (2001) and Konan and Maskus (2003), for example, note that not only can this generate much greater welfare gains, it can also reduce aggregate adjustment costs over time—through avoiding outcomes in which factors of production must move repeatedly across sectors (as will, by definition, occur if goods are liberalized first and then services/investment, or vice versa). They also note that because many services continue to be less tradable than goods, there is greater scope for employment opportunities to be created as a result of allowing greater competition in services markets, thus helping to absorb labor from other sectors as prices change due to trade reform.

Source: World Bank staff.

as members of coalitions, and it is not clear that these constraints impede compromise. If the effects on the multilateral round are negligible, it does seem that all players appear to be quickening their efforts to seek new preferential agreements. The outcome of the game of RTA-based competitive liberalization is likely more RTAs.

One negative incentive effect created by preferences—reciprocal RTAs or voluntary programs—is that members' desire to safeguard their preferential access to the regional market may result in less support for MFN-based trade reforms. This incentive effect has long been recognized; it was one of the arguments made against the Generalized System of

Preferences when they were initially proposed in the 1960s. Indeed, unilateral preference programs, especially the more comprehensive and meaningful schemes adopted in recent years, such as the EU's Everything But Arms (EBA) program and the United States' African Growth and Opportunity Act (AGOA), potentially make matters worse, because their value to recipients depends on the existence of trade barriers against imports from other countries—with the greatest rents generated by programs that distort markets the most, such as in the sugar market. Maintaining preference margins—whether for RTA partners or beneficiaries under unilateral preference programs—is not the answer. What is needed is a willingness on the part of developed countries to move away from preferential access as an instrument to assist lower-income partner countries and to move toward greater reliance on direct transfers of technical and financial assistance (Stoeckel and Borrell 2001). This has the advantage of allowing high-income countries to target their trade-related development assistance to those countries most in need, something the system of preferences cannot do.

Multilateral Disciplines on Regional Arrangements

Efforts to deal with the implications of RTAs within the multilateral trading system are long standing. The primary disciplines are laid out in Article XXIV of the GATT—others are discussed in box 6.5. They permit RTAs if: (1) external trade barriers do not rise (Article XXIV:5); (2) all tariffs and other regulations of commerce are removed on substantially all exchanges of goods between the partner countries within a reasonable length of time (Article XXIV:8); and (3) notification is made to the WTO Council.

The first criterion is intended to limit the negative impact of an RTA on nonmembers.[14] The second condition might at first seem counterintuitive—after all, the more extensive is the liberalization with an RTA, the more

detrimental it is likely to be to nonmembers. But the rationale here was in fact different; as noted by Finger (1993), the objective was to ensure that participants in RTAs are serious. In other words, while more trade in an RTA hurts nonmembers, pursuit of numerous partial RTAs can severely undermine the incentives for multilateral trade negotiations and create opportunities for special interests (farmers, specific industries) to carve out special arrangements. As a counterexample, if a restrictive interpretation (say 99 percent of all trade) of this criterion were agreed to and enforced, it is likely that the appetite for RTAs would be substantially diminished.

Determining whether the GATT or General Agreement on Trade in Services (GATS) tests are met is left for the Committee on Regional Trade Agreements (CRTA). Before the creation of the WTO, the GATT Council usually created a working party to evaluate whether its conditions were satisfied. Under the WTO, the CRTA was established for this task. The GATT experience in testing reciprocal preferential trade agreement (PTAs) against Article XXIV was very discouraging. Starting with the examination of the treaty establishing the EEC in 1957, almost no examination of agreements that were notified under Article XXIV led to clear conclusions or specific endorsements that the GATT requirements had been met. Only one working party could agree that a regional agreement fully satisfied the requirements of Article XXIV (the Czech-Slovak Customs Union).

There had been a conscious political decision made by GATT contracting parties in the late 1950s not to scrutinize the formation of the EEC because the EEC member states had made it clear that if the EEC treaty was found to be inconsistent with Article XXIV, they would withdraw from GATT (Snape 1993). Given that the EEC did not meet all the requirements of Article XXIV—agricultural trade was not liberalized—it created a precedent. It is also true that the criteria and language of Article XXIV are ambiguous. Legitimate differences of opinion are possible

Box 6.5 RTAs and WTO disciplines

The fundamental building block of the multilateral system is the principle of nondiscrimination. This is enshrined in Article I of the original text of the GATT signed in 1947. But from the start, there have been exceptions. One such provision is Article XXIV of the GATT, which permits WTO members to enter into preferential trade agreements (RTA) that extend trade concessions to RTA participants not offered to nonparticipants, as long as certain criteria are satisfied—in particular, regarding the scope of the RTA. Second, rules covering preferential agreements that deal with trade in services are set out in Article V of the GATS. Finally, developing countries may, if they wish, invoke the provisions of the 1979 Decision on Differential and More Favourable Treatment, Reciprocity and Fuller Participation of Developing Countries (the so-called Enabling Clause) to exchange tariff and, to a certain extent, nontariff preferences among them. Unlike Article XXIV, the Enabling Clause does not require that internal barriers be removed on "substantially all" trade among participants in those arrangements. MERCOSUR was notified to GATT under this provision, not under Article XXIV. The

Enabling Clause also legitimizes non-reciprocal programs such as the Generalized System of Preferences (GSP).

The task of verifying the WTO compliance of RTAs notified under GATT Article XXIV and GATS Article V is entrusted to the CRTA. The CRTA was established in 1996, in particular to (1) oversee, under a single framework, all regional trade agreements, and (2) consider the implications of such agreements and regional initiatives for the multilateral trading system and the relationship between them. RTAs among developing countries, when notified under the Enabling Clause, are not, in principle, subject to review by the CRTA. As was the case under the GATT, however, the CRTA has been unable to carry out effectively its functions of examining the consistency of RTAs with the rules, and overseeing their implementation. The reason for this is essentially a fear of setting a precedent and opening up agreements to dispute settlement proceedings. The CRTA has thus far been unable to conclude the examination of any of the 110 RTAs currently under scrutiny and has a backlog of about 35 RTA reports to prepare.

regarding issues such as the definition of "substantially all" trade; how to determine whether the external trade policy of a customs union has become more restrictive on average; and what a reasonable time period is for the transition toward full implementation of an RTA (Hoekman and Kostecki 2001).

In the Uruguay Round some of these issues were clarified: Specific criteria were adopted to assess whether a customs union's external tariff satisfies Article XXIV; a 10-year maximum for the transition period for implementation of an agreement was imposed; and, as mentioned, a standing committee was created to oversee RTAs. None of these changes had any effect on the ability of WTO members to agree on whether an RTA conformed to WTO requirements. Most observers would agree that existing WTO disciplines and enforcement mechanisms have no teeth, and are not

particularly effective at controlling, limiting, or shaping the growth and coverage of RTAs. At the Fourth Ministerial Conference in Doha, ministers agreed to launch negotiations to clarify and improve the disciplines and procedures under the existing WTO provisions that apply to RTAs, taking into account the developmental aspects of these agreements.

The Doha Agenda negotiations on rules for preferential trade agreements have been conducted on two tracks, one focusing on transparency issues and the other addressing the substantive disciplines. Transparency is generally less contentious, and includes:

- **Administrative overload in reviewing proposals.** Review of long, detailed, and often unclear RTA documents imposes a substantial workload on committee members. One possible solution would be an expanded "first review" by WTO staff based on clear and objective criteria; this would require a significant expansion of resources allocated by the Secretariat.

- **Notification of RTAs to the WTO.** The WTO has been notified of around 300 agreements (of which about 140 are currently in force), and another 60 or so are in advanced stages of negotiation (see chapter 2). Many of these are for RTAs among developing countries. Moreover, few RTAs have been designated as "interim arrangements," even though most RTAs have been implemented in stages.

- **Data and information requirements.** There is no clarity on the type, quantity, and level of detail to be provided when the WTO is notified of an agreement. Developing countries often lack the capacity to undertake this task. While some members want more detail, it is understood that unduly straining the capacity in developing countries should be avoided. Some suggest that WTO assistance could be provided for the notification process if necessary.

- **Review of South-South agreements.** The Enabling Clause does not provide for any consistency examination. Current practice is for RTAs formed between developing countries (and notified under the Enabling Clause) to be reported to the Committee on Trade and Development (some developing countries have chosen to notify the WTO of agreements under Article XXIV). Countries have raised the issue of reporting Enabling Clause Agreements to a single body, the CRTA.

- **Services.** Some of the requirements of the provisions of Article V of GATS are unclear (e.g., in terms of the departure from MFN obligations in key areas such as transparency, emergency safeguards, and administration of domestic regulations).

- **Process.** Some delegations want notification of RTAs to occur before they are

implemented. Others support issuing a final report that does not pass or fail a RTA, but allows members to register concerns. Finally, some delegations want greater diligence in encouraging RTA participants to file biennial reports on the implementation of RTAs.

Although no early harvest on transparency issues was undertaken for the 2003 Cancun Ministerial, negotiations for a (provisional) application of strengthened surveillance mechanisms are considerably advanced. Such mechanisms would require more detail in the RTA notification procedures and might involve an enhanced role for the Secretariat in preparing an assessment of each RTA that would be provided to WTO members.

Informal discussions on the substantive rules began in June 2004, and there are many issues under consideration. The fact that WTO rules on RTAs relate to several other regulatory areas (some of which are under negotiation)—including rules of origin, trade facilitation rules on trade remedies, the GATS—adds to the complexity. Issues under consideration include:

- **Product coverage of RTAs.** One central issue is whether to make more specific the requirement that "substantially all" trade be covered in each RTA. Lack of clarity regarding this criterion is viewed by many as a source of the CRTA's inability to reach clear-cut conclusions on WTO compatibility for most RTAs. Many RTAs exclude agriculture, which is a major problem. Some have proposed that "substantially all" trade should be defined as a percentage not only of actual trade but also of all the six-digit tariff lines listed in the Harmonized System. This approach could ensure that the standard is set high, but that there is also sufficient flexibility to set aside product areas that remain sensitive for one reason or another. A related issue concerns how (if at all) such a criterion would be applied to RTAs already notified—would they be subject to the same percentage, or grandfathered in under the existing imprecise criterion? Although inherently arbitrary, a more specific coverage criterion could help to move the review process for RTAs along. Schiff and Winters (2003) suggest adopting a coverage criterion of 95 percent of the value of trade after 10 years of operation of the agreement, rising to 98 percent after 15 years. This would require that at least some sensitive products be included (e.g., agriculture), but not all, and would imply that over time the set of excluded products would decrease.

- **Policy coverage of RTAs.** GATT Article XXIV.5 requires that duties and other regulations of commerce applied by members of a RTA are not more restrictive than those existing prior to its formation. In assessing the impact of a RTA, there is no agreement on what this covers. In particular, it is unclear to what extent it covers policies such as safeguards, anti-dumping measures, mutual recognition agreements, or rules of origin—and if they are covered, how they should be evaluated. Many RTAs continue to allow for the use of antidumping and safeguards on intra-member trade—that is, conflict with the supposedly free trade objective of RTAs. Only a few RTAs have abolished the reach of antidumping (the EU, ANZCERTA, Canada-Chile). Alternatively, some RTAs preclude the use of safeguards on goods originating in partner countries—for example, Canada and Mexico were exempted from the recent U.S. steel safeguard action. This increases the negative effect of the action for nonmembers.

Whether rules of origin are a regulation of commerce has been a key source of disagreement for decades. The rules of origin are relevant not just for normal trade flows, but also play a role in the application of safeguards and other contingent trade policies. Issues related to rules of origin were already being discussed in the early 1970s in working parties that were considering RTAs. Thus in connection with the 1972 free trade agreement between the EEC and European Free Trade in Europe (EFTA) member states, the United States argued that the rules of origin would harm nonmembers.[15] Not surprisingly, preferential rules of origin are being discussed in the current Doha talks, although expectations are low that there will be agreement on common disciplines. Discussions on harmonization of nonpreferential rules of origin have been under way for almost 10 years and have yet to be concluded.[16] In any event, these harmonized rules of origin will not apply to regional agreements or to GSP schemes. Because rules of origin facilitate the fine tuning of preferential liberalization at the product level, many countries do not want to see constraints imposed on their policy freedoms in this arena.

Many proposals have been made in the WTO for stronger rules for RTAs. One suggestion is that all RTA members be required to extend their preferential concessions to the rest of the world within a specific time frame (Srinivasan, 1998).[17] Another suggestion is to minimize the adverse discriminatory consequences of RTAs by requiring (or exhorting) members to allow any developing country to "opt in" on the same terms as existing members, perhaps after a certain time period. This goes back to Viner (1950). As noted, virtually every existing RTA has geographic restrictions on membership and has features that require negotiation, so the practical promise of such open regionalism is limited. Other suggestions do not make good economic sense (see Schiff and Winters, 2003).

Many observers have concluded that the quest for stronger rules is unlikely to succeed because many RTAs will not satisfy the rules, which will, in turn, lead countries to prefer the status quo. Schiff and Winters (2003) conclude their discussion of regionalism and the WTO with a section called "Rules Are Not the

Answer." From this perspective, the primary function of the WTO is to act as a negotiating forum to bring down the discrimination created by RTAs. The importance (and feasibility) of this depends, in part, on the motivation of governments to pursue RTAs.

Making Open Regionalism Work for Development

Defining the role of the WTO

Numerous observers and analysts of RTAs, who are interested in enhancing their compatibility with the global trading system, propose that WTO disciplines be applied more stringently. Years of discussion in the GATT/WTO on the interpretation of existing criteria, and the many papers proposing more specific criteria have had no impact on the spread or content of RTAs. Improving the enforcement of Article XXIV or strengthening/changing WTO disciplines on regionalism is unlikely to fare any better.

Whether it is helpful to articulate more specific criteria delimiting what "substantially all" trade means, or tightening up disciplines on "other regulations of commerce," depends in large part on the feasibility of attaining a consensus on specific criteria. Given the plethora of RTAs that are in force, and the share of global trade notionally covered through such agreements, a strong case can be made that the horse has already bolted from the barn—shutting the barn door will make little difference. The problem is a political one; any number of countries will oppose stronger rules because they are already members of RTAs that would violate them. Indeed, even if groups of developed countries—such as the EU—make a case that their agreement satisfies whatever criteria might be proposed, or that their model should become the benchmark, other countries could legitimately argue that if it was acceptable for the EEC to pass muster in the 1960s and 1970s, it would be hypocritical to impose stronger rules on all WTO members today.

Nonetheless, WTO members should look for ways that existing disciplines on RTAs can be reinforced and new disciplines introduced to enhance their development impact. One area where knowledge is much more extensive now, compared to when the original GATT rules were written, regards rules of origin. It is clear that complex and restrictive rules of origin limit the benefits of RTAs for developing country participants and divert trade in intermediate products. Rules of origin that differ across agreements complicate world trading conditions and contribute to the emergence of hub-and-spoke patterns. Thus there would be substantial benefits from an agreement that promoted common, simple, less restrictive, and easy-to-apply rules of origin. That being said, the delays and problems in achieving the objectives defined in the Uruguay Round for the nonpreferential rules of origin are not propitious in this case.

From a development perspective, the most useful and immediate step for the WTO is to improve transparency. Information and analysis are important inputs for a well-functioning trading order. Greater monitoring and assessment of the impacts of RTA-related policies would allow more informed and proactive engagement by civil society (think tanks, nongovernmental organizations, consumers, and taxpayers) in the policy formation and negotiation process. It is true that to reduce protection and protectionist pressures, those that lose (pay) need to be aware of the costs of such policies. The suppliers of and the clients for such analysis and information are not necessarily governments, but the constituencies in individual countries who are affected by policy. In order for trade agreements to promote good policy-making in member countries, stakeholders must be able to be active in the domestic policy formation process.

This could be achieved by augmenting the capacity of the WTO Secretariat and the CRTA to review, document, and analyze the effects of RTAs. That is, WTO attention in this area should focus on gathering information and analysis. Efforts could concentrate on addressing such questions as: Are RTAs being implemented? How? What is the effect on member countries and on nonmembers? How much trade is covered by the RTA (and is it "substantially all")? Ideally, stronger surveillance would involve those responsible for implementing each RTA and, in the process, empower them to engage policymakers and stakeholders. Such surveillance and analytical monitoring should extend to South-South RTAs—which should all be notified to the CRTA.

Strengthening information exchange and mutual (multilateral) dialogue, (including through the establishment of formal monitoring mechanisms), would facilitate cooperation on new regulatory issues. If existing or proposed policies could be evaluated using objective criteria on their ability to achieve the stated national objectives, countries and stakeholders could assess their efficacy and, if needed, adjust the policies. Greater analysis of the effects of trade discrimination—both unilateral preferences and RTAs—should be part of this agenda.

Information of this type would help RTA stakeholders to hold governments accountable for outcomes and to assist nonmembers by providing data that could feed into demands in the context of WTO negotiations.[18] As argued by Hoekman and Kostecki (2001) among others, the primary means through which the WTO can impose limits on RTAs is by providing a venue for negotiation to reduce MFN barriers, which will automatically limit the discrimination against outsiders that is inherent in RTAs.

Priorities for the industrial countries

The major industrial countries must strike a difficult balance in their pursuit of bilateral and regional deals with developing countries. On the one hand, there are legitimate reasons to pursue such initiatives, rather than relying only on multilateral channels. The ongoing EU effort to deepen relations with a wider Europe is an important example. Cooperation among a smaller number of countries may

also be the most effective solution to mitigating environmental externalities, addressing nontrade issues such as labor migration (legal or illegal), or attaining national security objectives. But it must be recognized that the aggressive pursuit of RTAs with developing country partners in all corners of the globe serves the cause of global liberalization poorly if it delays or halts altogether the progress toward multilateral liberalization.

Fostering development is increasingly identified as a key rationale for North-South RTAs. In part this reflects economic interests—growing markets abroad are expanding export markets—and in part it is due to the recognition that there is a correlation between sustained economic growth in partner countries and national security. From this vantage point, several recommendations emerge.

The highest priority should be to ensure that the Doha Development Agenda is completed in a manner that provides new market access to exporters in developing countries. In addition to their interests in development, the large countries have an important historical and systemic responsibility to ensure that the world trading system remains as open as possible.

Supporting open regionalism by encouraging partner countries to adopt low external barriers would create momentum toward integration with the world, establish a more efficient development path, and reduce the adverse negative implications of RTAs on nonmembers. Because these countries are less likely to be preferred RTA partners of the United States and the EU, they will continue to have an incentive to engage at the WTO level.

Adopting the widest possible product coverage and greatest market access expansion would increase the development impact. This means that agricultural trade policies should be included in RTAs. Excluding agriculture from RTAs—the dominant practice at present—does not promote development. Although inclusion of agricultural market access will increase the incentives for small countries to seek RTAs with the large players, it will also increase the

Box 6.6 Tunisia's Association Agreement with the European Union

In July 1995, Tunisia signed the Association Agreement with the European Union (AAEU). The agreement, which came into effect in March 1998, would liberalize trade for industrial goods over a 12-year period and ultimately create a free-trade zone. Trade in agricultural goods and services was left out for future negotiations. By the mid-1990s, Tunisia had already become a successful exporting country, thanks to the establishment, in 1972, of a special offshore system for exporting enterprises that mitigated the anti-export bias of the highly protective trade regime.* Exports of manufactured goods had increased from 4 percent of GDP in 1975 to 20 percent by 1994. Free market access to EU markets under the AAEU further enhanced Tunisia's export performance, with manufactured exports increasing to 25 percent of GDP in 2002.

The AAEU gave momentum to trade liberalization in Tunisia. Average MFN tariffs were reduced from 33 percent in 1994 to 26 percent in 2003. However, Tunisia still posts the second highest average MFN tariffs in the broader EU neighborhood, including in the EU accession countries. For example, only Morocco, with a tariff rate of 30 percent, has a higher border barrier, but countries as diverse as Turkey, Bulgaria, Ukraine, Lebanon, and Moldova have tariffs of 10 percent or lower.

High MFN tariff differentials in the presence of EU preferential access risks diverting trade away from the lowest cost sources, denying Tunisian producers and consumers the benefit of less expensive imports from outside the preferential trade zone with the EU. As a result of high MFN tariffs and geographical proximity, about 75 percent of Tunisia's trade is dependent on the European market—especially in EU neighborhood countries.

A trade strategy linked to the domestic reform agenda would help Tunisia fully realize the development promise of deeper trade integration. First, ambitious reduction of MFN tariffs for industrial goods would prevent trade diversion. Second, removing beyond-the-border obstacles to trade—by reducing the still-high trade logistics costs—would enhance firms' ability to exploit export opportunities and improve their competitiveness; liberalization of backbone services, especially in transport, ICT, and finance, are also essential. Third, once the free-trade zone with the EU is fully implemented in 2007, preferential tax treatment of exporting firms will become much harder to justify, because both offshore and onshore firms will be equally exposed to foreign competition. The regulatory framework of investment incentives and trade facilitation will thus have to become more even. The EU could also liberalize market access for Tunisian agricultural exports in products in which Tunisia is competitive. Unless market access is improved, the scope for farmers to shift into these products will remain limited, and sectoral adjustment in agriculture will continue to be impaired.

---

*This system covers companies located anywhere in the country and it grants duty-free imports of capital and intermediate goods, exemptions from the VAT and excise taxes, and exemption from the corporate income tax for the first 10 years of operation.

Source: World Bank staff.

downside of RTAs for large agricultural producers in the developing world. The latter will then have a greater incentive to push for WTO-level MFN reforms; the marginal increases in competition from preferred partners may help overcome the domestic interests opposed to reforms through a process of gradual, piecemeal expansion of access to agricultural markets.

Industrial countries negotiating North-South RTAs should adopt liberal cumulation provisions in their rules of origin. Because the least-developed countries (LDCs) already have nearly free access to OECD markets, North-South RTAs will erode such preferences. Cumulation will ensure that rules of origin do not impose an additional burden on these countries. For member countries, liberal rules of origin will enhance the benefits of North-South RTAs. A demonstrated willingness of industrialized countries to put partner country interests before those of national industry groups (who prefer restrictive rules of origin) would show that development objectives are being taken seriously in RTAs.

Industrial countries could also enhance the development credentials of their RTAs by taking action to abolish antidumping and similar instruments of contingent protection. There is a plethora of evidence that antidumping is straightforward protectionism and that insofar as there is a rationale for intervention, other policy instruments can be used (i.e., competition policy). A number of RTAs—ANCERTA, Canada-Chile, the EU itself—have proceeded down this path, which illustrates that it is feasible.[19]

Industrial countries should exercise caution regarding their demands for new regulatory policies in RTAs. Behind-the-border, regulatory policies are critical for a positive impact on development outcomes, but getting the rules right—ensuring that rules are calibrated to development capacities and do not detract from other, more pressing priorities—is as essential as it is difficult to orchestrate. Applying regulatory norms in RTAs on a nondiscriminatory basis will avoid creating another complex set of discriminatory preferences. In other words, RTAs will be supportive of development if the negotiation and implementation process is designed to ensure that such priorities are set appropriately, and the preconditions for benefiting development are in place. Many RTAs are far from satisfying this prescription.

Increasing the effectiveness of development assistance for trade can help. Aid is an important part of the equation motivating RTA negotiations, especially for agreements with the EU. Export growth in many LDCs and other small and low-income countries is limited by the lack of supply capacity and the high-cost business environment. Firms in these countries may also find it difficult to deal with the regulatory requirements that apply in export markets. Health and safety standards, for example, are often regulatory barriers to entry; the standards can be excessively strict and the compliance costly, which weighs disproportionately on producers in low-income countries. Development assistance can help to build

the institutional and trade capacity needed to benefit from increased trade and better access to markets. This assistance will be more effective when it is focused more broadly on supply capacity, and when it addresses the adjustment costs associated with reforms. Recently attention has been given to expanding programs that provide aid for trade, but only when trade issues are integrated into a nation's overall development priorities. Although priorities will differ, in many cases assistance will be needed to address trade-related policy and public investment priorities. More could be done to replace preferential access as the primary carrot for RTAs with financial transfers. It has been argued at length (e.g., Hoekman, Michalopoulos, and Winters 2004), that trade preferences should not be a permanent feature of the global trading system. Appropriately designed aid would offer a similar result to preferences and at a lower overall cost.

Challenges for developing countries: A three-pronged strategy

Developing countries would benefit from adopting a coherent three-part strategy that integrates unilateral, multilateral, and regional initiatives. A number of middle-income countries have enunciated a clear set of priorities and objectives regarding regional and multilateral efforts, and have the technical and negotiating capacity to pursue them; however, many developing countries show less evidence of a coherent strategy on how to use RTAs to maximum advantage.

At the *multilateral* level, the Doha Agenda negotiations are the best instrument for most developing countries to reduce the discrimination they face from the prevailing web of RTAs. Doha is also critical insofar as it provides the greatest potential new market access for the greatest number of the world's poor. It is also the only venue in which key policy areas such as agricultural support policies or antidumping can be negotiated in a comprehensive and substantive manner. As with the high-income countries, completing the Doha deal is the highest priority.

18. Clearly there would be budgetary implications associated with a stronger surveillance role, and a precondition is that WTO members accept that the Secretariat be given the independence to undertake the analysis and form an explicit judgment of the effects of specific agreements. However, if the required resources or willingness for the WTO to undertake the task cannot be found, this in itself would be a good indication of the importance that is accorded by WTO members to the spread of RTAs.

19. See Hoekman (1998) for a discussion.

References

Aghion, Philippe, Pol Antras, and Elhanan Helpman. 2004. Negotiating Free Trade. NBER Working Paper 10721, National Bureau of Economic Research, Cambridge, MA.

Baldwin, Richard. 1993. A Domino Theory of Regionalism. CEPR Discussion Paper No. 857. Center for Economic Policy Research, Washington, DC.

Bhagwati, Jagdish. 1991. *The World Trading System at Risk.* Princeton, NJ: Princeton University Press.

Bhagwati, Jagdish, and Arvind Panagariya. 1996. *The Economics of Preferential Trading Agreements.* Washington, DC: AEI Press.

Dee, P., and J. Gali. Forthcoming. The Trade and Investment Effects of Preferential Trading Arrangements. In *NBER East Asian Seminar in Economics 14 Proceedings.* Chicago: University of Chicago Press.

De Melo, Jaime, Arvind Panagariya, and Dani Rodrik. 1993. Regional Integration: An Analytical and Empirical Overview. In *New Dimensions in Regional Integration,* eds. J. De Melo and A. Panagariya. New York: Cambridge University Press.

Finger, J. Michael. 1993. GATT's Influence on Regional Agreements. In *New Dimensions in Regional Integration,* eds. J. De Melo and A. Panagariya. New York: Cambridge University Press.

Harrison, Glenn, Thomas Rutherford, and David Tarr. 2002. Trade Policy Options for Chile: The Importance of Market Access. *World Bank Economic Review* 16(1).

Hoekman, Bernard. 1998. Preferential Trade Agreements, In *Brookings Trade Forum 1998,* ed. Robert Lawrence. Washington, DC: Brookings Institution.

Hoekman, Bernard, and Denise Konan. 2001. Deep Integration, Nondiscrimination and Euro-Mediterranean Free Trade. In *Regionalism in Europe: Geometries and Strategies After 2000,* eds. Jurgen von Hagen and Mika Widgren. Kluwer Academic Publishers.

Hoekman, Bernard, and Michel Kostecki. 2001. *The Political Economy of the World Trading System,* 2d ed. New York: Oxford University Press.

Hoekman, Bernard, Constantine Michalopoulos, and L. Alan Winters. 2004. Special and Differential Treatment of Developing Countries: Moving Forward After Cancún. *The World Economy* 27: 481–506.

Konan, Denise, and Keith E. Maskus. 2003. Quantifying the Impact of Services Liberalization in a Developing Country. Policy Research Working Paper 3193, World Bank, Washington, DC.

Krishna, Pravin. 1998. Regionalism and Multilateralism: A Political Economy Approach. *Quarterly Journal of Economics* 113: 227–51.

Lawrence, Robert Z. 1991. Emerging Regional Arrangements: Building Blocks or Stumbling Blocks? In *Finance and the International Economy 5: The AMEX Bank Review Prize Essays,* 23–25, ed. Richard O'Brien. New York: Oxford University Press.

Levy, Philip. 1997. A Political-Economic Analysis of Free-Trade Agreements. *American Economic Review* 87(4): 506–19.

Limão, Nuno. 2003. Preferential Trade Agreements as Stumbling Blocks for Multilateral Trade Liberalization: Evidence for the U.S. Paper. University of Maryland, College Park.

Mansfield, and Reinhardt. 2003. Multilateral Determinants of Regionalism: The Effects of GATT/WTO on the Formation of Preferential Trading Arrangements. *International Organization* 57(4): 829–862.

Milward, Alan. 1992. *The European Rescue of the Nation State.* Berkeley: University of California Press.

Patterson, Gardner. 1966. *Discrimination in International Trade: The Policy Issues, 1945–1965.* Princeton, NJ: Princeton University Press.

Saggi, Kamal. 2004. Preferential Trading Arrangements and Multilateral Tariff Cooperation. Southern Methodist University Working Paper. Dallas.

Saggi, Kamal, and Halis Murat Yildiz. 2004. Bilateral Trade Agreements and the Feasibility of Multilateral Free Trade. Southern Methodist University and Ryerson University Working Paper. Dallas.

Schiff, Maurice. 1997. Small is Beautiful: Preferential Trade Agreements and the Impact of Country Size and Market Share. *Journal of Economic Integration* 12: 359–87.

Schiff, Maurice, and L. Alan Winters. 2003. *Regionalism and Development.* New York: Oxford University Press.

Schott, Jeffrey. 2004. Assessing US FTA Policy. In *Free Trade Agreements: US Strategies and Priorities,* ed. Jeffrey Schott. Washington, DC: IIE (Institute for International Economics).

Snape, Richard. 1993. History and Economics of GATT's Article XXIV, In *Regional Integration and the Global Trading System*, eds. K. Anderson and R. Blackhurst. London: Harvester-Wheatsheaf.

Srinivasan, T. N. 1998. *Developing Countries and the Multilateral Trading System: From GATT to the Uruguay Round and Beyond*. New York: Harper Collins.

Stoeckel, Andrew, and B. Borrell 2001. *Preferential Trade and Developing Countries: Bad Aid, Bad Trade* Canberra: RIRDC (Rural Industries Research & Development Corporation).

Tojo, Yoshiaki. 2004. The WTO and FTAs. Presentation at the JEF-IIE Conference, 16 March.

U.S. GAO (United States General Accounting Office). 2004. International Trade: Intensifying Free Trade Negotiating Agenda Calls for Better Allocation of Staff and Resources. Report to Congressional Requesters, Washington, DC.

Viner, Jacob. 1950. *The Customs Union Issue*. New York: Carnegie Endowment for International Peace.

Winham, Gilbert. 1986. *International Trade and the Tokyo Round Negotiation*. Princeton, NJ: Princeton University Press.

Winters, L. Alan. 2000. Regionalism versus Multilateralism. In *Market Integration, Regionalism and the Global Economy*, eds. R. Baldwin, Daniel Cohen, André Sapir and Anthony J. Venables. London: Centre for Economic Policy Research.

————. 2001. Post-Lomé Trading Arrangements: The Multilateral Option. In *Regionalism in Europe: Geometries and Strategies After 2000*, eds. Jurgen von Hagen and Mika Widgren. Kluwer Academic Publishers.

World Bank. 2000. *Trade Blocs*. Washington, DC: World Bank.